THE MILITARY SNIPER

WELCOME

Stealth, nerves of steel, and single purpose. These are the attributes of the sniper, whose role in the military is clearly defined. The sniper, patient in his concealment, waits for the moment to pull the trigger. The crack of his rifle shatters the silence, and the target collapses.

Welcome to the world of the sniper, a single soldier whose training, skill and fieldcraft cause those potentially in his sights to shudder. The sniper has the ability to halt an enemy force many times his own size, to create confusion, inflict immediate casualties, and break the spirit of a wary and weary opposing force.

The sniper owes his existence to the evolution of the sighted and rifled shoulder arm. Unlike its predecessor, the smoothbore musket, the rifle transformed the battlefield with its accuracy. The grooves twisted into its barrel caused the bullet to spin and maintain its trajectory, allowing truer flight at longer distances. During the 17th century, the rifle became prominent with the game hunters of Britain and continental Europe, and fulfilling that purpose it further migrated into the military during the wars for empire and colonial domination.

Although the introduction of the rifle to the military was somewhat gradual due to the cost of such weapons and the time-consuming process of loading and firing under the stress of combat, its eventual preeminence was inevitable. During the American Revolution, the colonial frontiersman hunter proved its worth in battle. While tactics dictated that ranks of opposing riflemen were to fire at one another in volley, the minuteman, so named because he dropped his plough and took up his rifle at a minute's notice, proved the devastating capability of the relatively recent technology in the context of a new type of warfare. Using the cover of rocks, trees, the windows of houses, and darkness of the forest, these irregular militiamen complemented the Continentals who opposed the British Redcoats.

Through the decades, the role of the sniper became magnified, as did his reputation as a deadly adversary and force multiplier. From the Napoleonic Wars to the American Civil War, the sniper came into his own. Stories of the sniper's prowess abound, and with them emerged a grudging and then healthy respect for his ability to dominate the area immediately around him. And, of course, technology constantly improved, impacting the lethality of the skilled sniper plying his craft.

The trenches of World War I, the urban warfare, street combat, and island fighting of World War II, the thick jungle of Vietnam, the barren, windswept landscape of the Falklands, and the dust and searing sun of the desert have found the sniper in action. His deployment has caused the adversary to pause, considering the risk of movement, a slight appearance in the open, the raising of a head to survey the field, or that unsuspecting moment when the rifle cracks and the target is liquidated.

The modern sniper, often working in a team with a spotter alongside, continues to rely on the rifle, the telescopic sight, and his ability to remain hidden from sight, utilizing the fieldcraft of camouflage and the ghillie suit along with the essential stealth and coolness that are timeless attributes.

The sniper has literally held the ability to change the course of history. Neither general not private is immune from his sharp eye and steady hand. The sniper is consigned to war in the shadows, in his hide, or camouflaged so thoroughly that he is undetectable. In this volume, however, we take a glimpse into the ethereal world of the expert marksman. He plies his trade in silence and with singular determination, revealing his position only as he must and then melting into the mist, the depth of the forest, or the maze of buildings that offer obscurity.

Join us in this exploration of the world of the military sniper, his evolution from the hunting rifle with open sights to the incredible technology of the telescopic sight, infrared and night vision equipment, and the rifles made solely for his singular purpose in the modern military. All the while, we acknowledge the human element, the sniper's nature, his rhythmic respiration, and his finger on the trigger.

Michael E. Haskew

ABOVE: British and French snipers in full combat gear stride toward positions during a joint field exercise.
(Open Government License Author Bill Jamieson via Wikipedia)

CONTENTS

6 THE SNIPER'S ORIGIN
The saga of the sniper is entwined with the deployment of the shoulder-fired musket and the development of the rifle.

7 AMERICAN REVOLUTION
The sniper and the rifle influenced the course of history on the battlefield during the American war for independence.

11 COMMENTARY ON THE EARLY RIFLE
Military men who experienced the effectiveness of the rifle in the field advocated for is extensive use in the early 19th century.

12 NAPOLEONIC WARS TO THE CRIMEA
Greater recognition of the sniper's role and advancing technology changed the conduct of warfare.

16 DEATH OF ADMIRAL NELSON
A French sharpshooter shot and killed the greatest hero in the history of the Royal Navy during the Battle of Trafalgar in October 1805.

17 THE AMERICAN CIVIL WAR
Snipers were active with both the Union and Confederate armies, influencing the course of several battles during the conflict between North and South.

24 OLD JACK
At age 57, Od Jack Hinson sought vengeance against the Union army for the killing of his two sons and shot at least 100 Yankees.

25 THE BOER WARS
The British army fought tough, resourceful Boer settlers in a struggle for dominance in South Africa, encountering proficient enemy snipers.

27 WORLD WAR I
Opposing snipers duelled in the trenches and from concealed positions, taking a heavy toll in lives while employing powerful rifles and optical enhancements.

34 FRANCIS PEGAHMAGABOW
The highest scoring Allied sniper of the Great War, Peghamagabow was Canadian and a member of the Native American Ojibwe tribe.

35 THE GHILLIE SUIT
A classic method of concealment invented by Scottish game wardens, the ghillie suit is prevalent among modern snipers.

36 THE WINTER WAR
Finnish sniper Simo Hayha taught the Soviet Red Army a terrible lesson in sniper warfare during their invasion of his homeland.

40 WORLD WAR II IN THE WEST
Snipers took a heavy toll during the fighting in the North African desert, up the Italian book, and across France into the Third Reich.

50 EDGAR RABBETS
Private Rabbets delayed the German onslaught toward Dunkirk in the spring of 1940, assisting thousands of British and French soldiers in their evacuation.

ABOVE: Commodore Oliver Hazard Perry transfers his flag during the Battle of Lake Erie. American sharpshooters swept the decks of British ships during the battle. (Public Domain)

ABOVE: California Joe was a celebrated sniper of the Union Army during the American Civil War. (Public Domain)

51 HENRY SCHAUER
Private First Class Henry Schauer of the US 15th Infantry Regiment killed five German snipers in combat at Cisterna, Italy, in 1944.

52 CAPTAIN CLIFFORD SHORE
Author of the classic book With British Snipers to the Reich, Captain Clifford Shore gained a wide range of experience with the craft during World War II.

53 WORLD WAR II IN THE EAST
Locked in a death struggle, the armies of Nazi Germany and the Soviet Union put their snipers to deadly use in the open country and urban settings.

63 GERMAN ARMY SNIPER SCHOOL
From mid-1942, The German Army established sniper schools in response to the success of the Soviet snipers encountered during Operation Barbarossa.

64 LYUDMILA PAVLICHENKO
The most successful female sniper of World War II, Lieutenant Pavlichenko was credited with 309 kills. She visited the US, Canada and Great Britain during the war.

65 ZAITSEV THE TEACHER
Zaitsev was not only a top scoring sniper, but also an instructor of new snipers during the Battle of Stalingrad.

ABOVE: An American soldier takes aim from the cover of a tree during the Battle of Oriskany during the Saratoga campaign of the Revolutionary War. (Public Domain)

ABOVE: German sniper Ernst Junger wrote of a deadly encounter during World War I. (Public Domain)

66 BRUNO SUTKUS
German sniper Bruno Sutkus spent years in prison and exile in the Soviet Union and later trained troops of the Lithuanian army.

67 WORLD WAR II IN THE PACIFIC
During the Pacific War, the sniper fought in the jungle, the mountains, and on tropical islands across thousands of miles.

76 LEE-ENFIELD SNIPER RIFLE
The Lee-Enfield family of rifles served the British army for well over half a century, and the Rifle No. 4 Mk I (T) emerged during World War II.

77 MARINE CORPS SNIPER SCHOOLS
The US Marines began sniper training as war loomed in 1940 and established snipe schools during the war years.

79 KOREAN CONFLICT AND THE COLD WAR
Sniper operations and equipment matured substantially during the post-World War II era, expanding their presence in the world's militaries.

87 ZHANG TAOFANG
A renowned communist sniper during the Korean Conflict, Zhang Taofang displayed amazing ability with a rudimentary rifle and equipment.

88 IAN ROBERTSON
Australian soldier Ian Robertson was an accomplished sniper in Korea but also took many other compelling shots – with a camera.

89 THE MILITARY SNIPER IN FILM
Feature films have portrayed the drama of the military sniper experience through the years, bringing home to viewers the intensity of the sniper craft.

91 THE VIETNAM WAR
An unseen adversary and jungle terrain made the sniper an indispensable weapon during the lengthy Vietnam War.

98 APACHE
Possibly apocryphal, the story of Carlos Hathcock and the Viet Cong sniper Apache is nevertheless compelling.

99 CHUCK MAWHINNEY
Marine Sergeant Chuck Mawhinney was the top scoring sniper of his service branch during the Vietnam War.

100 THE FALKLANDS WAR
British forces ejected the invading Argentines from the islands in 74 days, while the sniper took his toll amid the inhospitable climate and terrain.

101 THE GULF WAR AND HOTSPOTS
Coalition forces removed Iraqi invaders from Kuwait, while unrest erupted around the globe, reinforcing the role of the sniper in urban and battlefield combat settings.

103 THE BARRETT M82 LIGHT FIFTY
The .50-calibre Barrett Light Fifty sniper rifle is a long-distance anti-material and anti-personnel weapon, deadly in the hands of a trained sniper.

104 IRAQ AND AFGHANISTAN
Snipers performed their duties in urban, mountainous, and desert combat settings during two decades of operations in Iraq and Afghanistan.

109 CRAIG HARRISON
British sniper Craig Harrison rendered invaluable service during the fighting in Afghanistan and made a record distance kill shot.

ABOVE: Canadian sniper Private L.V. Hughes waits patiently in his hide for a German victim. (Public Domain)

110 ROB FURLONG
Canadian Corporal Rob Furlong received the US Bronze Star medal for heroism in Afghanistan and made an extraordinary long-distance sniper kill.

111 CHRIS KYLE
The subject of the book and motion picture American Sniper, US Navy SEAL Chris Kyle lived the combat life in Iraq and died tragically.

112 THE MILITARY SNIPER TODAY
The mission and the menace of the sniper remain present around the world amid changing interpretations, technology, and rules of engagement.

114 THE MILITARY SNIPER'S VIEW
The role of the military sniper is continually evaluated and redefined as it exists in modern warfare.

ABOVE: A British soldier fires downrange during training for Operation Desert Storm. (Public Domain)

ISBN: 978 1 80282 768 2
Editor: Michael Haskew
Senior editor: Paul Sander
Senior editor, specials: Roger Mortimer
Email: roger.mortimer@keypublishing.com
Cover design: Steve Donovan
Design: SJmagic DESIGN SERVICES, India
Advertising Sales Manager: Brodie Baxter
Email: brodie.baxter@keypublishing.com
Tel: 01780 755131
Advertising Production: Debi McGowan
Email: debi.mcgowan@keypublishing.com

SUBSCRIPTION/MAIL ORDER
Key Publishing Ltd, PO Box 300, Stamford, Lincs, PE9 1NA
Tel: 01780 480404
Subscriptions email: subs@keypublishing.com

Mail Order email: orders@keypublishing.com
Website: www.keypublishing.com/shop

PUBLISHING
Group CEO and Publisher: Adrian Cox
Published by
Key Publishing Ltd, PO Box 100, Stamford, Lincs, PE9 1XQ
Tel: 01780 755131 **Website:** www.keypublishing.com

PRINTING
Precision Colour Printing Ltd, Haldane, Halesfield 1, Telford, Shropshire. TF7 4QQ

DISTRIBUTION
Seymour Distribution Ltd, 2 Poultry Avenue, London, EC1A 9PU
Enquiries Line: 02074 294000.

We are unable to guarantee the bona fides of any of our advertisers. Readers are strongly recommended to take their own precautions before parting with any information or item of value, including, but not limited to money, manuscripts, photographs, or personal information in response to any advertisements within this publication.

© Key Publishing Ltd 2023
All rights reserved. No part of this magazine may be reproduced or transmitted in any form by any means, electronic or mechanical, including photocopying, recording or by any information storage and retrieval system, without prior permission in writing from the copyright owner. Multiple copying of the contents of the magazine without prior written approval is not permitted.

THE SNIPER'S ORIGIN

The two men climbed to the roof of the Lichfield Cathedral. From there, a panoramic view of the surrounding countryside unfolded. Brothers John and Richard Dyott were committed to the Royalist cause, and the date was March 2, 1643. They had reached the central spire of the structure and from the battlements surveyed the siege lines of the Parliamentarian forces that were besieging the Royalist garrison.

In the distance, the two men saw the figure of an officer standing in a doorway and watching the operations of a cannon crew. As the officer stepped into the open, John Dyott, whom history says was deaf and mute, concentrated solely on the target several hundred yards in the distance, Robert Greville, 2nd Baron Brooke, commander of the Parliamentarian forces. Dyott drew a

ABOVE: Robert Greville, 2nd Baron Brooke, is considered by many historians to be the victim of the first sniper shot. (Public Domain)

deep breath and fired his musket. Seconds later, Greville fell to the ground, killed instantly by a ball through the left eye.

This story, while its foundation in fact is sometimes questioned, has been considered through the years as the first documented sniper kill. Some historians aver that the incident never occurred, others that John Dyott's ball was deflected and struck Greville on the ricochet. Still, others maintain the this was the beginning and that the sniper of the modern era traces his lineage to that day during the First English Civil War.

Perhaps, it should be noted that the incident, real or imagined as the practical beginning of the sniper's saga, did occur in step with the evolution of the shouldered firearm. The matchlock musket made its appearance on the battlefield in the 14th century, and the rudimentary models

ABOVE: Two musketeers operate their cumbersome matchlock muskets during the Thirty Years' War of the 17th century. (Public Domain)

available were heavy, difficult to manage in the midst of combat, and terribly inaccurate. Their resounding reports probably did more to strike fear into the opposition than the actual discharge of their projectiles.

However, like all technology, the design and effectiveness of the musket began to steadily evolve, and by the 17th century it had become the predominant weapon on the contemporary battlefield. Smoothbore muskets were available in quantity, and standard weaponry such as swords and pikes became secondary as opposing armies stood some distance apart and loaded and fired, blazing away at one another until one side had had enough. Typically, the rate of fire was around four shots per minute, and though accuracy had been prized since the day of the bow and arrow the open iron sights of the musket were quite limited in use.

Rifling was invented toward the end of the 15th century and initially used in heavy artillery. However, recognition of the simple fact that the principles of the flight of a projectile would hold true on a smaller scale, led to the introduction of rifling the barrels of shouldered firearms. Independent gunsmiths were considered among the finest artisans, and they turned out quality smoothbore muskets, rifled muskets, and finally "rifles." But the advent of mass production proved the game changer, allowing rifles to be produced in quantities sufficient enough to arm large military units.

ABOVE: Lichfield Cathedral was the site of the fabled first sniper kill during the First English Civil War. (Creative Commons Bs0u10e01 via Wikipedia)

By the 18th century, the rifle appeared in increasing numbers in the ranks of the world's armies, and though the flintlock musket was also in common use, it eventually gave way to the more accurate and deadly rifle, capable of increasing range, accuracy and lethality. While the smoothbore was scarcely capable of hitting a target beyond 80 to 100 yards distant, the rifle, in the hands of a skilled shooter, might strike home at 300 yards or more.

The era of revolution and the wars for empire became the proving ground for the rifle and the dawn of the age of the sniper.

ABOVE: Muskets are visible in this woodcut of a battle during the Thirty Years' War. (Public Domain)

THE MILITARY SNIPER

AMERICAN REVOLUTION

The rifle and the sniper came into their own during the American Revolution, and through the lens of history it is apparent that both exerted their influence on the future course of events.

In June 1775, the Continental Congress enthusiastically ratified the raising of 10 companies of frontiersmen and militia that would be designated as sharpshooters in the Continental army. Most likely that action was spurred by the first exchanges of hostile fire that had taken place at Lexington and Concord just a few weeks earlier.

Indeed, the British regulars who had started out on the evening of April 18, 1775, were scarcely aware of the type of opposition they would face. The colonials that responded to the alarm that British troops were advancing toward the village of Concord, Massachusetts, to seize caches of weapons and ammunition were already skilled in the art of marksmanship. Subsisting on the crop yield of their farms and their ability to supplement the table with game, they knew the capabilities and characteristics of their Kentucky long rifles like the proverbial back of the hand.

As the British retired from Concord toward the safety of Boston, they were harried without letup by the colonial minutemen who took up positions behind rocks and trees and fired their rifles from the windows of houses along the route of march. A reinforcing column led by Brigadier General Hugh Percy came up to support the hard-pressed soldiers retreating from Concord, and it was subjected to terrific fire as well, forcing the regulars to repeatedly halt on the dirt road, disperse into the neighbouring fields and forests in pursuit of the sharpshooters, and then resume their arduous trek.

Percy later wrote of the harrowing experience, "As it began now to grow pretty late and we had 15 miles (24 kilometres) to retire, and only 36 rounds, I ordered the grenadiers and light infantry to move first; and covered them with my brigade sending out very strong flanking parties which were absolutely very necessary, as there was not a stone wall, or house, though before in appearance evacuated, from whence the rebels did not fire upon us. As soon as they saw us begin to retire, they pressed very much upon our rear guard, which for that reason, I relieved every now and then. In this manner, we retired for 15 miles under incessant fire all around us, till we arrived

ABOVE: Colonial militia and British regulars clash during the battles of Lexington and Concord, April 1775. (No Restrictions via Wikipedia)

at Charlestown, between 7 and 8 in the evening and having expended almost all our ammunition."

He continued, "During the whole affair, the rebels attacked us in a very scattered, irregular manner, but with perseverance and resolution, nor did they ever dare to form into a regular body. Indeed, they knew too well what was proper, to do so. Whoever looks upon them as an irregular mob, will find himself very much mistaken. They have men amongst them who know very well what they are about, having been employed as rangers against the Indians and Canadians, and this country being very much covered with wood, and hilly, is very advantageous for their method of fighting."

When the long day of Lexington and Concord was over, the British had suffered 73 killed and 174 wounded, many of them during the difficult retirement. Even as they were surrounded in the Boston area during the weeks that followed, the British were not immune from attack. Years after the war, author Charles Winthrop Sawyer wrote, "In the army around Boston the riflemen were employed as sharpshooters to pick off any British soldiers or officers who were incautious in exposing themselves. This they did to perfection."

ABOVE: Artist Don Troiani painted this image of the brief fight at Lexington as the British proceeded toward Concord. (Public Domain)

AMERICAN REVOLUTION

ABOVE: Colonial minutemen and British regulars clash at the North Bridge in Concord on April 19, 1775. The British were harried by sharpshooters in their retreat. (Public Domain)

ABOVE: General Hugh Percy, Second Duke of Northumberland, paid grudging respect to the colonial militia and sharpshooters after Lexington and Concord. (Public Domain)

One of the best-known regiments of sharpshooters in the Continental army was Morgan's Riflemen. General Daniel Morgan, born in New Jersey, was unanimously chosen to raise the regiment from the population of Frederick County, Virginia. By July 14, 1775, just weeks after the congressional endorsement, Morgan had recruited 96 soldiers in 10 days. He trained them thoroughly and marched them 600 miles (970 kilometres) northward at a remarkable pace to support the siege of Boston. He deployed them as snipers, and they took such a toll on British officers whom they spied in an unguarded moment that an outcry was heard from the British that such tactics were outrageous.

Even General George Washington, supreme commander of the Continental army, became concerned and temporarily withheld supplies of gunpowder from Morgan's men. Still, Washington was already quite familiar with the concept of frontier fighting. Twenty years earlier during the French and Indian War, he had barely escaped with his life and heroically commanded British soldiers and militia during the retreat from the Monongahela River with the remnants of an ill-fated expedition under the command of General Edward Braddock. In July 1755, the British had proceeded toward Fort Duquesne in western Pennsylvania but met with disaster when their column of 2,400 redcoat soldiers was ambushed by 900 French and Native American fighters. Braddock was among the dead, and more than half his command was killed or wounded in the debacle.

In December 1755, Parliament approved the formation of the 62nd Royal American Regiment, initially four battalions of sharpshooters to fight in British North America in the form and fashion that the opposing French and Native Americans had displayed so effectively. Renumbered the 60th Regiment of Foot in 1757, the unit remained separate in the British Army as the King's Royal Rifle Corps for the next two centuries.

During the Saratoga campaign in the autumn of 1777, Morgan's Riflemen made a significant contribution to the American victory. Their number had grown to exceed 500, and an incident at the Battle of Bemis Heights brought home the shattering realization of the sniper's reach. In the heat of battle, Morgan spotted a British officer, conspicuous among the troops he led, and recognized his opponent as Brigadier General Simon Fraser.

Twenty years after the fateful day at Bemis Heights, Morgan recounted his memory to Richard Brent, a Virginia Congressman. According to Brent, Fraser was vigorously directing his troops and demonstrated "all activity courage and vigilance, riding from one part of his division to another, and animating the troops by his example… Morgan took a few of his best riflemen aside; men in whose fidelity, and fatal precision of aim, he could repose the most perfect confidence, and said to them: 'that gallant officer is General Fraser; I admire and respect him, but it is necessary that he should die – take your stations in that wood and do your duty.' Within a few moments General Fraser fell, mortally wounded."

Rifleman Timothy Murphy had climbed a tree, aimed his double-barrelled rifle, and fired three shots from 300 to 500 yards distant. Witnesses recalled that the first shot severed the crupper of Fraser's horse. The second creased the horse's mane. The third struck the general, who was borne from the field to a nearby house, where he died that evening.

Morgan told a British officer in late 1781, "Me and my boys had a bad time until I saw

ABOVE: Soldiers of Morgan's Rifles fire at the advancing British during the Battle of Bemis Heights. (Public Domain)

THE MILITARY SNIPER

ABOVE: A superb tactician, General Daniel Morgan defeated the British under Lieutenant Colonel Banastre Tarleton at the Battle of Cowpens. (Public Domain)

that they were led by an officer on a grey horse – a devilish brave fellow. Then, says I to one of my best shots, says I, you get up in that there tree, and single out him on the horse. Dang it, 'twas no sooner said than done. On came the British again, with the grey horseman leading; but his career was short enough this time. I jist tuck my eyes off him for a moment, and when I turned them to the place where he had been – pooh, he was gone."

Fraser was said to have told those gathered around his deathbed that he actually saw the sniper who took his life a fleeting moment later, perched in a tree and drawing the deadly bead. Murphy also shot and killed Sir Francis Clerke, 7th Baronet, an aide to General John Burgoyne. According to some accounts, Clerke was delivering a message to Fraser to withdraw and was killed minutes after Fraser was shot, while others relate that Clerke was struck down several days later.

ABOVE: Courageous British General Simon Fraser was shot by American sniper Timothy Murphy during the Saratoga campaign. (Public Domain)

Other feats of marksmanship occurred during the American Revolution and were remembered in histories of the conflict written in the ensuing years. Sawyer recounted, "There is mention of a British soldier shot at 250 yards (228 metres) when only half his head was visible; of ten men, three of whom were officers, killed one day while reconnoitring; of a rifleman who, seeing some British on a scow at a distance of fully half a mile, found a good resting place on a hill and bombarded them until he potted the lot."

Of course, the craft of skilled marksmanship was not reserved only for the upstart colonists. Scottish Major Patrick Ferguson of the King's 70th Foot was acknowledged as the finest marksman in the British army. He was authorized to raise a company of sharpshooters, although this was some time after the Revolution had been underway. Ferguson had made his own improvements to the French Chaumette screw-breech rifle, far more accurate, easier

ABOVE: The dashing Lieutenant Colonel Banastre Tarleton met defeat at Cowpens in January 1781. (Public Domain)

to load, and considerably lighter than the standard issue Brown Bess musket carried by the British rank and file. He equipped his 100 men with it. Their elite status was also evident in the green jackets they wore – perhaps in response to the American concealment tactic that found the scarlet coats of the British soldiers to be fine targets – and they intended to fight more like the rebel backwoodsmen equipped with their Kentucky long rifles.

Ferguson is personally responsible for one of the most significant sniper shots in history, and it was one which he declined to take. The story of the event differs from one account to another, but its consequences are nevertheless far-reaching. In September

ABOVE: Major Patrick Ferguson spared the life of General George Washington at Brandywine Creek in 1777. (Creative Commons via Wikipedia)

1777, a British army numbering approximately 12,500 men landed at the upper Chesapeake Bay and marched into Pennsylvania with Ferguson's command guarding the flank, says one account. Another simply states that Ferguson was somewhere along the banks of Brandywine Creek outside the rebel capital city of Philadelphia.

On one September morning, possibly the 7th, Ferguson spotted movement. Some historians say that he ordered three of his best marksmen to investigate, while others merely assert that he was on his own. Regardless, soon enough a mounted soldier dressed in the unform of a French hussar came into view. He was closely followed by a tall American officer wearing a cocked hat and riding a bay horse. In one account, Ferguson ordered his three snipers to dispatch the enemy riders but then decided to stand down because he felt such an ambush was unchivalrous.

It further says that he shouted at the American officer, who turned and looked in his direction but then rode on. With a second shout, Ferguson aimed his own rifle at the American, who turned again momentarily and then continued to canter away to safety. Ferguson lowered his weapon.

"On my calling, he stopped," Ferguson later wrote, "but after looking at me proceeded. I again drew his attention and made signs to him to stop, but he slowly continued on his way. I could have lodged half a dozen balls in or about him before he was out of my reach, but it was not pleasant to fire at the back of an unoffending individual, who was acquitting himself very coolly of his duty, so I let him alone."

During the Battle of Brandywine four days later, Ferguson's right elbow was shattered by a rebel musket ball. After he was treated for his wound, the officer wrote, "One of the surgeons who had been dressing the wounded rebel officers came in and told me

AMERICAN REVOLUTION

ABOVE: Major Patrick Ferguson falls wounded from his horse during the Battle of Kings Mountain (Public Domain)

ABOVE: Major Patrick Ferguson was a skilled marksman and chivalrous British officer. (Public Domain)

that they had been informed that General Washington was all that day with the light troops and only attended by a French officer in hussar dress, he himself dressed and mounted in every point as described. I am not sorry that I did not know at the time who it was."

While there are those who doubt the veracity of this story, there are reports of a letter that surfaced after the fact, written from Washington to the Continental Congress, which states that he had indeed been reconnoitring the area that day and was in company with the Polish Count Casimir Pulaski, dressed in the uniform of a hussar and newly arrived to serve as an aide to the general prior to taking up his own command in the rebel army.

Had Ferguson taken aim and shot George Washington dead on the banks of Brandywine Creek in 1777, would the outcome of the American Revolution have been altered? Such a question will never be answered with certainty. However, it is tantalizing to consider.

And what of Major Patrick Ferguson? He had previously demonstrated the improvement that his breechloading rifle offered, loading and firing at a rate of seven rounds per minute, more than twice that of the standard soldier handling the Brown Bess. After the incident on Brandywine Creek, he was tasked with a night raid against American naval privateers who had come ashore on the coast of New Jersey. With 400 men, Ferguson sailed into Little Egg Harbor, rushed ashore, and destroyed ships and dock facilities while putting the homes of rebel sympathizers to the torch.

A few days later, Ferguson received word that Pulaski was hunting his force. Turning the tables, Ferguson and 250 British soldiers attacked the rebel encampment under cover of darkness, killing 50 before Pulaski's dragoons mounted a counterattack, forcing them to retire. The Americans later protested bitterly that their dead had been massacred, but Ferguson retorted, "It being a night attack, little quarter could of course be given."

The incident was not forgotten, and Ferguson continued to campaign into the Carolina back country. By the autumn of 1780, he had convinced hundreds of Loyalists to take up arms against the rebels. Sharp skirmishes ensued, and Ferguson is said to have pursued his adversaries with zeal while trying to spare non-combatants any harm. Nevertheless, when necessary he was forthright in threatening retribution. He once sent a prisoner to a rebel commander with a warning to "desist from opposition to British arms or we will march our army over the mountains, hang your leaders, and lay your country waste with fire and sword."

Thereafter, the rebels, known as overmountain men, concentrated their forces to meet Ferguson and his Loyalists at the Battle of Kings Mountain, near the frontier between North and South Carolina. On October 7, 1780, Ferguson was conspicuously dressed in his black and white plaid duster, riding a white charger confidently from one end of his line to the other and blowing a silver whistle that his men could hear above the din of battle.

When his men were virtually overrun, Ferguson cut down white flags of surrender and ordered them to keep fighting. He was a tempting target, and it is said that Robert Young, an overmountain sharpshooter, spotted Ferguson and muttered, "I'll try and see what Sweet Lips can do."

Young raised his rifle and shot Ferguson from his horse, his foot still in the stirrup as he was dragged toward the enemy line. One rebel stepped up to demand his surrender, but Ferguson drew his pistol and shot the man where he stood. Ferguson was then shot at least six more times. Some reports state that his body was desecrated in retaliation for perceived atrocities before it was buried near the spot where he died.

The American victory at Kings Mountain was turning point of the revolution, even as the sniper and the rifle emerged as forces to be reckoned with on the battlefield.

ABOVE: Daniel Morgan, clad in white, stands near General Horatio Gates as the surrender of the British army under General John Burgoyne is accepted at Saratoga. (Public Domain)

THE MILITARY SNIPER

COMMENTARY ON THE EARLY RIFLE

With the death of Patrick Ferguson, the ascendancy of the rifle in the British army paused for roughly 20 years. However, there were still those who advocated for its introduction as the standard shoulder arm for His Majesty's forces.

Those who had served in North America were among the proponents of the rifle's further development. They had seen it in action and experienced the weapon's accuracy in the hands of the skilled operator. Major George Hanger, 4th Baron Colerain, served as aide de camp to Sir Henry Clinton, the senior British commander, at the siege

ABOVE: Wearing his distinctive green uniform, a British soldier lies down to fire his Baker rifle in this 1803 image. (Public Domain)

ABOVE: Major George Hanger, 4th Lord Coleraine, wrote of the prowess of American marksmen during the revolution. (Public Domain)

ABOVE: This bronze relief honours Timothy Murphy, who shot General Simon Fraser at the Battle of Bemis Heights. (Public Domain)

of Charleston in 1776 and commanded the British Legion temporarily.

"I have many times asked the American backwoodsman what their best marksmen could do," wrote Hanger. "They have constantly told me that an expert rifleman can hit the head of a man at 200 yards. I am certain that provided an American rifleman was to get perfect aim at 300 yards at me standing still, he most undoubtedly would hit me, unless it was a very windy day."

Such sentiment was shared by others who had fought the Americans in the revolution, and in 1808 Captain Henry Beaufoy called upon his own experience to write a notable book on the origin, mechanical aspects, and deployment of the rifle. The book was titled Scloppeteria or Considerations on the Nature and Use of Rifled Barrel Guns. As well as serving the purpose of a practical guide Beaufoy lucidly argued that the age of the rifle would come, and along with it surely that of the sniper would follow.

Indeed, he predicted that the rifleman would become the central figure of the battlefield, and he was aware that the common British soldier who had faced American sharpshooters and snipers referred coldly to these lethal shooters as "widow makers."

Beaufoy wrote, "The Americans during their war with this country, were in the habit of forming themselves into small bands of ten or twelve, who, accustomed to shooting in hunting parties, went out in a sort of predatory warfare, each carrying his ammunition and provisions, and returning when they were exhausted. From the incessant attacks of these bodies, their opponents could never be prepared, as the first knowledge of a patrol in the neighbourhood was generally given by a volley of well-directed fire that perhaps killed or wounded the greater part."

He continued, "In short, rifles may be said, by the unerring flight of their shot, to constitute nothing less than an improved species of moveable battery, capable of being adapted to every and any situation, and consequently in hands trained and *familiarized* to their use, a military force of the highest importance."

Beaufoy later summed up the essence of the rifle's proliferation in battle – simply that it was in its earliest day a weapon that struck fear into the hearts of the enemy – even when it was employed by a single adversary, a sniper hidden in the bush.

"It has been readily confessed by old soldiers," Beaufoy related, "that when they understood they were opposed by riflemen, they felt a degree of terror never inspired by general action, from the idea that a rifleman always singled out an individual, who was almost certain of being killed or wounded."

By the dawn of the 19th century and the height of the Napoleonic Wars, the smoothbore musket remained the primary shoulder arm of the British soldier. However, just as Henry Beaufoy's report was being considered the rifle and the sharpshooter were being employed – albeit in relatively small numbers – to deadly effect.

NAPOLEONIC WARS TO THE CRIMEA

For the better part of two decades, Great Britain was at war with Napoleonic France during the late 18th and early 19th centuries. They fought on land and at sea, from the Iberian Peninsula across western and northern Europe to the eastern Mediterranean, and during that period the sniper and the rifle increased their influence in battle amid steadily advancing technology.

In 1800, the British Army established the Experimental Corps of Riflemen, undoubtedly in response to the experience in the American Revolution. A single battalion of the 60th Foot had previously received rifles, but the mission of the corps, which months later evolved into the three battalions of the 95th (Rifle) Regiment of Foot, was significantly different from that of the rank and file. For starters, these riflemen were outfitted with green uniforms and black leather kit, while the standard infantry retained their Brown Bess muskets and ubiquitous redcoat uniforms. It was the first British attempt at camouflage, a grudging acknowledgment of the reality of the battlefield as concealment offered a definite advantage.

The riflemen were trained to skirmish, exhibit initiative, and to select individual

ABOVE: The death of General Colbert, shot by rifleman Thomas Plunkett of the 95th (Rifle) Regiment of Foot, is depicted in this painting by artist Victor Schnetz. (Creative Commons via Wikipedia)

ABOVE: British riflemen fire their Baker rifles during the Peninsular War in this period image. (Public Domain)

targets as they presented themselves. Such was the essence of the sniper, taking on a specific target, while the sharpshooter might more or less fire at a target of opportunity. The idea of deliberately aiming a weapon, rather than pointing and firing as the traditional infantrymen had done, was something new. In addition, the British army adopted the Baker rifle in 1802, the first British-made standard issue rifle in its history. Although it would take some time to field enough of the weapons to place them in common use, the 95th (Rifle) Regiment of Foot were given the Baker as soon as it was available in sufficient quantity.

During the Peninsular War, the 95th Rifles found opportunities to demonstrate the value of their training and of the army's investment. While retreating toward the town of Corunna, Spain, on January 3, 1809, the 1st Battalion was serving as the rear guard and deployed in defence of a key bridge near the town of Cacabelos. From his vantage point, rifleman Thomas Plunkett spotted the commanding officer of the pursuing French vanguard.

Author Stuart Hadaway wrote in his book *Rifleman Thomas Plunkett: A Pattern for the Battalion*, "The French commander, a dashing and talented young general called Auguste-Marie-Francois Colbert, seeing the rest of the 28th Foot and six guns of the Royal Horse Artillery formed up on the ridge of the far side of the Cua, withdrew his men to be reformed. Paget [British commander Sir Edward] also pulled his forces back, placing the 28th across the road on the far side with the 52nd and 95th formed up on either side in positions to pour flanking fire onto the bridge. It was this position that Colbert unwisely, and fatally, decided to assault. Forming his cavalry into a column of fours he charged for the bridge.

"Seeing Colbert charging ahead of his men, distinctive because of his uniform and grey horse, Plunkett raced ahead of the line and onto the bridge. Throwing himself onto his back and resting his Baker rifle on his

ABOVE: Rifleman Thomas Plunkett kills the French General Colbert with his Baker rifle at long distance. (Public Domain)

crossed feet with the butt under his right shoulder in the approved manner, Plunkett fired at and killed Colbert. Apparently, having reloaded quickly, Plunkett then shot a second Frenchman who had ridden to Colbert's aid before dashing back to the British line."

Plunkett's shot was astounding. Estimates of its distance reached 800 yards (730 metres). Colbert was struck above the left eye and was dead within 15 minutes.

The French army had not ignored the concept of the sniper either. Its highly trained corps were known for their mobility and rapid deployment. On May 5, 1807, a German officer observed the efficiency of the French and noted, "Each Marshall of the French Empire has a body of Two Thousand men of sharpshooters attached to his Corps d'armee. Such sharpshooters, all of which being expert and skilled men…are always sure to hit their mark, at a distance of one hundred fifty paces. In any cases, when the whole army is concentrating for a general battle, the several bodies of sharpshooters, belonging to the Corps of each Marshall, are formed in one separate Corps by itself, consisting together of 16,000 men.

"Now, on whatever point, the Commander in Chief, is of intention… to break through the opposing army, on such point or spot this select corps of 16,000 men is always sure to be placed and posted. As it is, this body of sharpshooters of 16,000 men may within a short time destroy double the quantity, say an opposing army of 30 to 40,000 men…."

During the fateful Battle of Waterloo, a Private Wheeler of the 95th Rifles was among the defenders of the farmhouse of La Haye Sainte. Wheeler spent 19 years in the British army and never forgot that harrowing day of June 18, 1815. In 1951, historian B.H. Liddell-Hart edited his letters and noted that the private had been "ordered with two men to post ourselves behind a rock or large stone, well studded with brambles…This was somewhat to our right and in advance.

"About an hour after we were posted we saw an officer of Huzzars sneaking down to get a peep at our position. One of my men was what we term a dead shot, when he was within point-blank distance. I asked him if he could make sure of him. His reply was 'To be sure I can, but let him come nearer if he will, at all events his death warrant is signed and in my hands if he should turn back.' By this time, he had without perceiving us come up near to us. When Chipping fired, down he fell and in a minute we had his body with the horse in our possession behind the rock."

While the British army was further engaged with the United States during the War of 1812, the Battle of New Orleans was fought on January 8, 1815, actually after the terms of peace had been concluded at Ghent, Belgium. One of the memorable figures to emerge from this action, besides General Andrew Jackson and the pirate Jean Lafitte, was Kentucky rifleman Ephraim McLean Brank, who joined one of three companies raised in Muhlenberg County, in the west of the state.

An anonymous British officer gained firsthand knowledge of Brank's prowess with the Kentucky long rifle and wrote of the experience: "We marched in solid column in a direct line, upon the American defences… What attracted our attention most was the figure of a tall man standing on the breastworks dressed in linsey-woolsey, with buckskin leggings and a broad-brimmed hat that fell around his face almost concealing his features. He was standing in one of those picturesque graceful attitudes peculiar to those natural men dwelling in forests. The body rested in the left leg and swayed with a curved line upward. The right arm was extended, the hand grasping the rifle near the muzzle, the butt of which rested near the toe of his right foot.

"With his left hand he raised the rim of his hat from his eyes and seemed gazing intently on our advancing column. The cannon of the enemy had opened up on us and tore through our ranks with dreadful slaughter; but we continued to advance unwavering and cool, as if nothing threatened our program. The roar of the cannon had no effect upon the figure before us; he seemed fixed and motionless as a statue.

"At last, he moved, threw back his hat rim over the crown with his left hand, raised his rifle and took aim at our group. At whom had he levelled his piece? But the distance was so great that we looked at each other and smiled. We saw the rifle flash and very rightly conjectured that his aim was in the direction of our party. My right-hand companion, as noble a fellow as ever rode at the head of a regiment, fell from his saddle. The hunter paused a few moments without moving the gun from his shoulder. Then he reloaded and resumed his former attitude.

ABOVE: This French soldier is a sharpshooter, or voltigeur, in the army of Napoleon Bonaparte. (Public Domain)

ABOVE: The British army adopted the flintlock, muzzleloading Baker rifle in 1802. (Public Domain)

NAPOLEONIC WARS TO THE CRIMEA

ABOVE: Ephraim McLean Brank, a Kentucky rifleman, left a lasting impression on the British at the Battle of New Orleans. (Public Domain)

ABOVE: Andrew Jackson strikes a heroic pose as British and American troops fight hand to hand during the Battle of New Orleans. (Public Domain)

Throwing the hat rim over his eyes and again holding it up with the left hand, he fixed his piercing gaze upon us, as if hunting out another victim.

"Once more, the hat rim was thrown back, and the gun raised to his shoulder. This time we did not smile, but cast our glances at each other, to see which of us must die. When again the rifle flashed another of our party dropped to the earth. There was something most awful in this marching to certain death. The cannon and thousands of musket balls played upon our ranks, we cared not for; for there was a chance of escaping them. Most of us had walked as coolly upon batteries more destructive, without quailing, but to know that every time that rifle was levelled toward us, and its bullet sprang from the barrel, one of us must surely fall; to see it rest, motionless as if poised on a rack, and know, when the hammer came down, that the messenger of death drove unerringly to its goal, to know this, and still march on, was awful.

"I could see nothing but the tall figure standing on the breastworks; he seemed to grow, phantom-like, higher and higher, assuming through the smoke the supernatural appearance of some great spirit of death. Again, did he reload and discharge and reload and discharge his rifle with the same unfailing aim, and the same unfailing result; and it was with indescribable pleasure that I beheld, as we marched [towards] the American lines, the sulphurous clouds gathering around us, and shutting that spectral hunter from our gaze. "We lost the battle, and to my mind, that Kentucky Rifleman contributed more to our defeat than anything else; for which he remained to our sight, our attention was drawn from our duties. And when at last, we became enshrouded in the smoke, the work was completed, we were in utter confusion and unable, in the extremity, to restore order sufficient to make any successful attack. The battle was lost."

Indeed, the sniper, a backwoods hunter of game and then of men, had wreaked havoc in the ranks of British regulars. One man had so intimidated the British officers and soldiers that day that the discharge of their duties was more than they could muster.

While rifling had enabled the sniper's emergence on the field of battle, the invention of the percussion cap brought greater efficiency to the craft. The percussion cap consisted of a small metal cap manufactured from steel and later copper and made to fit the end of a tube that led to the firing chamber of the musket or rifle. It contained a mixture of fulminate of mercury and chloride of potash patented by Reverend A.J. Forsyth in 1807. When struck by the weapon's hammer, the unstable mixture ignited, sparking the powder in the firing chamber and discharging the weapon. The closed system virtually eliminated the problem of firing in inclement weather, when the open pan would often foul, causing the weapon to misfire. The percussion cap made the rifle more reliable, decreased the time required to load and fire, and eliminated the noxious cloud of burned powder that often irritated the sniper's eye. By the mid-19th century, it was in widespread use.

The rifled musket, produced in large numbers via the improved machinery characteristic of the Industrial Revolution, also became prominent in the 19th century, employing the percussion lock which displaced the flintlock system. The rifled musket was exponentially more accurate than its predecessor, the smoothbore musket,

ABOVE: French soldiers storm the gates of La Haye Sainte during the Battle of Waterloo, June 18, 1815. (Public Domain)

ABOVE: Reverend A.J. Forsyth patented the explosive mixture of the percussion cap in 1807. (Public Domain)

ABOVE: French officer Claude-Étienne Minié revolutionized warfare with his conical-shaped bullet. (Public Domain)

ABOVE: Pictured in 1890, Lieutenant Colonel David Davidson developed a basic telescopic rifle sight during the Crimean War. (Public Domain)

and when paired with Minié ball, a cone-shaped projectile, rather than the round ball, the weapon became a deadly killing machine. The Minié ball, actually a hollow-based bullet, was designed by Frenchman Claude-Étienne Minié. When the rifle was fired, the base expanded to catch the grooves of the barrel quickly and fill the entire space, substantially increasing muzzle velocity.

In the mid-1850s, the British army began to issue the Enfield rifle, a muzzleloader that would undoubtedly enable riflemen to fire more accurately at greater distances. However, the Enfield was not available in sufficient quantity before soldiers were fighting in the Crimea and in suppression of the insurrection in India at mid-century.

During the Crimean War of 1853-1856, the British and Russian adversaries experienced trench warfare that foreshadowed that of the Western Front during World War I half a century later. While the siege of the port of Sevastopol was underway, Lieutenant Colonel David Davidson of the 1st City of Edinburgh Rifle Volunteers fashioned a basic telescopic rifle sight after watching a detachment of sharpshooters in action.

It is probable that the term "sniper" emerged during this period in India, as soldiers referred to the snipe, a particularly difficult game bird to bring down, and began to use the word in conjunction with those who were successful during the hunt of the elusive fowl. It then migrated to widespread use, describing those dead-eyed shooters on the battlefield.

One particularly troublesome individual gained the lasting enmity of the British soldiers in the so-called Residency of the city of Lucknow in northern India. Most of the town was under the control of the rebellious Sepoys, and their sharpshooters had claimed many unsuspecting British soldiers. The deadliest of these was given the nickname "Jim the Nailer" or "Bob the Nailer," depending on which account is consulted. The Nailer was thought to be an African who did actually load his rifle with nails. So harassed were the British that they once dug a tunnel beneath the house where the Nailer was supposedly secreted and blew the structure up with explosives.

Another witness claimed, "The only way fire could be returned was from concealment. The garrison came gradually to encourage the assailants to occupy a point and to have confidence in occupying it. But they marked well the direction; and during the night they bored holes in that direction. in the morning the enemy would come up by twos and threes to occupy their chosen post. Then the muskets would be discharged. The result was almost inevitably successful…But there was a wily marksman whom this guileful device entirely failed to snare. Choosing his coign with infinite subtlety and care, he would await the appearance of a likely target with an unblinking watchfulness that dawn-chill or the heat of the noonday sun in no way seemed to affect.

"Unseen, undetectable, he would remain inactive for hours at a stretch. But if a gleam of scarlet tunic or white cap cover came to reward his vigil, then his swift, unerring shot took toll with a deadly precision that scorned the waste of a single cartridge… In wry tribute to his outstanding skill, the sweating men of the garrison dubbed him 'Jim the Nailer.' To give the exact tally of his score against the Residency's garrison is as impossible as to cloak him with a specific identity or pronounce upon his ultimate fate. For with the relief of Lucknow, no more was heard of him."

ABOVE: The relief of Lucknow ended Bob or Jim the Nailer's reign of terror during the Indian Insurrection. (Public Domain)

DEATH OF ADMIRAL NELSON

The climactic naval battle of the Napoleonic War of the Third Coalition occurred at Trafalgar on October 21, 1805. It was a resounding victory for the British Royal Navy over the combined fleets of France and Spain, but it came at a terrible price.

The sniper was not limited to warfare only on land, and it was common practice when going into battle to station riflemen amid the masts and rigging of warships to harass the enemy sailors on the upper decks and perhaps pick off an opposing officer. The Royal Navy typically included a detachment of marines aboard ships for that purpose.

During the Battle of Trafalgar, Admiral Horatio Nelson, the greatest commander in the illustrious history of the Royal Navy, was conspicuous on the quarterdeck of his flagship, HMS Victory. Even as Victory was locked in mortal combat with the French ship of the line Redoubtable, Nelson's secretary, John Scott, was killed by a cannon shot. Moments later, Vice Admiral Sir Thomas Hardy, flag captain aboard Victory, was startled when a shell fragment dented one of his shoe buckles as he stood beside Nelson, who commented, "This is too warm work to last long."

Soon enough, the bullets of French sharpshooters began to hiss past, sometimes cutting down a marine who was discharging his duty. Nelson did not waver and continued to issue orders as Victory came under fire from four enemy warships. Shortly after 1pm, Nelson suddenly fell toward the deck, supporting himself with one hand before collapsing. Hardy rushed to his side, and the stricken admiral murmured, "Hardy, I do believe they have done it at last…my backbone is shot through."

A French rifleman secured in the mizzen mast of Redoubtable had fired the shot that entered Nelson's left shoulder, passed through a lung and the spine, and finally lodged below his right shoulder blade, from only 50 feet (15 metres) distant. Two seamen and a marine sergeant major carried Nelson below decks, but along the way he asked them to pause in order to give direction to the midshipman manning the Victory's tiller. He asked that a handkerchief be placed over his face to avoid inciting panic among the crew, still hotly engaged in battle.

Nelson told the ship's surgeon, Dr. William Beatty, "You can do nothing for me. I have but a short time to live." He drifted in and out of consciousness, at times mumbling, "fan, fan, rub, rub, drink, drink…." Hardy came below to see the admiral and heard him whisper faintly, "Thank God I have done my duty."

ABOVE: Opposing warships lie alongside one another during the melee that was the Battle of Trafalgar in October 1805. (Public Domain)

ABOVE: A French sharpshooter aboard the ship of the line Redoubtable fired the shot that fatally wounded Admiral Horatio Nelson at Trafalgar. (Public Domain)

Nelson died at approximately 4:30pm; his last words were, "God and my country." He had lived long enough to hear the news of his great victory over the French and Spanish fleets, but the single shot of a single rifleman had ended the career of the illustrious hero at the age of just 47.

Other instances of riflemen participating in naval engagements occurred during the Age of Sail. At the Battle of Lake Erie during the War of 1812 on September 10, 1813, the American riflemen in the rigging of the ships under the command of Admiral Oliver Hazard Perry were said to have swept the decks of the opposing British ships so thoroughly that they provided a decided advantage in their victory.

ABOVE: Admiral Horatio Nelson lies mortally wounded on the quarterdeck of HMS Victory during the Battle of Trafalgar. (Public Domain)

THE MILITARY SNIPER

ABOVE: In this painting by artist Winslow Homer, a Union sharpshooter ensconced in a tree, takes aim at a distant target. (Public Domain)

THE AMERICAN CIVIL WAR

The American Civil War served as a proving ground for the rapid advances accomplished in the technology of shouldered firearms. The percussion cap made the rifled musket primed and ready to fire at a moment's notice regardless of weather conditions, while the Minié ball increased accuracy and lethality by a substantial margin. The introduction of rudimentary sights contributed as well.

Nevertheless, there remained a smattering of muskets, rifled muskets, calibres and ammunition. The British and American armies did not adopt percussion arms until the 1840s, many of them converted from smoothbore patterns. At the same time, the recognition of the rifle and the capabilities of the sniper gained attention. During the 1846-1848 US war with Mexico, the Model 1841 "Mississippi" rifle proved its worth.

"The unerring aim of our Mississippi rifles, acting in concert, cast terror and dismay among the cowardly and unprincipled foe," wrote an American observer. At the same time, author N. Bosworth wrote in his book A Treatise on Rifle, Musket, Pistol and Fowling Pieces in 1846, "The rifle in the hands of one who has studied its properties, will throw a ball with an accuracy that would surprise a large portion of those who are in the habit of using it. What we seriously want is more knowledge among the soldiery, both of guns and gunpowder."

The capabilities of the rifle and the sniper came into sharp focus just a few years later with the eruption of the American Civil War. Without doubt, battlefield tactics had not kept pace with the enhanced lethality of the weapons carried by ordinary infantrymen, and the horrific casualties that resulted from battles such as Shiloh, Antietam, Fredericksburg, Gettysburg, Chickamauga, and others bear mute and terrible testimony to this fact. Then, the presence of the sniper added another dimension to the conduct of warfare, sometimes with telling results.

ABOVE: Soldiers of Berdan's Sharpshooters take cover behind sheaves of wheat during the Battle of Malvern Hill, 1862. (Public Domain)

www.keymilitary.com 17

THE AMERICAN CIVIL WAR

ABOVE: Hiram Berdan formed the famous sharpshooter units that bore his name during the American Civil War. (Public Domain)

ABOVE: Truman Head, a prolific sniper for the Union, was better known as California Joe. (Public Domain)

The first shots of the Civil War were fired on Fort Sumter, in the harbour of Charleston, South Carolina, on April 12, 1861. After the Confederates occupied the fort, they withstood a blockade and naval bombardment from Union gunboats and ironclads, as well as continuing Union efforts to recapture Sumter and to take Charleston.

One of the Confederate soldiers occupying Fort Sumter scanned the horizon from the masonry structure's parapet on December 5, 1861. He spotted a Union soldier exposed while working around Battery Gregg near the mouth of the harbour. The rebel took aim and shot the Union soldier from a distance of 1,390 yards. It is likely that he used the British-made .45-calibre (11.43mm) Whitworth rifle to make the shot. The Whitworth, with its innovative hexagonal rifling, was highly prized by Confederate sharpshooters, particularly when paired with a telescopic sight. Its effective range extended to 1,000 yards (910 metres), and it was capable of hitting targets up to 1,500 yards (1,400 metres) distant. While the Whitworth was a muzzleloader, the breechloading rifle became popular among Union troops, particularly the Sharps rifle, introduced in 1848.

During the course of the Civil War, both the Union and Confederate armies formed units of sharpshooters which were equipped with the best weapons for their intended purpose. The sharpshooters were regularly chosen for their demonstrated marksmanship skills, and competitions were sometimes held for positions and for the best rifles.

By the outbreak of the war, Hiram Berdan, a New Yorker schooled in mechanical engineering and the inventor of his own repeating rifle and specialized ammunition, began raising two regiments of sharpshooters for the Union Army of the Potomac. Already known around the country as a tireless self-promoter and a crack shot, Berdan recruited the best marksmen he could find, and the competition was rigorous. Each would-be sharpshooter was required to score 10 consecutive rounds within a target only 10 inches (25.4cm) in diameter from a distance of 200 yards (183 metres). Their .52-calibre (13.2mm) breechloading Sharps rifles fired a prepared cartridge including paper or thin cloth containing the powder charge and projectile.

Berdan appreciated the value of concealment, particularly in light of the sharpshooter's role, while he also wanted his elite regiments to be recognizable as such. Therefore, the regiments, soon known as Berdan's Sharpshooters, were uniformed in wool frock coats and trousers of deep forest green, as opposed to the standard blue dress of the rest of the Union army. They wore green forage caps sometimes decorated with black ostrich plumes, leather gaiters that stretched above the knee to make negotiating the brambles and thickets of the forest easier, and brogan shoes. Their buttons were black rubber rather than the shiny brass that might attract the enemy's attention.

Berdan's Sharpshooters quickly gained a reputation for skill and stealth on the battlefield. Among their number were several individuals who earned lasting fame. Truman Head, for example, became known as California Joe, his exploits published in newspapers across the Union states. California Joe, who had invested in his own Sharps rifle and apparently lied about his age when he joined the regiment, was actually too old to serve according to regulations. His age at enlistment is estimated at roughly 52 years. California Joe, born either in rural New York or in Philadelphia, depending on which version of his sketchy story is read, had travelled west as a gold prospector and fur trapper, lured by the discovery of the precious metal and the Gold Rush of 1849.

In the autumn of 1861, California Joe enlisted in a Union regiment being raised in the state but decided that endless drill and training were not to his liking. He completed Berdan's tough qualifying program and joined Company C of the Sharpshooters after purchasing his Sharps rifle, the first that his regiment had seen and prior to the distribution of the government-supplied rifles. About that time, since he had no family, he also placed his considerable fortune, roughly $50,000, in trust for his fellow sharpshooters should he be killed in battle.

California Joe first made a name for himself during the siege of Yorktown, Virginia, in the spring of 1862. He watched as Confederate artillerymen brought a heavy 32-pound cannon forward and prepared to open fire on the Union lines. Just as one

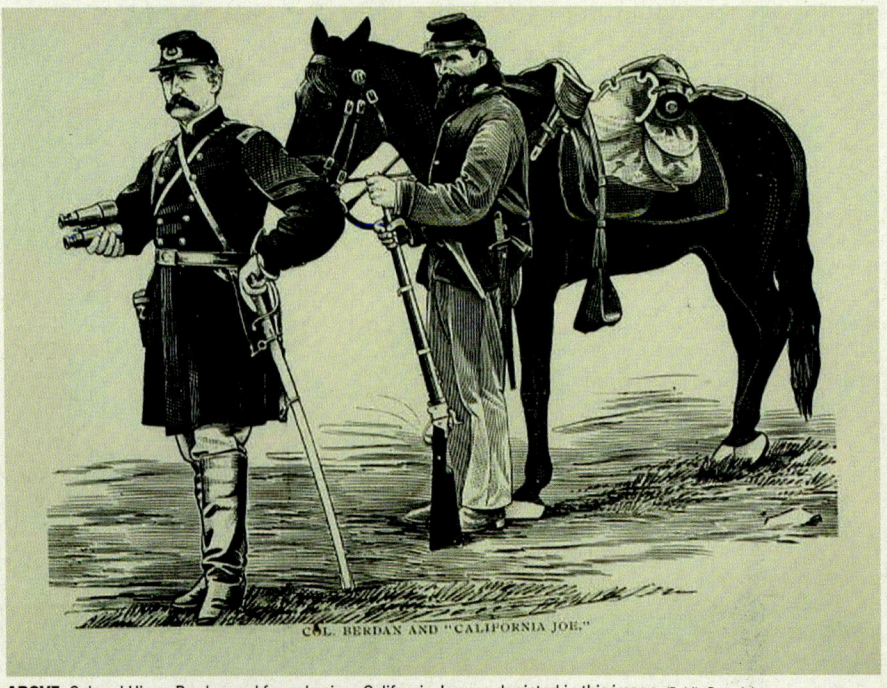

ABOVE: Colonel Hiram Berdan and famed sniper California Joe are depicted in this image. (Public Domain)

ABOVE: This monument to Berdan's Sharpshooters is located on the battlefield at Gettysburg. (Creative Commons veggies via Wikipedia)

of the rebels reached to swab the barrel, California Joe's rifle barked, and the rebel crumpled to the ground. For the rest of the day, anyone who attempted to remove the swab from the cannon barrel was shot down.

On another occasion, California Joe spotted a group of Confederate horsemen, one of them standing out while wearing a white shirt. He remarked to his fellow sharpshooters that white targets were his specialty, and seconds later the rebel was shot from his saddle. One Northern newspaper reported that California Joe had "shot a man out of a tree two miles off, just at daybreak, first pop."

By the summer of 1862, the aged California Joe was having problems with his vision, possibly because of prolonged use of the telescopic sight attached to his Sharps rifle. Failing health prompted him to write a succinct letter, which read: "Mr. Lincoln – I have done some service to the country, and my eyesight is ruined doing duty. I would like to be discharged. California Joe." Whether the president was involved in the process is not known, but California Joe received his discharge. He died in San Francisco in 1875, and his funeral included full military honours with a 21-gun salute.

Another of Berdan's sharpshooters to emerge at Yorktown was nicknamed Old Seth. One morning Old Seth slipped into a vacant rifle pit near the Confederate lines and proceeded to pick off enemy artillerymen for two straight days. Fellow soldiers supplied him with food and ammunition as he methodically shot anyone who stepped toward a particular cannon.

Meanwhile, The Confederate Army of Northern Virginia responded to the Union threat against the rebel capital of Richmond, Virginia, and fought doggedly during the Peninsula Campaign in the spring of 1862. General John Bell Hood's Texas Brigade arrived at Yorktown with many accomplished marksmen in its ranks. Often, these men were distributed among various units rather than concentrated in a single company or regiment. Although the Whitworth rifle was relatively scarce, the British-made Enfield was readily available, and the Texans put it to deadly use.

ABOVE: This image of the interior of Fort Sumter reveals the parapet from which a Confederate sniper took a shot at Union artillerymen at Charleston harbour. (Public Domain)

Author Stephen W. Sears wrote, "When the Yankee sharpshooters grew too bold, the Texans would slip into the forward picket line for what they liked to call a little squirrel shooting. Soon their fire would drive the Federals out of the trees and other hiding places they favoured and back into their fortifications, where sharpshooting continued but on more even terms. The marksmen on both sides at Yorktown considerably exaggerated their prowess, especially to credulous newspaper correspondents, yet there was no doubt that because of them the prudent learned to keep their heads down. The story quickly got around, for example, of the Confederate soldier who woke up one morning in his cramped trench and unthinkingly stood up to stretch and was instantly shot through the heart."

Private John West, a Georgian serving in the Confederate Army of Northern Virginia, was one of the relative few rebel snipers to receive a prized Whitworth rifle early in the Civil War. He remembered being particularly adept at harassing Union gunners and for a time served as one of only 13 Whitworth carrying snipers in the entire army.

"Artillerymen could stand anything better than they could sharpshooting," wrote West, "and they would turn their guns upon a sharpshooter as quick as they would upon a battery. You see, we could pick off the

ABOVE: Union soldiers wait for engineers to bridge the Rappahannock River under Confederate sniper fire at the Battle of Fredericksburg. (Public Domain)

THE AMERICAN CIVIL WAR

ABOVE: Union General Amiel Whipple was mortally wounded by a Confederate sniper's bullet at the Battle of Chancellorsville. (Public Domain)

ABOVE: The Whitworth rifle, such as this example equipped with a telescopic sight, was highly prized among Confederate snipers. (Public Domain)

ABOVE: Union General John F. Reynolds was killed by a Confederate sniper on the first day of the Battle of Gettysburg, July 1, 1863. (Public Domain)

In December 1862, the reluctant Union General Ambrose Burnside led the Army of the Potomac with great ineptitude at the Battle of Fredericksburg. The Union forces suffered heavy casualties attempting to seize high ground at Marye's Heights from General Lee's well-protected Confederate riflemen of the Army of Northern Virginia, also subjecting themselves to merciless artillery fire as they moved from the Rappahannock River toward the high ground. But before the abortive assaults on Marye's Heights, the Federals were obliged to bridge the Rappahannock.

Before sunrise on the morning of December 11, Union engineers began constructing three pontoon bridges downstream from Fredericksburg across the swift-flowing Rappahannock, and three more directly opposite the city. Downstream from Fredericksburg, the bridging went virtually unmolested as artillery covered the operations and Confederate soldiers were not concentrated. However, the effort at Fredericksburg was continually harassed as a Mississippi brigade took up positions in buildings and the adjacent woods, striking down the Federal engineers from the shelter of windows and ditches with alarming accuracy as the sun rose higher in the morning sky.

When Union artillery fired on Fredericksburg, numerous buildings were destroyed and set afire, but Confederate snipers used the ruins for concealment and continued to take a heavy toll. As a result, Union soldiers spent two days fighting street to street and house to house in Fredericksburg before they were able to cross the Rappahannock in relative safety to assault Marye's Heights. The fighting was a harbinger of the urban warfare that would characterize many future conflicts.

At the Battle of Chancellorsville, Berdan's Sharpshooters duelled with their Confederate counterparts, and one lethal exchange occurred in the vicinity of Chandler's house, near the point of Union General Joseph Hooker's defensive line. General Amiel Whipple, commanding the 3rd Infantry Division, III Corps, Army of the Potomac, sat on horseback on the morning of May 4, 1863, silhouetted against the rising sun as he watched his soldiers improve their breastworks. A Confederate sniper began to regularly fire at the exposed men, and Whipple became quite annoyed. He started to scribble an order requesting a detachment of Berdan's men to come up and deal with the hazard.

Just as Whipple was finishing his message, the rebel's rifle cracked again, striking him in the stomach, passing directly through his belt buckle and exiting his back between the buttons of his frock coat. Mortally wounded, Whipple died three days later.

A lieutenant of Berdan's command came up and surveyed the surroundings. He quickly spotted the enemy sniper and killed him with a single shot. He moved toward the spot where the rebel had fallen, confirmed that he was dead, and retrieved a cap made of fox skin, the soldier's rifle, $1,600 in Confederate money, and $100 in Union cash.

At Chancellorsville, the two regiments of Berdan's Sharpshooters worked together, attacking the wagon train that trailed the column under the command of Confederate

gunners so easily. Myself and my comrade completely silenced a battery of six guns in less than two hours on one occasion. The battery was then stormed and captured. I heard General Robert E. Lee say he would rather have those 13 sharpshooters than any regiment in the army."

West also recalled his efforts to use deception. "We frequently resorted to various artifices in our warfare," he said. "Sometimes we would climb a tree and pin leaves all over our clothes to keep their colour from betraying us. When two of us would be together and a Yankee sharpshooter would be trying to get a shot at us, one of us would put his hat on a ramrod and poke it up from behind the object that concealed and protected us, and when the Yankee showed his head to shoot at the hat the other one would put a bullet through his head. I have shot them out of trees and seen them fall like 'coons. When we were in grass or grain we would fire and fall over and roll…from the spot whence we fired and the Yankee sharpshooters would fire away at the smoke."

ABOVE: A Confederate sniper's bullet fatally strikes Union General John F. Reynolds in the heat of battle at Gettysburg. (Public Domain)

THE MILITARY SNIPER

ABOVE: This modern photo shows the sniper hide where photographers Timothy O'Sullivan and Alexander Gardner staged a famous death study at Gettysburg. (Creative Commons Judiasim12345 via Wikipedia)

ABOVE: Union General John Sedgwick was shot dead by a Confederate sniper after admonishing a soldier for his reluctance to move about during the Battle of Spotsylvania. (Public Domain)

A contemporary observer described Berdan as "most unscrupulous and totally unfit for command," while some of his own officers complained that he was a dishonest coward. Berdan resigned his commission in the Union army on January 2, 1864, and worked as an engineer and inventor. A recommendation for promotion to temporary major general of volunteers had failed ratification by the US Senate. Berdan died unexpectedly in 1893, aged 68.

The epic Battle of Gettysburg, fought July 1-3, 1863, in Pennsylvania, brought the sniper sharply into focus. In fact, a single shot had consequences that shaped the course of the three days that ended General Lee's second invasion of the North and forced his Army of Northern Virginia to retreat. Early in the fighting, Union cavalrymen under General John Buford held off Confederate infantrymen of General Henry Heth's division who had come to the little town in search of shoes for its ill-clad soldiers.

As the battle grew in intensity and both sides committed larger numbers of troops, General John F. Reynolds reached the field and took command of the Union forces engaged. As he encouraged the men of the 2nd Wisconsin, a regiment of the fabled Iron Brigade, Reynolds shouted, "Forward men forward for God's sake and drive those fellows out of those woods!"

General Thomas J. "Stonewall" Jackson during its flanking march that threw the Union lines into confusion. Even so, one of the sharpshooter regiments managed to trap the 23rd Georgia Infantry in the unfinished cut of a railroad line, killing three and forcing the remaining 296 Georgians to surrender rather than face the withering and accurate fire of massed sharpshooter rifles. "It was a most splendid affair, and the praise of the Sharpshooters was in everybody's mouth," wrote Union Lieutenant George Marden after the battle.

Berdan's Sharpshooters took particular pride in their accomplishments, and one of them wrote to his wife, "Our Sharp Shooters play mischief with them [Confederates] when they come out in daylight." However, their illustrious leader, Hiram Berdan, ended his military career before the Civil War came to a close. He had led Union infantry brigades in the great battles of Chancellorsville and Gettysburg, but many considered his claims of personal heroism and shooting skill to be unbelievable.

ABOVE: This postwar image of the jumble of boulders known as Devil's Den on the Gettysburg battlefield was taken in 1909. (Public Domain)

Determined that his troops take control of Herbst's Woods, Reynolds seemed unconcerned that bullets from Confederate snipers in the surrounding trees whizzed about him. Moments after riding into the fray, Reynolds, astride a majestic black charger, glanced toward the spire of the Lutheran seminary some distance away and serving as a Union observation post. Just then, a bullet struck behind his right ear. He collapsed from his horse.

Private Charles Veil, Reynolds' aide, witnessed the incident, and author Harry Pfanz wrote in *Gettysburg – The First Day*, "Veil vaulted from his horse and ran to Reynolds, who was lying on his left side and had a bruise above his left eye. Veil thought that he was stunned. He grasped the general under the arms; Capts. Robert W. Mitchell and Edward C. Baird joined him. Each took a leg, and they carried the general from the perils of the woods…They did not realize that their general was dead, but they surely knew he was out of the fight…They carried his body on a stretcher to the George House on the Emmitsburg Road. There Veil remembered seeing the general's wound for the first time; he recalled it as a small hole at the base of his skull that did not bleed."

With the death of Reynolds, one of the most capable battlefield commanders in the Union army, General Abner Doubleday and then General Oliver O. Howard were the senior Union officers in the fight for several hours on the first day at Gettysburg. Neither had the command presence or the tactical vision to conduct the battle to the fullest advantage for the Army of the Potomac. Eventually, General Winfield Scott Hancock reached the field and took command, but the loss of Reynolds was a severe blow that shaped the course of the pivotal battle of the Civil War.

After the opposing lines were established and both the Union and Confederate armies concentrated at Gettysburg, horrific fighting ensued. The Confederates occupied a jumble of large boulders and brush known to the local population as Devil's Den, and their sharpshooters proceeded to pick off Union officers that showed themselves on the heights of Little Round Top several hundred yards distant across Plum Run and the "Valley of Death." In the aftermath of the battle, photographers Timothy O'Sullivan and Alexander Gardner reached Gettysburg before the dead were collected for burial. Their wagon trundled over to Devil's Den, where they captured one of the most famous photographs of the war.

The image titled "The Home of A Rebel Sharpshooter, Gettysburg" was probably posed. It depicts the body of a Confederate soldier, killed by a shell fragment, lying behind a wall of stacked stone that he supposedly had built as a sniper hide. However, the rifle shown in the photo does not appear to be one that was regularly used for the purpose of sharpshooting, while the same body is used in other staged scenes from the dismal battlefield.

At the Battle of Spotsylvania on May 9, 1864, General John Sedgwick, in command of the VI Corps of the Army of the Potomac, was personally supervising the deployment of several artillery pieces. Confederate snipers were regularly firing on the artillerymen, and the soldiers around Sedgwick took cover as they heard the reports of the rebel rifles. Sedgwick was not deterred in his task, but an aide to General George G. Meade, commander of the Union army, watched the drama of a sniper's shot unfold.

ABOVE: President Abraham Lincoln peers toward Confederate positions from the parapet at Fort Stevens while he is being pulled back to safety. (Public Domain)

ABOVE: Captain Oliver Wendell Holmes, Jr., is believed to have shouted at President Lincoln to take cover at Fort Stevens. (Public Domain)

Lieutenant Colonel Theodore Lyman wrote a letter of explanation to General Meade relating that Sedgwick had "…noticed a soldier dodging the bullets as they came over. Rising from the grass, he went up to the man, and, laying his hand on his shoulder, said, 'Why, what are you dodging for? They could not hit an elephant at this distance.' As he spoke the last word, he fell shot, through the brain by a ball from a telescopic rifle."

The deadly bullet, probably fired by a Confederate sniper with a Whitworth rifle, had struck General Sedgwick in the left eye, and he died instantly. The distance was estimated at 800 yards (730 metres).

Two months later, President Abraham Lincoln came quite close to a brush with death at the hands of a Confederate sniper.

ABOVE: Staff officers gather around the dying General John Sedgwick after he was shot by a rebel sniper at the Battle of Spotsylvania. (Public Domain)

THE MILITARY SNIPER

ABOVE: A Confederate sharpshooter takes aim toward a distant target in this sketch. (Creative Commons Century Magazine via Wikipedia)

In mid-July 1864, a strong Confederate detachment under General Jubal Early raided in the North, putting the city of Chambersburg, Pennsylvania, to the torch and then threatening Washington, D.C. The defences of the capital city were beefed up, and President Lincoln decided to see the situation for himself. Along with his wife, Mary Todd Lincoln, the president and his entourage travelled to the outskirts of the city to visit Fort Stevens, part of the works that ringed the capital. While it was probable that General Early's snipers could see the unfinished dome of the Capitol building looming in the distance, it is certain that they were capable of hitting targets within range of their Whitworths.

Quite interested in the troop and artillery dispositions, Lincoln climbed to the top of a parapet, his tall, rail-thin frame crowned by a stovepipe hat conspicuously exposed. In a diary entry, the president's secretary John Hay, described the events that ensued on July 11, 1864, and the next day when Lincoln came out a second time. "The President concluded to travel around the defenses… At three o'clock P.M. the President came in bringing the news that the enemy's advance was at Ft. Stevens on the 7th Street road. He was in the Fort when it was first attacked, standing upon the parapet. A soldier roughly ordered him to get down or he would have his head knocked off…The President again made the tour of the fortifications; was again under fire at Ft. Stevens; a man was shot at his side…."

It is likely that the soldier Hay referred to during the July 11 incident was future US Supreme Court Justice Oliver Wendell Holmes. Without nicety or any regard to who the individual atop the parapet was, Holmes roared, "Get down, you damn fool, before you get shot." The president heeded the warning and sat behind the parapet out of sight for a while, but the temptation to look over the field was too great. While distressed staff officers looked on in disbelief, Lincoln repeatedly stood up to acquire a better view. Those two days may well have been the last time a President of the United States was within range of enemy fire during wartime, and it must be stated that the sniper's round made no distinction between military and civilian targets, or those holding high office. Lincoln was probably lucky.

The sniper altered the course of the American Civil War, and in the process the concept of his craft became more ingrained in the tactical thinking of military planners. Meanwhile, improvements in the sniper's equipment proceeded apace. The famed scientist Alfred Nobel and others worked during the latter part of the 19th century to improve the efficiency of the black powder mixture that had been unchanged virtually since the dawn of the firearm nearly four centuries earlier. By the mid-1880s, smokeless gunpowder with enhanced explosive capability had been introduced in rifle cartridges.

At the same time, the proverbial sun was setting on the muzzleloading smoothbore musket. Breechloading rifles, magazine fed and operated by lever action, provided a much faster rate of fire and were cheaper to mass produce than the laborious process of the artisan who turned out the earlier single-shot muzzleloaders. In 1860, for example, Christopher Spencer introduced the lever-action, seven-shot Spencer repeating rifle, the world's first such repeating weapon utilizing a metallic cartridge. The Spencer was fed by a tubular magazine inserted into the butt of the rifle, and a skilled marksman could fire between 14 and 20 rounds per minute. It was an astonishing rate of fire compared to the muzzleloader, and Civil War soldiers began to call the Spencer the rifle that "could be loaded on Sunday and fired all week."

During the great westward settlement of North America, the lever-action .44-calibre Winchester Model 1873 rifle became known as the "Gun that Won the West." In Europe, the armies maintained a preference for single-shot breechloading rifles, including the Martini-Henry, a .45-calibre weapon introduced to the British Army in 1871 and existing in variants with it through the next half century, although it was replaced as standard issue by the bolt-action .303-calibre Lee-Metford in 1888, followed by the iconic Lee-Enfield. In Germany, Mauser developed the Model 1871, which was adopted by most of the armies of the German Empire the following year. The .43-calibre Model 1871 was replaced by the magazine-fed Gewehr 88, and then the ubiquitous 7.92mm (.30-calibre) Gewehr 98, the standard German army bolt-action rifle until 1935.

Each of these types was re-engineered, enhanced and customized for the sniper's employ and helped to assure his lasting role in modern warfare.

ABOVE: The Spencer repeating rifle revolutionized firepower on the Civil War battlefield. (Public Domain)

ABOVE: A Confederate sniper fires at Union soldiers from the upper window of a house. (No restrictions)

www.keymilitary.com

OLD JACK

Had they left his family alone, Old Jack may well have been a spectator only. However, when Union soldiers apparently acted to excess, spurred by the heat of the moment, they drank the bitter dram of vengeance.

John W. "Jack" Hinson was a well-to-do landowner, father of 10 children, and a one-time slaveholder. There are indications that he had freed all his slaves and they had chosen to remain at the plantation, Bubbling Springs, continuing to work for him. He voted with secessionists in several elections leading up to the Civil War, and two sons enlisted in the Confederate army as well. However, Hinson was content and probably hopeful of keeping to himself during the war years. That is, until two of his younger boys, George and Jack, aged 22 and 17, decided to go deer hunting in the forest that surrounded their home in upper west Tennessee one day in the autumn of 1862. The area was then known as the land 'tween the rivers, the Tennessee and Cumberland rivers, actually.

They left that day knowing that the Yankees and the rebels had been at one another in the vicinity. In fact, there had been quite a bit of "bushwhacking" going on as vigilantes and renegade soldiers killed and robbed indiscriminately. Often enough, the victims were soldiers of the blue-clad Union army. George and Jack were soon detained by a Union patrol and accused of bad intent, collaborating with the Confederates, and even spying for the rebels during the fight at nearby Fort Donelson some months earlier.

The brothers were tied to trees and summarily shot, their bodies dragged behind horses through the streets of the town of Dover, Tennessee, and then decapitated by the blade of a Yankee sabre. Afterward, the severed heads were placed into a burlap sack, carried to the gates of Bubbling Springs, and impaled on the posts as a warning to other would-be bushwhackers.

The Hinson family was horrified. When he saw what had happened to his sons, Jack, at the age of 57, chose his side. He vowed retribution and made good on his promise. Jack commissioned a gunsmith to make a purpose-built .50-calibre, percussion muzzleloading Kentucky rifle with a 41-inch hexagonal barrel reminiscent of the famous Whitworth rifle. It weighed 17 pounds and was said to be unadorned with much of anything that would pick up a glint of sunlight, possibly giving away a sniper's position. It was not meant to be fired from the shoulder, and when Old Jack put it to use, he propped it on a tree limb or used an iron tripod.

Soon enough, Old Jack was ready to settle the score. First, he drew a bead on the Yankee lieutenant who had ordered his sons killed and shot him from his saddle. Next, he located the sergeant who had gruesomely placed their heads on the columns and killed him as well.

For the rest of the war, Old Jack eluded attempts to apprehend him, and in the process, he is believed to have killed 100 or more Union soldiers and sailors aboard ships plying the waters of the Tennessee and the Cumberland. His aim was deadly, so it was said, from half a mile distant. He notched his rifle's stock with 36 cuts, and some historians speculate that this was specifically the tally of officers he felled. One thing is sure, Old Jack meted out retribution to the Union army many times over, firing from an unseen post,

ABOVE: Sniper Jack Hinson sought vengeance against the Union army for killing his sons. (Public Domain)

only the crack of that rifle to give him away. But then he was gone like the wisp of acrid smoke that followed each deadly round.

Jack Hinson, who lost seven children to violence or disease during the war, survived. He died in his bed on April 28, 1874, aged about 67. His rifle remains an heirloom owned by a Tennessee family. Whether Old Jack's thirst for vengeance was truly satisfied is unknown.

ABOVE: Months before Old Jack began his one-man war on the Yankees, a major battle was fought at nearby Fort Donelson. (Public Domain)

ABOVE: This aerial view depicts the land 'tween the rivers, the domain of sniper Old Jack Hinson. (Creative Commons terraprints.com via Wikipedia)

THE MILITARY SNIPER

ABOVE: A Confederate sharpshooter takes aim toward a distant target in this sketch. (Creative Commons Century Magazine via Wikipedia)

In mid-July 1864, a strong Confederate detachment under General Jubal Early raided in the North, putting the city of Chambersburg, Pennsylvania, to the torch and then threatening Washington, D.C. The defences of the capital city were beefed up, and President Lincoln decided to see the situation for himself. Along with his wife, Mary Todd Lincoln, the president and his entourage travelled to the outskirts of the city to visit Fort Stevens, part of the works that ringed the capital. While it was probable that General Early's snipers could see the unfinished dome of the Capitol building looming in the distance, it is certain that they were capable of hitting targets within range of their Whitworths.

Quite interested in the troop and artillery dispositions, Lincoln climbed to the top of a parapet, his tall, rail-thin frame crowned by a stovepipe hat conspicuously exposed. In a diary entry, the president's secretary John Hay, described the events that ensued on July 11, 1864, and the next day when Lincoln came out a second time. "The President concluded to travel around the defenses… At three o'clock P.M. the President came in bringing the news that the enemy's advance was at Ft. Stevens on the 7th Street road. He was in the Fort when it was first attacked, standing upon the parapet. A soldier roughly ordered him to get down or he would have his head knocked off…The President again made the tour of the fortifications; was again under fire at Ft. Stevens; a man was shot at his side…."

It is likely that the soldier Hay referred to during the July 11 incident was future US Supreme Court Justice Oliver Wendell Holmes. Without nicety or any regard to who the individual atop the parapet was, Holmes roared, "Get down, you damn fool, before you get shot." The president heeded the warning and sat behind the parapet out of sight for a while, but the temptation to look over the field was too great. While distressed staff officers looked on in disbelief, Lincoln repeatedly stood up to acquire a better view. Those two days may well have been the last time a President of the United States was within range of enemy fire during wartime, and it must be stated that the sniper's round made no distinction between military and civilian targets, or those holding high office. Lincoln was probably lucky.

The sniper altered the course of the American Civil War, and in the process the concept of his craft became more ingrained in the tactical thinking of military planners. Meanwhile, improvements in the sniper's equipment proceeded apace. The famed scientist Alfred Nobel and others worked during the latter part of the 19th century to improve the efficiency of the black powder mixture that had been unchanged virtually since the dawn of the firearm nearly four centuries earlier. By the mid-1880s, smokeless gunpowder with enhanced explosive capability had been introduced in rifle cartridges.

At the same time, the proverbial sun was setting on the muzzleloading smoothbore musket. Breechloading rifles, magazine fed and operated by lever action, provided a much faster rate of fire and were cheaper to mass produce than the laborious process of the artisan who turned out the earlier single-shot muzzleloaders. In 1860, for example, Christopher Spencer introduced the lever-action, seven-shot Spencer repeating rifle, the world's first such repeating weapon utilizing a metallic cartridge. The Spencer was fed by a tubular magazine inserted into the butt of the rifle, and a skilled marksman could fire between 14 and 20 rounds per minute. It was an astonishing rate of fire compared to the muzzleloader, and Civil War soldiers began to call the Spencer the rifle that "could be loaded on Sunday and fired all week."

During the great westward settlement of North America, the lever-action .44-calibre Winchester Model 1873 rifle became known as the "Gun that Won the West." In Europe, the armies maintained a preference for single-shot breechloading rifles, including the Martini-Henry, a .45-calibre weapon introduced to the British Army in 1871 and existing in variants with it through the next half century, although it was replaced as standard issue by the bolt-action .303-calibre Lee-Metford in 1888, followed by the iconic Lee-Enfield. In Germany, Mauser developed the Model 1871, which was adopted by most of the armies of the German Empire the following year. The .43-calibre Model 1871 was replaced by the magazine-fed Gewehr 88, and then the ubiquitous 7.92mm (.30-calibre) Gewehr 98, the standard German army bolt-action rifle until 1935.

Each of these types was re-engineered, enhanced and customized for the sniper's employ and helped to assure his lasting role in modern warfare.

ABOVE: The Spencer repeating rifle revolutionized firepower on the Civil War battlefield. (Public Domain)

ABOVE: A Confederate sniper fires at Union soldiers from the upper window of a house. (No restrictions)

OLD JACK

Had they left his family alone, Old Jack may well have been a spectator only. However, when Union soldiers apparently acted to excess, spurred by the heat of the moment, they drank the bitter dram of vengeance.

John W. "Jack" Hinson was a well-to-do landowner, father of 10 children, and a one-time slaveholder. There are indications that he had freed all his slaves and they had chosen to remain at the plantation, Bubbling Springs, continuing to work for him. He voted with secessionists in several elections leading up to the Civil War, and two sons enlisted in the Confederate army as well. However, Hinson was content and probably hopeful of keeping to himself during the war years. That is, until two of his younger boys, George and Jack, aged 22 and 17, decided to go deer hunting in the forest that surrounded their home in upper west Tennessee one day in the autumn of 1862. The area was then known as the land 'tween the rivers, the Tennessee and Cumberland rivers, actually.

They left that day knowing that the Yankees and the rebels had been at one another in the vicinity. In fact, there had been quite a bit of "bushwhacking" going on as vigilantes and renegade soldiers killed and robbed indiscriminately. Often enough, the victims were soldiers of the blue-clad Union army. George and Jack were soon detained by a Union patrol and accused of bad intent, collaborating with the Confederates, and even spying for the rebels during the fight at nearby Fort Donelson some months earlier.

The brothers were tied to trees and summarily shot, their bodies dragged behind horses through the streets of the town of Dover, Tennessee, and then decapitated by the blade of a Yankee sabre. Afterward, the severed heads were placed into a burlap sack, carried to the gates of Bubbling Springs, and impaled on the posts as a warning to other would-be bushwhackers.

The Hinson family was horrified. When he saw what had happened to his sons, Jack, at the age of 57, chose his side. He vowed retribution and made good on his promise. Jack commissioned a gunsmith to make a purpose-built .50-calibre, percussion muzzleloading Kentucky rifle with a 41-inch hexagonal barrel reminiscent of the famous Whitworth rifle. It weighed 17 pounds and was said to be unadorned with much of anything that would pick up a glint of sunlight, possibly giving away a sniper's position. It was not meant to be fired from the shoulder, and when Old Jack put it to use, he propped it on a tree limb or used an iron tripod.

Soon enough, Old Jack was ready to settle the score. First, he drew a bead on the Yankee lieutenant who had ordered his sons killed and shot him from his saddle. Next, he located the sergeant who had gruesomely placed their heads on the columns and killed him as well.

For the rest of the war, Old Jack eluded attempts to apprehend him, and in the process, he is believed to have killed 100 or more Union soldiers and sailors aboard ships plying the waters of the Tennessee and the Cumberland. His aim was deadly, so it was said, from half a mile distant. He notched his rifle's stock with 36 cuts, and some historians speculate that this was specifically the tally of officers he felled. One thing is sure, Old Jack meted out retribution to the Union army many times over, firing from an unseen post, only the crack of that rifle to give him away. But then he was gone like the wisp of acrid smoke that followed each deadly round.

Jack Hinson, who lost seven children to violence or disease during the war, survived. He died in his bed on April 28, 1874, aged about 67. His rifle remains an heirloom owned by a Tennessee family. Whether Old Jack's thirst for vengeance was truly satisfied is unknown.

ABOVE: Sniper Jack Hinson sought vengeance against the Union army for killing his sons. (Public Domain)

ABOVE: Months before Old Jack began his one-man war on the Yankees, a major battle was fought at nearby Fort Donelson. (Public Domain)

ABOVE: This aerial view depicts the land 'tween the rivers, the domain of sniper Old Jack Hinson. (Creative Commons terraprints.com via Wikipedia)

THE BOER WARS

When untested British soldiers arrived in South Africa during the Second Boer War, they were quickly advised to stay some distance away from officers and from white rocks. Their adversaries, the Boers, were known for their prowess with the magazine-fed Mauser rifle, and their favourite targets were officers, often conspicuous with their badges of rank and shiny medals, while large, white rocks offered excellent background for aiming a rifle at long distance against a silhouetted target.

ABOVE: Seconds before a Boer sniper's bullet ended his life, Major General Sir George Colley gestures during the Battle of Majuba Hill. (Public Domain)

The Boers, farming settlers primarily of Dutch and German descent who had come to South Africa years earlier, inevitably came into contact with the British, who had gained control of neighbouring territory during the Napoleonic Wars. While the Boers had established the Transvaal and the Orange Free State, the British occupied the southern region and the great port of Cape Town along with the colony of Natal in the east.

The two sides had fought a brief war, lasting only three months, in 1880-1881. The result had been an embarrassing rebuff for Britain. During the catastrophic British defeat at the Battle of Majuba Hill, the Boers killed 92 British soldiers, wounded 134, and captured 59 for the loss of only one man dead and five wounded. Among those killed was the British commanding officer, Major General Sir George Pomeroy Colley. As his line collapsed under the weight of a Boer frontal assault, Colley attempted to rally his men and conduct a fighting withdrawal, but he was shot through the head by a distant Boer sniper just as he turned to issue orders.

For two decades resentment and animosity smouldered, and then the discovery of gold in the Transvaal sparked the Second Boer War of 1899-1902. The overwhelming strength of the British army eventually prevailed, and Boer territory was consolidated into the Empire.

However, the result did not come about with ease. The Boers proved themselves in both conflicts to be excellent marksmen, and their skill with the rifle was grudgingly respected in British military circles. British observers noted the disparity of rifle skills and sometimes explained it as a phenomenon that had developed through the years with young Boer men becoming acquainted with firearms as a way of life while many British army recruits had never held a weapon until they entered the service.

Boer fighters utilized terrain, concealment, and knowledge of their surroundings to great advantage, and one British officer observed that his troops had come under rifle fire from the enemy at distances as great as 2,000 yards (1,829 metres). "War is not what it was when armies manoeuvred in sight of each other," he related, "and when 600 yards was the limit of artillery fire… That was old time fighting, and some sport about it too. Now Bill is killed at 2,400 yards, and Bill's pal hasn't an idea where the shot was fired. That is modern warfare."

Another officer groused with frustration, "Boers had only to keep at 2,000 yards from our cavalry in the hills and could shoot them down with impunity."

Truly, the Boers had lived their lives hunting in the veldt to supplement their crops with meat for the dinner table. They grew long beards to obscure their faces, while their clothing easily blended into the surrounding scrub land, and slouch hats were pulled low over their eyes as they used long-range sniping to slow advancing British

ABOVE: Boer fighters pose with their weapons and equipment prior to an operation. Often acting as snipers, they continually harassed British troops. (Public Domain)

ABOVE: British soldiers keep their heads down in a trench as smoke rises from the rifles of Boer snipers on distant high ground. (Public Domain)

THE BOER WARS

ABOVE: A British soldier risks drawing Boer sniper fire as he scans the horizon from a trench. (Public Domain)

ABOVE: Resolute Boer fighters pose for a photo somewhere in the Transvaal during the Second Boer War. (Creative Commons wellcomeimages via Wikipedia)

troop and supply columns. Those soldiers who failed to heed the warnings of the veterans suffered grievously.

One soldier wrote, "At first officers and men were very stupid about taking cover. I have seen men halted on a rise in full view of the enemy when a few paces forward or backward would have placed them in shelter, the reason being that to have taken this step would have broken the dressing of the line."

Such sentiments gave way soon enough to measures meant to counter the Boer sniper's skill set. In January 1900, the Lovat Scouts were formed as a Scottish Highland yeomanry regiment of the British army. Raised by Simon Fraser, 14th Lord Lovat, these men were crack shots, recruited from the gamekeepers and wardens of the Scottish Highlands. They were the first to wear the camouflage ghillie suit for concealment, and during the Great War two decades later became the first designated sniper unit of the British armed forces.

The Lovat Scouts engaged not only in sometimes turning the tables on the Boers with accurate sniper fire, but also in gathering intelligence and executing reconnaissance missions across enemy lines. After the initial call for volunteers, second and third contingents were raised and sent to South Africa before hostilities ceased. Famed British marksman Hesketh-Prichard once remarked of the Lovat Scouts, "Keener men never lived…If they reported a thing, the thing was as they reported it."

Earning a tremendous reputation, the Lovat Scouts were sometimes described as a unit that was half wolf and half rabbit. General Archibald Hunter, a senior army field commander during the Boer War, commented, "As scouts, spies, guides, on foot or on pony, as individual marksmen or as a collective body in the fighting line, they are a splendid band of Scotsmen, which is the highest compliment I can pay them."

The conduct of the Second Boer influenced the British development of sniper tactics that were employed during World War I. In the meantime, though, there were lessons learned. During one lengthy campaign, the British pursued Boer guerrillas under the command of General Christiaan de Wet and found the irregulars to be worthy opponents. "On each side of the line there were ditches," read one report of an encounter, "and at dawn on the seventh day of the investment, it was found that these had been occupied by snipers during the night, and that it was impossible to water the animals…About noon several companies of Scots and Welsh Fusiliers advanced from different directions in very extended order upon the ditches. Captain Baillie's company of the former regiment first attracted the fire of the burghers. Wounded twice the brave officer staggered on until a third bullet struck him dead. Six of his men were found lying beside him."

A Canadian contingent encountered similar resistance. "There was no chance to advance in the regular way without being shot down by the Dutch in position high above," a soldier later remarked. "It was advance, but not standing up, so the men grovelled along on their bellies, with the wicked Mausers snapping in front."

Indeed, it was hazardous for any soldier to venture into the open, even for a moment at times. While the 2nd Tower Hamlets Rifle Volunteers gained praise for their courage and at least 20 of their number were praised for their marksmanship, during the summer months of 1900, the regiment lost four of its number to Boer snipers while engaged in watering and grazing their horses.

The sniper, picking and choosing when to strike, was an ever-present threat, whether in the midst of a pitched battle or the momentary quiet at the edge of a stream or pasture.

ABOVE: British riflemen of the 17th Lancers fight at Modderfontein as they are assailed by Boer fighters. (Public Domain)

THE MILITARY SNIPER

WORLD WAR I

BELOW: Canadian soldiers advance into No Man's Land, the killing ground between opposing trench lines on the Western Front during World War I. (Public Domain)

The young soldier was barely more than a teenager, yet he was a veteran of the blood and carnage of the Western Front, the crucible of trench warfare that characterized World War I as the opposing armies of the Allies and the Central Powers confronted one another along a labyrinth of fetid earthworks that stretched from the North Sea to the Swiss frontier.

Paul Bäumer had watched each of his classmates die, and on his own fateful day, he spied a butterfly – something beautiful – amid the destruction of No-Man's Land. The creature was just out of reach, and so he stretched to touch it. In an instant, the French sniper's rifle cracked, and the boy from a small, charming German village crumpled to the ground – dead.

Such drama surely played out many times across the killing fields of World War I, and the victims were the flower of youth from both sides. On this particular day, the German High Command observed nothing of great importance taking place and issued a short status communiqué that read: "All Quiet on the Western Front."

Of course, this is the plotline of a well-known literary classic by author Erich Maria Remarque, based on his own experience during the Great War. Although fictionalized, it is representative of the soldier's experience in combat. In this case, art is reflective of life – and death. And it represents the cold, calculating craft of the sniper as well. Amid the war of attrition and the unprecedented loss of human life that occurred during the war of 1914-1918, the soldier endured the threat of death from artillery shells, machine-gun fire, rifle bullets, and poison gas. Each of these haunted him daily, and the perhaps the spectre of the sniper gripped his psyche most thoroughly.

The sniper brought swift death, and he was silent and stealthy until the moment of the trigger pull.

Although the sniper depicted in the above sequence is French, the German army had the upper hand in the craft early in the Great War. The German soldier was typically a fine marksman in his own right, but the best of them were those who had served as gamekeepers on the estates of the wealthy and hunted in the deep forests of central Europe prior to the outbreak of war.

Therefore, skilled marksmen were detailed down to the company level. German infantry battalions often contained sniper sections consisting of as many as 24 soldiers. The primary tool of their craft was the Scharfschützen Gewehr 98, or sharpshooter gun 98, a 7.92mm (.31 calibre) bolt action Mauser rifle.

Germany was long recognized as one of the world's great producers of precision optics, and factory-fitted telescopic sights of three power (3X) or better were supplied as well. During the early days of the war, the British were quite deficient in their optics, and an acute shortage resulted in a national appeal that rendered thousands of pairs of binoculars. The Germans were also well aware

ABOVE: A German sniper used this abandoned building as his hide during fighting on the Western Front. (No Restrictions via Wikipedia)

WORLD WAR I

ABOVE: British soldiers use a decoy head of papier maché to goad German snipers into revealing their positions. (Public Domain)

of their surroundings. While the British constructed their trenches with lines that were more or less straight, the Germans used irregular edges, swabbed paint of different colours onto their sandbags to break up the landscape, and piled anything they could find that might make themselves less conspicuous to enemy snipers, old sheet metal, branches, broken glass, or discarded bricks.

Soon after the war began, the German sniper developed a reputation for deadly accuracy, and on February 26, 1915, an American serving with troops of the British Commonwealth wrote to his father of a harrowing brush with death at the hands of a skilled enemy sniper. Alan Seeger explained, "I was shot a few days ago coming in from sentinel duty. I exposed myself for about two seconds at a point where the communication ditch is not deep enough. One of the snipers who keep cracking away with their Mausers at any one who shows his head came within an ace of getting me. The ball just grazed my arm, tore the sleeve of my capote and raised a lump on the biceps which is still sore, but the skin was not broken and the wound was not serious enough to make me leave the ranks. The Germans are marvellous. You hear their rifles only a few hundred metres off, you feel them about you all the time, and yet you can never see them. Only last night when the moon set behind the crest, it silhouetted the heads of two sentinels in their big trench on top."

Another American, Herbert McBride, enlisted in the Canadian army and amassed more than 100 sniper kills on the battlefield. He observed the German sniper at work and respected the man and his Mauser, which McBride said often struck at a relatively short distance of 200 yards (182 metres) but was capable of much longer effective range. McBride recalled, "At short ranges, due to the high velocity, it [the German bullet] does have an explosive effect and, not only the effect but, when it strikes, it sounds like an explosion…all of a sudden, you hear a 'whop' and the man alongside goes down.

If it is daylight and you are looking that way, you may see a little tuft sticking out from his clothes. Wherever the bullet comes out it carries a little of the clothing…the sound of a bullet hitting a man can never be mistaken for anything else…the effect of the bullet, at short range, also suggests the idea of an explosion, especially if a large bone be struck. I remember one instance where one of our men was struck in the knee and the bullet almost amputated the leg. He died before he could be taken to the dressing station."

When the war was over, McBride wrote a memoir of his time in the trenches titled *A Rifleman Went to War*. His observations and practical advice remained relevant for more than half a century and were applied by US Marine sniper instructors into the Vietnam War era.

British fortunes improved largely through the efforts of one man, a well-known individual prior to the Great War. Major Hesketh Vernon Hesketh-Prichard had been a champion cricketeer, big game hunter, explorer and author. He sought a commission in the Black Watch but was turned away because of his age – 37. Later, he secured a post as an assistant press officer with the War Office and shipped across the Channel to France. He was astonished to learn that German snipers were so effective that it was common for British regiments to lose an average of five men a day. One astounding tally recorded the loss of 18 men in a single day. To make matters worse, the Germans were rarely located, slipping away to a new hide without an opportunity to return fire.

Hesketh-Prichard introduced innovations such as the use of dummy heads made of papier maché to draw enemy fire and safeguards for observers who had been vulnerable to sniper shots through their vision loopholes. He investigated the

ABOVE: In this posed image German sniper teams ply their craft on the Western Front. (Creative Commons Mike Ax via Wikipedia)

ABOVE: The fatigue of war is evident in the faces of these two German snipers of the Great War. (Public Domain)

THE MILITARY SNIPER

ABOVE: German sniper Georg Herrenreiter is shown wearing the Iron Cross 2nd Class. The sniper claimed 121 confirmed kills. He died near Arras, France, in January 1916. (Public Domain)

ABOVE: This dummy soldier's head was used as a sniper decoy and survived the war. (Creative Commons Courtesy of York Museums Trust via Wikipedia)

ABOVE: Major Hesketh Hesketh-Prichard, in his late 30s during the Great War, is shown in uniform. (Creative Commons Eric Parker via Wikipedia)

ABOVE: Major Hesketh Hesketh-Prichard was the father of British sniper craft in World War I. (Public Domain)

strength of German armour plate and found it substantially stronger than that of the British and then worked to correct the situation. At first, his own military establishment was reluctant to embrace change, despite the disheartening number of casualties the German snipers were inflicting.

However, in August 1915 he was allowed to organize a sniper training school. By the end of the year, he was quite busy with many unit commanders requesting his services. He received a captain's commission in the British army and was mentioned in despatches in January 1916. Then, in August of that year he formalised the First Army Sniping, Observation and Scouting School near the town of Bethune, France. He taught a 17-day course that included camouflage, map reading, care and maintenance of the rifle, and accurate sighting and firing. Promoted to major in November, he successfully witnessed the formation of sniper battalions of 16 trained riflemen and two officers in the British army. In 1920, Hesketh-Prichard wrote an account of his wartime experiences titled *Sniping in France*.

The standard-issue British rifle of the period was the 7.7mm (.303-calibre) Short Magazine Lee-Enfield, while some snipers opted for the American-made Rifle No. 3 Mk I, a longer weapon that was commonly referred to as the P14. When the United States entered the war in April 1917, the primary infantry weapon was the 7.62mm (.30-06 calibre) Springfield Model 1903, while Canadian snipers often employed the 7.7mm (.303-calibre) Ross rifle, manufactured in their own country.

Hesketh-Prichard taught his would-be sniper charges to work in teams, sniper and observer, and to switch roles from time to time as fatigue would obviously affect the shooter's performance or the observer's visual acuity after surveying enemy trenches through magnification lenses. At times, both sides utilized viewing periscopes that protruded above the edge of a trench but allowed the observer to remain concealed below the enemy's field of vision. At times, sniper teams constructed elaborate nests reinforced with steel plates that included firing loopholes or even disguising themselves as trees or shrubs. The Lovat Scouts introduced the camouflaged ghillie suit, which covered a man head to toe.

Among other pioneers of British army sniper tactics was Major Frederick Maurice Crum, who served with the King's Royal Rifles and in May 1916 established a brigade-level sniper school at Acq. Crum wrote a treatise titled *Scouts and Snipers in the Trenches* during this period and recommended that 16 to 24 snipers be detailed to each infantry battalion in the army.

The disparity in sniping proficiency rapidly closed, and counter-sniper duels became more common. The sound of the single report often signalled an unexpected death. Sergeant Sandy MacDonald of the 5th Battalion, Seaforths, was a gamekeeper in civilian life and was said to be accurate up to 1,000 yards (914 metres). He was credited with 97 confirmed kills before he was lost in action at Beaumont Hamel in 1917.

Private Thomas Barratt of the 7th Battalion, South Staffordshire Regiment, was the only known sniper of the Great War to receive the Victoria Cross. He was presented the medal posthumously and died in action at Ypres, Belgium, on July 27, 1917. His citation, published in the London Gazette, read: "For most conspicuous bravery when as a scout to a patrol he worked his way towards the enemy's line with the greatest gallantry and determination in spite of continuous fire from hostile snipers at close range. These snipers he stalked and killed. later his patrol was similarly held up, and again he disposed of the snipers.

"When during the subsequent withdrawal of the patrol it was observed that a party of the enemy were endeavouring to outflank them, Private Barratt at once volunteered to cover the retirement, and this he succeeded in accomplishing. His accurate shooting caused many casualties to the enemy, and prevented their advance.

"Throughout the enterprise he was under heavy machine-gun and rifle fire, and his splendid example of coolness and daring was beyond all praise. After safely regaining our lines, this very gallant soldier was killed by a shell."

The top-scoring Allied sniper of World War I was Canadian Corporal Francis

WORLD WAR I

ABOVE: A British soldier of the Cheshire Regiment peers warily toward the edge of a trench on the Somme front, 1916. (Public Domain)

ABOVE: German sniper and author Ernst Junger posed for this portrait in uniform in 1920. (Public Domain)

Pegahmagabow, a Native American of the Ojibwe tribe, who is believed to have scored 378 kills. Another prolific sniper was Canadian Lance Corporal Henry Norwest. Before he was killed by a German sniper in August 1918, Norwest recorded 115 confirmed kills. However, his career very nearly did not materialize.

Norwest joined the army in January 1915 under his real name, Henry Louie, but was discharged for misconduct only three months later. Undeterred, he joined the army a second time using the surname of Norwest and received high praise for his courage during the capture of Vimy Ridge displaying "great bravery, skill and initiative in sniping the enemy after the capture of the Peak… By his activity he saved a great number of our men's lives."

One fellow soldier of the 50th Infantry Battalion was awed by Norwest's steely nerves and willingness to go in harm's way. He wrote, "Our famous sniper no doubt understood better than most of us the cost of life and the price of death. Henry Norwest carried out his terrible duty superbly because he believed his special skill gave him no choice but to fulfil his indispensable mission. Our 50th sniper went about his work with passionate dedication and showed complete detachment from everything while he was in the line… Yet when we had a rare opportunity to see our comrade at close quarters, we found him pleasant and kindly, quite naturally one of us, and always an inspiration."

Ernst Junger of the 73rd Hanoverian Fusiliers was one of only 13 infantry officers of the German army in World War I to receive the prestigious Pour le Mérite, popularly known as the Blue Max. During the years between the world wars, he became a noted author and wrote an account of his experiences in the Great War titled Copse 125.

Accompanied by his spotter, identified only as "H.," Junger stealthily slithered into No Man's Land. He recalled, "Suddenly a sound rang out – a sound foreign to this noontide scene, an ominous clicking as of a helmet or a bayonet striking the side of a trench. At the same moment I felt a hand grip my leg and heard a low-breathed whistle behind me. It was H., for he had passed those hours in the same alert attention as I.

"I pushed back with my foot to warn him, and at the same moment a greenish-yellow shadow flitted across the exposed part of the trench," Junger continued. "It was a tall figure in clay-coloured uniform, with a flat helmet set well down over his forehead and both hands grasping his rifle, which was slung from his neck by a strap. It must have been the relief as he came from the rear; and now it could only be a matter of seconds till the man he relieved passed across the same spot. I sighted my rifle on it sharply.

"A murmuring of voices arose from behind the screen of grass, broken now and again by suppressed laughter or a soft clanking. then a tiny puff of smoke ascended – the moment had come when the returning post lit a pipe or cigarette for the way back. And in fact, he appeared a moment later, first his helmet only, next his whole figure. His luck was against him, for just as he came in line of aim, he turned round and took his cigarette from his mouth – probably to add a word that occurred to him during the few steps he had come. It was his last, for at that moment the iron chain between shoulder, hand and butt was drawn tight and the patch pocket on the left side of his tunic was taken as clearly on the foresight as though it were on the very muzzle of the rifle. Thus, the shot took the words from his mouth. I saw him fall, and having seen many fall before this, I knew he would never get up again. He fell

BELOW: Australian soldiers charge Turkish trenches during the terrible ordeal at Gallipoli. (Public Domain)

ABOVE: Canadian Lance Corporal Henry Norwest was a prolific sniper on the Western Front. (Public Domain)

ABOVE: Australian sniper Billy Sing dueled his Turkish counterpart Abdul the Terrible at Gallipoli. (Public Domain)

first against the side of the trench and then collapsed into a heap that obeyed the force of life no longer but only the force of gravity."

The ill-fated 1915 expedition to the Gallipoli Peninsula was the brainchild of Winston Churchill, the First Lord of the Admiralty. Churchill envisioned a grand landing of British, Australian, New Zealand, and French soldiers on the shores of Ottoman Turkey coupled with a naval offensive that would wrest control of the Bosporus and the Dardanelles, threaten Constantinople, the Ottoman capital, and open a route of supply into the Black Sea to assist the allied Russians, who were then hard pressed. The operation began that spring, and before the fiasco was over in January 1916, the combined Allied forces had lost 250,000 casualties, including 46,000 killed, to the tenacious Turks.

During the months-long standoff, the Turks proved every bit as adept at sniper warfare as their German allies, and some British regiments suffered losses as high as 20 men in a single day. One of the artillery officers who observed the tactics of the Turkish riflemen was Colonel A.C. Ferguson.

He remembered, "After we had been ashore quite a long time and were well dug-in at 'Pifferpore,' we always had at least one casualty per night which always occurred in the same place, just opposite our mess. One night at dusk just after our Doctor had been talking about it, I noticed something white beside the road, just where the casualties occurred. I sent a man to see what it was and he came back with a piece of white cloth. That night there were no casualties at that spot, but the next night there was a piece of white paper there. I had this taken away, again no casualties. After that it was the Mess Orderly's job to look out for and clear away marks from there every evening at dusk and casualties ceased.

"The modus operandi apparently was, the sniper laid his rifle on or a little to one side of the mark. When he saw it obscured, he pulled the trigger, if the target was going one way he missed, if the other, he hit. There was so much rifle fire going on all round, he was not likely to be spotted from his firing position within our lines."

The Turks were proficient, however, and Ian Idriess, a well-known author who served with the Australian 5th Light Horse Regiment, wrote in his diary of the untimely death of one unfortunate soldier. "He was a little infantry lad, quite a boy, with snow hair that looked comical above his clean singlet. I was going for water. He stepped out of a dugout and walked down the path ahead whistling. I was puffing the old pipe, while carrying a dozen water bottles. Just as we were crossing Shrapnel Gully he suddenly flung up his water bottles, wheeled around, and stared for one startled second, even as he crumpled to my feet. In seconds his hair was scarlet, his clean white singlet all crimson."

Turkish Lieutenant Mehmed Fasih never forgot the spectacle of a sniper victim's corpse he encountered. "The top of his skull and brain are gone. Inside of head, completely empty. Part of spinal cord visible. Blue veins dangle. Roots of eyeballs exposed…The sight boggles the mind."

Just as on the Western Front, death came swiftly when the sniper was about. And one of the most prolific of the Great War was

ABOVE: Henry Norwest's rifle is on display at the Military Museums in Calgary, Alberta, Canada. (Creative Commons Rkonigs via Wikipedia)

WORLD WAR I

BELOW: Australian and New Zealand troops come ashore at Gallipoli in the spring of 1915. (Public Domain)

Billy Sing, another trooper of the Australian 5th Light Horse. Sometimes Idriess served as a spotter for Sing, who ended the war with 150 confirmed kills and an actual toll that was probably well over 200. He was known to have taken down nine Turkish soldiers in a single day. Sing was a master at counter-sniper tactics and had been a top tier kangaroo hunter and rifle club member at home in Queensland.

Sing became well known in the newspapers, and correspondent Brian Tate of the Brisbane Courier Mail wrote of an unnerving encounter. He related that Sing's success would provoke an inevitable response from the Turks, and one morning in August the Australian's confidence was shaken when Billy and his spotter, Trooper Tom Sheehan, were momentarily in the sights of a worthy adversary.

"A quick hazy puff of vapour from a weapon discharge, the unguarded tell-tale movement of an arm or body," wrote Tate. "A Turkish marksman with similar intent seized upon a sudden and inadvertent movement in the Australian sniping team and fired on them. His shot passed through Sheehan's telescope, end to end, wounding the Australian in both hands, before entering his mouth and coming out his left cheek. The almost-spent bullet travelled on, completing its pernicious run by striking Sing in the right shoulder…It was another week before Billy Sing was physically and psychologically able to…face the newly respected Turkish snipers once more."

When Sing reappeared, the Turks were more determined than before to end his career. From the diaries taken off their dead and the stories told by Turkish prisoners, it became known that the Turks had summoned their finest sniper to do the job. The ensuing duel with the dead-eyed enemy nicknamed Abdul the Terrible is quite literally the stuff of legend. According to Tate, each time Abdul the Terrible received word of a victim of Sing, he went to the scene and measured the angles of bullet trajectory. Each time the lines pointed to a position on Harris Ridge at Chatham's Post.

Accordingly, a pattern emerged, and Abdul the Terrible was certain that he had located the favoured hide of the deadly Australian. Although numerous targets passed through his sights, Abdul declined

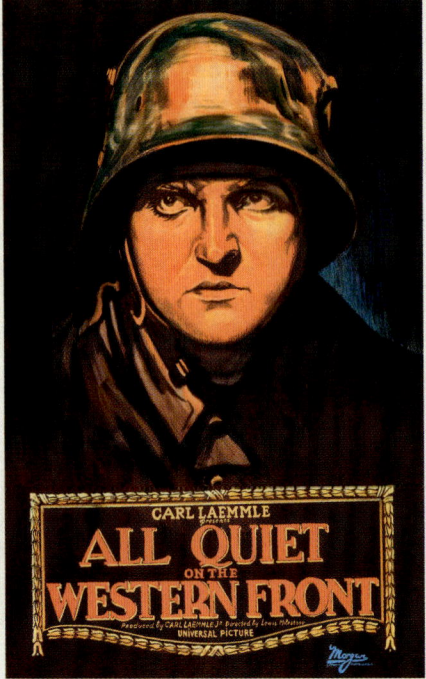

ABOVE: This poster advertises the 1930 film sensation All Quiet on the Western Front. (Public Domain)

ABOVE: Following his capture in 1917, a Turkish sniper sits dejectedly while waiting for disposition. (Public Domain)

THE MILITARY SNIPER

ABOVE: Turkish soldiers shelter in a trench along the front line at Gallipoli in 1915. (Public Domain)

ABOVE: Allied soldiers guard a captured Turkish sniper who is wearing heavy camouflage. (Public Domain)

soldiers and capturing 132 with some assistance from others who had accompanied him on a mission to silence troublesome machine-gun positions during the Meuse-Argonne offensive. York became a national hero in the United States and received the Medal of Honor for his exploits. His story was later made into a 1941 feature film with actor Gary Cooper in the title role.

History portrays the sniper as a willing agent of his army, a cold and steady angel of unerring death. However, there are times when one pauses, and sniper R.A. Chell recalled his first experience on sniper duty in the autumn of 1915.

"After about 15 minutes quiet watching – with my rifle in ready position – I saw a capless bald head come up behind the plate. The day was bright and clear and I hadn't the slightest difficulty in taking a most deliberate aim at the very centre of that bright and shiny plate – but somehow I couldn't press the trigger: to shoot such a 'sitter' so deliberately in cold blood required more real courage than I possessed. After a good look round he went down and I argued with myself about my duty. My bald-headed opponent had been given a very sporting chance and if he were fool enough to come up again I must shoot him unflinchingly. I considered it my duty to be absolutely ready for that contingency.

"After about two minutes," Chell concluded, "he came up again with added boldness and I did my duty. I had been a marksman before the war and so had no doubt about the instantaneousness of that man's death. I felt funny for days and the shooting of another German at 'stand-to' the next morning did nothing to remove those horrid feelings I had."

After examining his role, his duty, and his condition, the sniper may hesitate at times, perhaps even turn away from a sure shot. But often enough, he kills.

By the end of World War I in 1918, the sniper had confirmed his menacing role on the field of battle.

to fire. He waited for Billy Sing, and one morning Abdul's quarry arrived in company with his spotter.

"As Sing settled himself in," wrote Tate, "the observer began his day's first semi-alert yawning frontal sweep with his telescope. Almost immediately the man's movement abruptly ceased and he whispered to his sniper that he already had a target. Sing took the telescope and, glancing towards a point indicated by his spotter, he stared ahead – in the face and rifle-muzzle of Abdul the Terrible. Carefully taking up his rifle, Sing made a final check that nothing would betray their position; then gently eased the loophole cover back and cautiously pushed the weapon forward. The Turk also saw Sing and began his own firing sequence. As he settled the rifle into his shoulder, Abdul drew in a breath and steadily sighted it on Sing. At that moment, a bullet struck the Turk between the eyes."

After the epic confrontation on the sun-drenched hills of Gallipoli, Billy Sing was evacuated with the rest of the Allied forces and ordered to the Western Front, where he was conspicuous in clearing an area called the Polygon Woods of German snipers and received the Belgian Croix de Guerre for his extraordinary effort. After the war, he returned to his native Australia, working unsuccessfully as a sheep farmer and gold miner. The hero fell into obscurity and died of a ruptured aorta in a boarding house in Brisbane on May 19, 1943, at the age of 57. At the time of his death, his only possessions were a small hut on a mining claim that was worth about £20 and five shillings that were found in his room.

American Sergeant Alvin C. York emerged from World War I as a hero of epic proportion. Born in rural Tennessee, York had grown up on a farm and became a dead shot with a rifle. On October 8, 1918, he was credited with killing at least 25 German

ABOVE: An Australian soldier uses a periscope to observe enemy lines and has his rifle attached to the apparatus. (Public Domain)

FRANCIS PEGAHMAGABOW

A Native American of the Caribou Clan, Ojibwe tribe, Francis Pegahmagabow was a legendary hero of World War I, not only among his people, but all of Canada and the Allied nations. He was a mystic shaman, heroic message runner, and above all a deadly sniper wielding the Canadian-made Ross rifle.

By the time the Great War ended, Pegahmagabow had become one his country's most highly decorated war veterans, and the tales of his courage brought the magnitude of his service sharply into focus as the dealer of death to 378 German soldiers in confirmed kills, while at least another 300 are believed to have fallen under his deadly aim.

Born on March 9, 1891, on the Shawanaga First Nation reserve at Parry Sound, Ontario, on the eastern shore of Georgian Bay, Francis Pegahmagabow was the son of Michael Pegahmagabow, who soon left the reserve and reportedly died a short time after Francis came into the world. Francis's mother, Mary Contin, left the reserve as well and may have also died soon afterward. The boy was abandoned, but another Ojibwe, Noah Nebimanyquod, stepped in to raise Francis, whose native name was "The Wind That Blows Off." Noah taught Francis the skills of silently stalking game and honing marksmanship that would one day mean death without warning for his country's enemies. In Noah's care, the boy was introduced to traditional tribal spiritualism and the Roman Catholic faith.

Francis left school at the age of 12 and began working in lumber yards and fishing camps. He then worked for the provincial Department of Marine and Fisheries on the Great Lakes and became a marine firefighter. In 1913, he developed a serious case of typhoid fever and nearly died. He was

ABOVE: Francis Pegahmagabow was among the Canadian soldiers who fought with distinction at Passchendaele in World War I. (Public Domain)

ABOVE: Pictured in uniform, Corporal Francis Pegahmagabow was one of the most highly decorated indigenous soldiers in the history of the Canadian Army. (Public Domain)

attended by nuns of the Sisters of St. Joseph in Parry Sound, and the experience of recovery reinforced his Catholic beliefs.

In 1914, Francis enlisted in the Canadian army nine days after the Commonwealth declaration of war – even though as a Native American he was exempt from military service.

Once in Europe, Warrant Officer Pegahmagabow wasted no time. Nicknamed "Peggy" by his fellow soldiers, he gained their admiration as a fearless messenger, and stories of his service, though sketchy, included episodes of the mysticism in which he had grown up. He saw visions.

"During one period of the war in France I was a runner," Francis recalled years later, "and had as my fellow runner a Norwegian named Oscar Lund. One evening we saw a black dog with a luminous mouth carrying what appeared to be a paper tied to its neck. Believing it to be a scout for the Germans Lund reported it to the adjutant, who took me with him in a motorcycle to look for it. However, we did not see it again."

On another occasion the clouds of a chlorine gas attack were roiling toward Canadian positions, and an officer offered up a cigarette – containing tobacco of course – to see if Pegahmagabow could save the situation

ABOVE: Wearing his medals from the Great War, Francis Pegahmagabow is pictured in 1945. (Public Domain)

from rapidly deteriorating. This time, he lit the cigarette and invoked the spirit of the east wind to prevent the gas from approaching any closer. The west wind spirit was then asked to blow the killing fumes back from whence they came. The clouds of death abruptly changed course, wafting toward the trenches filled with German troops.

Soldiers who witnessed these spiritual connections were awe struck, and numbers of them began to seek Pegahmagabow's company. His legend continued to grow not only for this mystique, but also for his amazing courage and coolness under fire.

A fellow soldier marveled at Francis's willingness to regularly put his life on the line and face danger. "Pegahmagabow went looking for it," he recalled. "He preferred to work alone, in the dark, even infiltrating an enemy trench to stand among its occupants for the fun of it." And when he worked as a sniper, Pegahmagabow waited – quiet and immobile – until an enemy soldier filled the sights of his Ross rifle.

Seriously wounded more than once, Francis Pegahmagabow was always committed to return to his unit, ending the war with the Military Medal and two bars among other awards. He worked as a Native American activist after the war and died in 1952 at the age of 61.

THE GHILLIE SUIT

The stealthy game wardens who kept watch on the estates of their wealthy employers in the highlands of Scotland were known as ghillies, and with the outbreak of the Boer War, Simon Fraser, 14th Lord Lovat, raised a special unit of snipers from among these hearty men. With the coming of World War I, the Lovat Scouts were again involved in service to their country.

Not only did they engage in hazardous reconnaissance missions, but they were also effective snipers, who employed camouflage and concealment to dramatic effect. The most noteworthy innovation that the Lovat Scouts brought to the battlefield in the Great War was the ghillie suit, derived from those worn in the highlands by wardens on duty to arrest poachers and other interlopers. The ghillie suit found effective application during wartime, and it remains among the equipment of choice for snipers to this day.

The word "ghillie" found its roots in the Scottish Gaelic language and translates literally as servant or lad. In Scottish folklore, the fairy Gille Dubh was a wispy being that inhabited the highlands and proved elusive to those who would capture him, camouflaged in a cloak of leaves and flora that concealed his features. Australian snipers adapted their own version of the ghillie suit and nicknamed it the "Yowie," in reference to a mythical creature similar to the Yeti or Bigfoot who lived in the wilderness of their native land.

When Lovat's Scouts introduced the ghillie suit to the battlefield in World War I, fieldcraft took a leap forward. The concept, though, was simple. The suit itself was typically fashioned from mesh or thin cloth adorned with leaves or burlap strips, random earth toned cloth, small limbs, and anything that would help the sniper to blend into his surroundings sufficiently. A hood or veil made the costume complete, and the sniper would then be capable of hiding in plain sight. Snipers from other armies quickly saw the value of the ghillie suit and adapted it for their own use. It survives today, as the modern sniper takes advantage of its high potential to provide the camouflage necessary for the sniper to survive and strike.

The British military establishment warmed to the art of sniper warfare by 1917 and included advice on numerous aspects of it in a field manual that December titled Scouting and Patrolling. It stressed the importance of proper concealment.

"The sniper should make use of veils, sniper suits, camouflage, etc., when available," it read, "and scout officers should keep themselves up to date with the latest ideas. The study of protective colouring is interesting and of value; but it must be impressed on the sniper that, however well his disguise may conform with his surroundings, if he does not at the same time learn to keep still, or, move only with stealth and cunning, he is likely to disclose his position. Great patience and constant practice in moving very slowly are required. Disguises may be improvised by using grass, leaves, etc., and by smearing the hands and face to harmonise with the surroundings. A regular outline of any shape attracts attention."

The ghillie suit not only assisted the sniper in plying his trade, but also served to promote the standardization of the sniper role in modern warfare. By the end of World War I, sniper training had been formalized in each of the largest combatant armies, and the ghillie suit enhanced the sniper's value even more.

ABOVE: A hunter wears a simple ghillie suit, which may easily be adapted to wartime sniper use. (No Restrictions via Wikipedia)

ABOVE: Simon Fraser, 14th Lord Lovat, founded the Lovat Scouts, proponents of the ghillie suit. (Public Domain)

ABOVE: The ghillie suit obscures this modern sniper, and the fieldcraft technique has been practiced for more than a century. (Public Domain)

ABOVE: Finnish soldiers man a Maxim machine gun as they lie in wait for a Red Army column to come within range. (Public Domain)

THE WINTER WAR

The brief Winter War between the Soviet Union and Finland was sparked by Soviet intimidation and Finnish defiance. It lasted slightly longer than three months, from November 30, 1939, to March 13, 1940, ending when the Soviets prevailed and their land grab took Finnish territory.

But during that time, the overmatched Finnish military taught the invaders bitter lessons in winter warfare. Finnish ski troops ravaged Soviet columns with small arms fire and then melted away into the snowy landscape, while their accomplished snipers struck terror in the hearts of the Red Army, from the rank and file to senior field officers.

Estimates of total Soviet casualties in the weeks-long war reach a staggering 400,000, and the Finnish sniper did his utmost to make the Red Army pay for every yard of territory gained. The most prolific Finnish sniper was Simo Hayha, who earned the nickname of the "White Death" and may well have become the most successful sniper in history with more than 505 confirmed kills.

Hayha recorded his own estimate of his tally, around 500, and called it his "sin list" in a memoir of his war experience that was written just after he was wounded and withdrawn from combat after just 100 days. However, the volume remained undiscovered until 2017.

Born in southern Finland near the Russian frontier, Hayha stood only five feet, three inches tall. He became an accomplished farmer, hunter and endurance skier, and by the time the Winter War broke out, the 33-year-old was an expert with the Model 28-30 7.62mm (.30-calibre) rifle, a variant of the Soviet-made Mosin Nagant, firing across rudimentary iron sights. He received sniper training in 1938 as the Finns prepared for war with the Soviets and was reported to have hit a target 150 metres distant 16

ABOVE: Simo Hayha, the Finnish sniper dubbed the 'White Death,' smiles for a photographer. (Public Domain)

ABOVE: A Finnish ski soldier sits ready to engage the invading Red Army of the Soviet Union during the Winter War. (Public Domain)

THE MILITARY SNIPER

ABOVE: After an ambush by Finnish ski troops, a Soviet column lies destroyed and scattered in March 1940. (Public Domain)

straight times in a single minute utilizing his bolt-action rifle.

Serving 98 days with Infantry Regiment 34 of the Finnish Army, he was wrapped in a white snow suit for concealment and preferred to work alone in temperatures that regularly plunged below minus 20 degrees Celsius. Carrying provisions for a single day, usually only sugar cubes and small pieces of bread for the "hunting time," he would lie in wait for the unsuspecting Soviet soldier to venture into his field of vision. Hayha's kill rate averaged five Soviet soldiers per day. He hid with snow in his mouth so that his breath would not give his position away and targeted the enemy who was rarely clad in camouflage uniform. Although he had access to telescopic sights, he preferred the use of the iron sights because he believed they provided a more accurate picture of the target. Operating in the area of Kollaa, north of Lake Ladoga, he managed to kill an estimated 138 soldiers in just 22 days.

Finnish propaganda made the most of the great sniper's exploits, and Hayha became a national hero, scourge of the Red Army, and an extraordinary dealer of death. Although some authorities question the accuracy of his total since a true count would have been problematic in wartime conditions, his own commanding officer estimated his body count at more than 500.

During one duel with a Red Army counter-sniper, Hayha caught a glint of sunlight off the adversary's telescopic sight and pinpointed his location. The daring Finn simply waited the enemy sniper out. And when the Russian rose in the twilight to go back to his camp, Hayha shot him dead. On December 21, 1939, he is believed to have disposed of four Red Army soldiers each hour during a six-hour period. Considering the fact that only six hours of daylight were available for good visual contact in the remoteness of the northern hemisphere winter, the achievement is astounding.

Years later, Hayha commented, "I just shot every time I saw an enemy. I didn't care if he was a commander or not." His record of confirmed kills in a single day was 25.

The Soviets came to fear Hayha so acutely that they place a bounty on his head and dispatched their own snipers to stalk him – unsuccessfully. If reports of Hayha's presence in a certain area were received, Red Air Force bombers were sometimes sent on missions to bomb the location in the hopes of killing him, to no avail.

For all his prowess as a sniper, Hayha became the quarry himself just 11 days before the Winter War ended in 1940. A Soviet soldier spotted him and fired a single explosive bullet that ripped into his jaw and wounded him severely. Given up for dead, his body was piled with the corpses of other casualties. However, his commanding officer was notified and refused to depart without accounting for the hero.

The officer sent a soldier to search for Hayha, and when he noticed the muscular movement of a leg amid the pile of dead, Hayha was pulled free and rushed to a hospital. He remained in a coma for 11 days but recovered, bearing the scars of the encounter for the rest of his life and fortunate to be alive. Newspapers in both Finland and the Soviet Union carried erroneous reports of Hayha's death, and when he became aware of them, he wrote a letter to the editor of a Finnish newspaper to dispel the rumour. Shortly after the war ended, he was promoted from corporal to the rank of 2nd lieutenant.

Due to his wounds, Hayha underwent 26 reconstructive operations and was unable to serve during the subsequent Continuation War, as World War II was called in Finland. Often asked about the secret to his incredible sniping success, he consistently responded with a single word, "practice." During an interview decades after his exploits in the Winter War, Hayha was asked whether he held any regret for taking so many lives. He replied, "I did what I was told to do as well as I could. There would be no Finland unless everyone else had done the same."

For his service in the Winter War, Simo Hayha was awarded a farm by the Finnish government. He lived peacefully to the age of 96, occasionally participating in civilian marksmanship contests and breeding dogs as a pastime. He passed away in the town of Hamina, Finland, in 2002.

Reports of another prolific Finnish sniper during the Winter War have been questioned as mere myth, a confusion with the story of Hayha, or outright false propaganda. However, it is worthy of mention that a soldier named Suko Solkka was said to have recorded more than 400 kills against the Red Army in the three-month conflict. Although there are few, if any, recorded documents that mention Solkka by name, it is said that he once shot a Soviet soldier with his Mosin Nagant sniper rifle at an incredible distance of 600 yards (528 metres) after several days of stalking the enemy in the field.

ABOVE: After recovering from his terrible wound, Simo Hayha posed for this portrait. (Public Domain)

ABOVE: Clad in sniper gear with rifle at his side, Simo Hayha prepares for another foray against the Red Army. (Creative Commons Julius Jaaskelainen via Wikipedia)

YOUR GAZINE

SAVE 18% WHEN YOU SUBSCRIBE!

FREE GIFT WORTH £5!

Aeroplane traces its lineage back to the weekly The Aeroplane launched in June 1911, and is still continuing to provide the best aviation coverage around. *Aeroplane* magazine is dedicated to offering the most in-depth and entertaining read on all historical aircraft.

shop.keypublishing.com/amsubs

FREE GIFT WORTH £16.99!

Classic Land Rover is an exciting monthly magazine dedicated to Series and the classic Land Rovers. Written by enthusiasts, it is the complete guide to buying, owning, running, driving, repairing, modifying and restoring pre-nineties Land Rovers and Range Rover classics.

shop.keypublishing.com/clrsubs

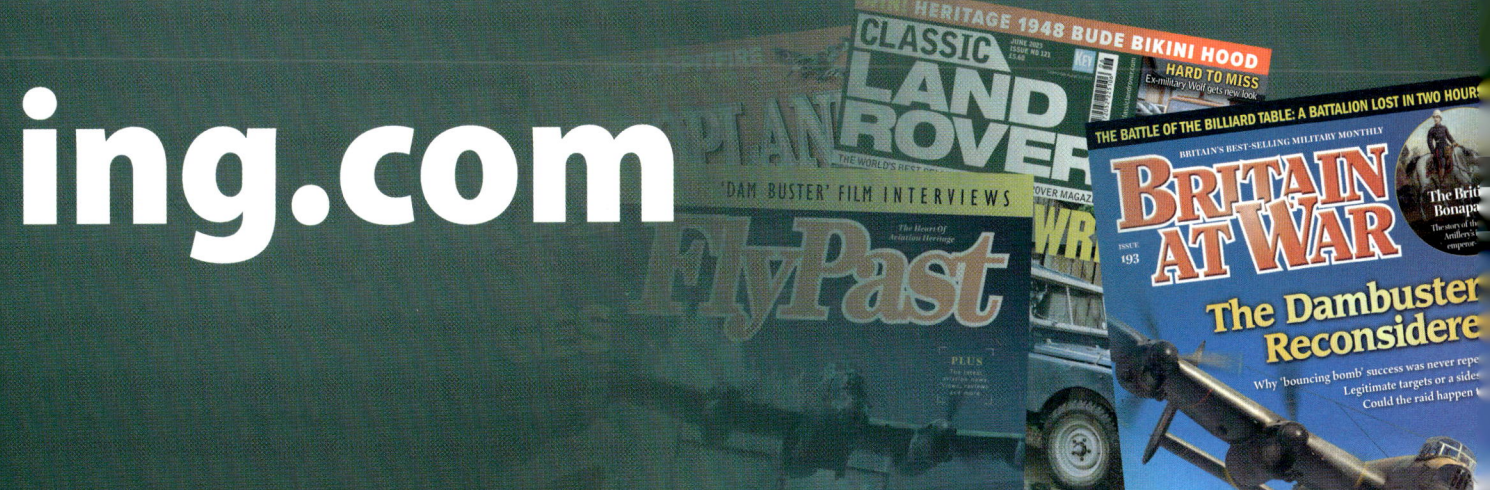

ing.com

WORLD WAR II IN THE WEST

ABOVE: A British sniper in full ghillie suit camouflage lies in wait as the barrel of his Enfield rifle protrudes. (Public Domain)

Between the world wars, the victors and the vanquished were left to consider the terrible cost of armed conflict. The sniper's role in the Great War was more or less a footnote amid the mind-numbing casualty figures and the tremendous destruction of property that had occurred. Nevertheless, a generation later the world was plunged again into catastrophic conflict.

The rise of Nazi Germany and the territorial designs of Adolf Hitler initiated a conflagration the likes of which had never been contemplated. When the Nazis invaded Poland on September 1, 1939, nearly six long years of warfare followed. As if he were choosing a target from a long dormant hide, the sniper again emerged. This time with renewed relevance on the battlefield and even in an attempt to alter the course of political events.

By August 25, 1944, Paris, one of the world's great cities, had been under the heel of Nazi occupation for four long years. Allied armies had landed in Normandy and fought the Germans for weeks before breaking out of their beachhead and streaming toward the City of Light. As liberation day approached, Parisians took to the streets, the buildings, and the open spaces of the city and fought the Germans in anticipation of the arrival of the Allied armies.

Tanks of the Free French 2nd Armoured Division rolled into Paris on that day, and collaborators were rounded up to receive street justice. Meanwhile, General Charles de Gaulle, leader of the Free French, arrived in the capital city on August 26. In the spring of 1940, de Gaulle had escaped the Nazi occupation, fleeing to London to organize his movement and carrying the honour of France in the satchel case by his side.

Now, de Gaulle had returned in triumph, and at 3pm, a dizzying victory parade stepped off down the Champs Elysées. At the head of the tumultuous procession, the tall, stately figure of de Gaulle strode resolutely. Moments later, the leader reached the Place de la Concorde, and a shot rang out. The crowd scattered, seeking shelter wherever possible. Escorts looked about for the location of the sniper, but he eluded detection.

No matter. De Gaulle kept walking, undeterred and as if nothing out of the ordinary had happened. More rifle reports were heard. Still, the leader, in full uniform, kept walking.

When de Gaulle reached the plaza before the Cathedral of Notre Dame, more rifle shots crackled loudly. Again, the spectators scattered. And again, Charles de Gaulle was a tower of strength. Ignoring the danger, he walked crisply down the aisle in full view of those attending, and took his seat nearly 200 feet (60 metres) from the entrance. Those who witnessed the event were awe struck, but de Gaulle, after such an agonizing period

ABOVE: A German sniper peers through binoculars while hiding in a French forest.
(Creative Commons Bundesarchiv Bild via Wikipedia)

THE MILITARY SNIPER

ABOVE: This interwar photo depicts black soldiers of the US army participating in sharpshooter training. (No Restrictions via Wikipedia)

of uncertainty in the life of his country, was not about to allow a single rifleman to steal the moment.

Reporters from Great Britain and the United States could scarcely believe what they had seen, and de Gaulle had, in a rather dangerous and peculiar way, made the sniper a weapon of his own propaganda and persuasion. A BBC commentator offered, "He walked straight ahead in what appeared to me to be a hail of fire, without hesitation, his shoulders flung back. It was the most extraordinary example of courage that I've ever seen."

Granted, it was against all-natural law and impulse for a man to stand in or near the sights of a sniper and go unflinchingly about his duty. But the point was made, and one observer commented that at that moment de Gaulle had "France in the palm of his hand."

While the science of killing had taken a tremendous leap forward during the Great War, the financial burden and terrible human toll had caused most of the treasuries of the former warring nations, victors and vanquished, to recoil in its wake. The nations curbed military spending and reduced the size of standing armies. Germany was compelled to shoulder the blame for the catastrophe with the terms of the Treaty of Versailles and saddled with war reparations of such immense proportion that the debt could not be repaid fully until the 1980s.

The sniper was muzzled, and only the Soviet Union appears to have maintained a relatively competent, cohesive, and highly-trained sniper force during the 1930s. In Germany, a memorandum from the Chief of Army Command dated December 5, 1931, succinctly stated, "Telescopic sight carbines should be used up. Parts for mounting the telescopic sight as well as spare parts will no longer be kept in stock. Telescopic sight carbines in need of repair will be exchanged for rifles."

In the United States, no formal army sniper training existed, and only a few US Marines were designated as skilled in the art. The British army curtailed its sniper commitment, reducing the number of such soldiers to only eight men in a battalion.

Nevertheless, with the outbreak of hostilities in 1939, military establishments did reawaken, albeit slowly, to the value of the sniper on the battlefield. The early Nazi victories in Poland, Denmark, Norway, France and the Low Countries produced a flurry of sniper activity, and it was clear that the sniper was capable of more than shooting enemy soldiers from a distance. He could very well serve as an early warning "picket," provide intelligence as to enemy troop dispositions and movement from an advanced and concealed position, and relay coordinates for artillery or air strikes against targets of high value.

Sniper schools were organized, and within months of the beginning of hostilities the trained sniper again proliferated. In Germany, numerous training programs were initiated by the army and the field infantry units of the Luftwaffe, while a dedicated sniper school was established at Zossen. The Waffen SS, or armed SS, instituted a sniper training program as well. Hitler repudiated the Versailles Treaty and began to rearm Germany overtly in 1935. At the time, the standard issue shoulder arm of the Wehrmacht was the Karabiner 98K rifle, a shorter version of the venerable Mauser Gewehr 98 of World War I. Later, the Gewehr 41 and Gewehr 43, both 7.92mm (.31-calibre) semiautomatic weapons became available with sniper applications when fitted with telescopic sights, but most German snipers preferred the 98K during World War II.

ABOVE: A sniper of the Canadian Perth Regiment hides in an Italian farmhouse in January 1944. (Public Domain)

In Great Britain, a sniper school was opened at Bisley in 1940, and the celebrated Lovat Scouts were detailed as trainers, following their legacy from the Great War. Other sniper schools came along through the war years, and the standard British sniper rifle remained the P14 or Mk I until it was eclipsed thoroughly by the Enfield No. 4 Mk I.

In the United States, only a brief course at Camp Perry, Ohio, was operating as the nation avoided entanglement in World War II until the Japanese attack on Pearl Harbor on December 7, 1941. The American sniper rifle standard was embodied in the 7.62mm (.30-06 calibre) Springfield Model

ABOVE: A Polish soldier of the Carpathian Brigade undergoes sniper training in Palestine in 1940 (Public Domain)

WORLD WAR II IN THE WEST

ABOVE: This sniper of the Seaforth Highlanders of Canada waits patiently under cover in Foiano, Italy, 1943. (Public Domain)

ABOVE: Lance Corporal Jacob Feinbuch of the Jewish Brigade prepares his rifle for action in Mezzano, Italy. (Public Domain)

1903 A-1, which was later augmented with the A-4 variant in the European theatre. The M-1 Garand, the standard US army rifle issued beginning in 1936, was a semiautomatic 7.62mm (.30-calibre) weapon modified for sniper use in its C and D variants that included telescopic sights, cheek rest, heavier barrel, and a cone-shaped flash suppressor. Sniper training grew in the US army although there was no formal program in World War II. The Marine Corps maintained a programme with its first scout snipers trained at San Diego, California, in early 1943.

By the end of World War II, the British army had trained and deployed roughly 5,000 snipers, and these soldiers excelled in their craft. They were taught to identify a potential target through four components – shape, shadow, shine, and silhouette. Commando forces were active early in the conflict and found themselves in the thick of the fighting as Allied forces tested the strength of Hitler's Atlantic Wall, a string of fortifications that stretched from the North Sea to the Spanish frontier to deter a seaborne invasion of occupied Europe. Although Nazi propaganda touted the fortifications as impregnable, a major Allied raid was conceived, principally by Lord Louis Mountbatten, to test its defensive capability.

A dress rehearsal for the invasion of Nazi-occupied France, Operation Jubilee involved more than 10,000 Allied troops in a strong raid against the French port city of Dieppe. The primary troops designated to execute the raid were Canadian, accompanied by No.3 and No.4 Commando of the British army and about 50 US Army Rangers. Launched on August 18, 1942, the raid was a disaster, as the incoming Allied troops were attacked by German E-boats, the element of surprise lost as a German convoy spotted their craft as they crossed the English Channel.

The planned preliminary bombardment had been reduced significantly, and when approximately 5,000 Canadian troops stormed ashore, they were met with heavy small-arms fire that killed and wounded many as they stepped onto the beach. The sand was found to be unsuitable for the deployment of Allied tanks, and many of these were quickly knocked out or foundered. No.3 Commando lost about half its strength on the run in, its mission to silence a German battery on the east end of the landing beaches at Berneval, while No.4 Commando was to destroy the battery in the west at Varengeville.

Allied intelligence reports that suggested only a lightly defended stretch of coastline proved tragically incorrect, and more than 4,000 Allied soldiers were killed, wounded, or taken prisoner.

Nevertheless, No.4 Commando pressed on and succeeded in its mission against the

ABOVE: A sniper from New Zealand scans the horizon from the ruins of Cassino in Italy, 1944. (Public Domain)

THE MILITARY SNIPER

ABOVE: Vigilant for German snipers, an American soldier points his M-1 rifle in the direction of a disturbance during hazardous mopping up operations in Cisterna, Italy, 1944. (Public Domain)

ABOVE: British army cadets sport sniper camouflage during training in the summer of 1943. (Public Domain)

that lay the barbed wire round the howitzers. It was carelessly laid wire which gave our men little trouble, but the battery defenders knew how to fight. To get at them the attackers had to cross open ground under fire from carefully concealed snipers. There fell two Commando officers, one seriously wounded, and several men…Sniping from his office window was Hauptmann [Captain] and Batterie Führer Schoeler, the battery C.O. A trooper kicked in the door, sprayed him with tommy gun bullets. 'Couldn't take him prisoner,' he said. 'It was him or me.'"

No.4 Commando included three sniper teams, and Captain Mills-Roberts ordered two snipers to take positions within 250 yards (228 metres) of the Varengeville battery. The officer and the snipers climbed into the loft of a barn, and from there they could clearly observe the activities of the German gun crews.

"The first sniper's bullet was to be a signal for all-out fire to be opened on the Germans and Mills-Roberts gave the order to proceed," wrote Robert Atkin in his book Dieppe 1942. "The marksman settled himself on a table, taking careful aim. These Bisly chaps are not to be hurried. At last the rifle cracked. It was a bullseye and one of the Master Race took a toss into the gun pit. His comrades looked shocked and surprised. It seemed rather like shooting one of the members of a church congregation from the organ loft."

ABOVE: Lord Lovat leads his command ashore in Normandy on D-Day. He is shown in the lower left adjacent to a column of soldiers. (Public Domain)

ABOVE: Lord Lovat led his scouts during the Dieppe Raid and the Normandy landings. (Public Domain)

six 150mm guns at Varengeville. Attacking in two groups, led by Lord Lovat himself and by Captain Derek Mills-Roberts, they made good their escape despite encounters with strong German defences and the ever-present threat of the enemy sniper. One soldier remembered an incident as he wrote his thoughts on Operation Jubilee 48 hours after he returned to safety in Britain.

"'Like to come up and see what's going on above?' said the signals officer. We climbed the steps. 'I can't guarantee there won't be any German snipers about,' he added cheerfully, as we walked along the bottom of a gully… He was right, as I found out a little later as I passed several times up and down the gully carrying messages or mortar shells. Snipers seemed to be the Germans' favourite defence immediately along the coast. They were responsible for most of our remarkably few casualties…Just as I got back to the gully stairs a bullet or two began to whistle past. 'That saucy sniper,' said a Navy signaller, 'is too bloody cocky.'"

The soldier added, "Beyond the woods… there was a stretch of open field, and beyond

WORLD WAR II IN THE WEST

ABOVE: A weary Lord Lovat is pictured with survivors following the disastrous Dieppe Raid in 1942. (Public Domain)

ABOVE: A German sniper wears a camouflage hood as he prepares to move to a hide.
(Creative Commons Bundesarchiv Bild via Wikipedia)

Atkin continued, "The Germans reacted quickly. A flak tower on stilts sprayed the wood with tracer and mortars caused casualties among the Commandos around the perimeter wire. The flak tower was silenced by an anti-tank rifle and soon the raiders brought into action their own 2-in mortar (50.8mm) operated by Troop Sgt-Major Jimmy Dunning with spectacular results. The third shot struck a stack of cordite which ignited with a mighty explosion. Gleefully, the Commandos sniped at the battery crews frantically trying to extinguish the fires started by the explosion. The most daring was L/Cpl Dick Mann who, his hands and face painted green, crawled forward over open ground with a telescopic rifle and sniped at the crews from a fully exposed position."

Though the Dieppe Raid ended in costly failure, the experience provided valuable lessons that were put into practice two years later with the Allied landings in Normandy on D-Day, June 6, 1944.

Meanwhile, four days after the Japanese raid on Pearl Harbor, Adolf Hitler committed one of his greatest blunders of World War II. In support of his treaty cohorts, Hitler rose before the Reichstag on December 11, 1941, and declared war on the United States, an industrial colossus that would supply much of the military hardware and manpower that would eventually spell the destruction of the Third Reich.

The United States, however, was not fully prepared to wage war, and several months were required to bring the American military to the point of engagement with the Germans. On November 8, 1942, the first American soldiers landed on the shores of North Africa, alongside their British partners, in the execution of Operation Torch. The combined landings at Casablanca, Oran, and Algiers placed the Axis forces in North Africa in a vice as these Allied armies moved north and east. Simultaneously, the British and Commonwealth soldiers of Eighth Army, under General Bernard Montgomery, moved inexorably westward across more than 1,000 miles of desert, chasing the Axis enemy, once commanded by General Erwin Rommel – the vaunted Desert Fox – from the Egyptian frontier to Tunisia following their great victory at El Alamein.

By the spring of 1943, the Allies had trapped the German and Italian armies in North Africa in a pocket along the Tunisian coast of the Mediterranean Sea, compelling the surrender of 267,000 enemy soldiers. But during the intervening months, the sniper was active throughout the desert war.

One American soldier whose unenviable task was to string telegraph lines remembered a narrow escape. Norton Hubbard was a combat lineman in the US Army Signal Corps, who wrote a memoir of his wartime experiences titled The Hero Next Door. Hubbard recalled climbing a pole one day and wrote, "A signalman's task was complicated by land mines, snipers and poor rations. I was shot at by a sniper near Mateur. I was on a telegraph pole and he hit the insulator about a foot from my head on the other side of the pole. I dropped to the ground and went through a railroad tunnel and didn't go back."

One army nurse tending wounded at a US hospital in the city of Arzew, Algeria, was continually forced to duck and cover as German sniper bullets whizzed through her building, breaking windows and striking the walls. Street fighting and clearing houses of the enemy were commonplace in North Africa, and some snipers hid so well that they went undiscovered for days. Not until the time and place of their choosing did they open fire to spread chaos, and often death.

The particular nurse decided one day that she had simply had enough. "The Army nurses who participated in the North African invasion at first had little conception of the realities of battle and were unfamiliar with military procedures," recorded the History of the Nurse Corps in World War II. "One nurse at Arzew Hospital became so incensed at snipers firing into the windows of the hospital and endangering the patients that she had to be forcibly restrained from going outside to 'give them a piece of her mind.'"

By the autumn of 1943, the Allies had completed the liberation of Sicily and landed against stiff resistance on the Italian mainland at Salerno. The subsequent Italian campaign was an arduous trek, and fighting was still going on there during the last days of World War II. General Mark Clark, commander of the Allied Fifth Army, ridiculed a comment from Prime Minister Winston Churchill that the offensive would be against the "soft underbelly" of Nazi-occupied Europe and said bluntly that it was rather a "tough old gut."

ABOVE: The crack of a German sniper's rifle scatters a crowd in Lyon, France, in this September 1944 image. (Public Domain)

At times the opposing lines were locked in stalemate, similar to the old Western Front ordeal of World War I, and the situation became a prime environment for the sniper team to harass the enemy. In their classic book One Shot-One Kill, authors Charles Sasser and Craig Roberts recorded the memory of one sniper's Italian encounter.

"We snipers adopted a tactic the Nazis sometimes used," recalled US Army Sergeant John Fulcher. "Slipping from our lines before daylight, we located a hill or ridge within range of a road or trail inside enemy-occupied territory, divided it into sectors for each two-man team – sniper and spotter – and then settled down to wait for whatever came along… I spotted troops coming at the end of the road where it hazed into the horizon. I nudged my partner and nodded in their direction.

"Through binoculars, I could tell they were green replacements. Their uniforms were still a crisp gray-green; their jackboots kicking up little spurts of dust still shone. They left a cloud of dust hanging in their wake… As cool as could be, I cross-haired the officer and shot him through the belly. He looked momentarily surprised. He plopped down on his butt in the middle of the road. The report of the shot reached him as he fell over onto his back. He was dead by the time I brought my rifle down out of recoil and picked him up again in my scope. His legs were drumming on the road, but he was dead. His body just didn't know it yet.

"The other krauts were so green they didn't know enough to scatter for cover until my partner got in his licks by knocking down one more. Even then, they behaved more like quail than combat troops. They hid in the drainage ditches and in some shell craters, their heads bobbing up…I figured I could have drilled two or three more, but I held my fire. It wouldn't do to be pinpointed, even by green troops…

ABOVE: French civilians take cover behind armoured vehicles of the Free French 2nd Armoured Division as a German sniper opens fire in Paris, August 1944. (Public Domain)

The company reorganized without making an attempt to find us… As soon as the Germans swept around a distant bend in the road, they were greeted by the twin Crack! Crack! of two more rifle shots as they entered another Yank team's sector."

When the Allies bogged down at Monte Cassino and the Gustav Line at the end of 1943, they launched a daring amphibious operation to outflank the strong German positions and perhaps even capture Rome. Operation Shingle involved a major landing at the port city of Anzio, and it required that ground commanders exhibit initiative in exploiting the element of surprise. However, Major General John P. Lucas hesitated, and the American VI Corps was bottled up in the Anzio beachhead for five months.

Again, an attritive standoff developed, and the sniper came to the fore during the following weeks. One such sniper who earned praise from his sergeant was Robert J. Kindig of the US 45th Infantry Division. The sergeant called Kindig a one-man army during a fight for a position dubbed the Overpass, and before the sniper was wounded by shrapnel from a mortar round that also destroyed his rifle, he managed to strike fear into the enemy.

ABOVE: French soldiers march a group of captured German snipers, flushed from their hides, into captivity in November 1944. (Public Domain)

"Kindig recalled that he and his buddies tried digging foxholes near the Overpass," wrote author Flint Whitlock in his book Rock of Anzio. 'You'd dig down about a foot and hit water, so we never had much protection…I was in a foxhole near the company command post when the Germans let loose with an artillery barrage. One of their shells landed right next to my foxhole and caved it in on me. The shell didn't go off; it was a dud.'

"Kindig had been issued a brand-new rifle with a telescopic sight and was performing sniper duties. 'We had barbed wire out there and the Germans were trying to get over it and under it and around it. I was on the outskirts with that sniper rifle and they were coming up through some drainage ditches at us. I picked them off before they could get around to us.'" When Kindig was through with the advancing Germans, he had stalled their movement, and 25 bodies lay a distance from his concealed position.

ABOVE: Soldiers of the US 7th Infantry Regiment prepare to rush a house where German snipers have holed up in Guiderkirch, France. (Public Domain)

WORLD WAR II IN THE WEST

ABOVE: French soldiers prepare to return fire against German soldiers in Paris in the shadow of the Arc de Triomphe. (Public Domain)

With the tide of war turning, The Western Allies mounted Operation Overlord, the invasion of Normandy, on June 6, 1944. Overlord was the largest amphibious operation of its kind up to that time, and the assault against Hitler's Fortress Europe was conducted across five beaches code named Gold, Juno, Sword, Utah, and Omaha. Resistance was particularly robust at Omaha, where elements of the US 1st and 29th Infantry Divisions fought for hours to gain a toehold and General Omar Bradley, commanding the assault troops, briefly considered withdrawing them for redeployment to another sector.

By afternoon, the immediate crisis had passed, and American and British troops began their tough eastward offensive toward the frontier of the Third Reich while the Soviet Red Army pressed inexorably toward the west. Still, German defenders were persistent. Their artillery boomed, machine guns barked, and skilled snipers slowed the advance of the British, Canadian, and American soldiers through coastal towns and into the Norman hedgerow country, or bocage.

Just off Omaha Beach, Sergeant Bob Slaughter of the 29th Division recalled the determination of the defenders. "Snipers, machine guns, and 88s interrupted movement on the road to Vierville. The column took cover and waited for an officer or noncom with the initiative to collar a few riflemen and clear the obstacle…Following an exchange of fire, three or four enemy soldiers appeared waving white flags, hands over heads, yelling 'Kamerad!' With them appeared a young French female civilian whom we suspected of collaboration. Thinking that she was one of the deadly snipers, we didn't treat her or the other prisoners gently. I doubt they made it back to the beach alive." Weeks after the ordeal on D-Day, Slaughter barely escaped death from an unseen sniper a second time as a German bullet ripped through the brim of his helmet and grazed his forehead, causing profuse bleeding.

Unlike the ordeal the Americans confronted at Omaha Beach, their landings at Utah Beach to the west were virtually unopposed, in part because of strong currents that pulled the landing craft away from the designated invasion point. Nevertheless, once the US 4th Infantry Division got ashore and began to push inland, the German snipers kept heads down. Captain John C. Ausland, an artillery liaison officer, wrote a letter to his family describing the opening hours of his experience in France.

"…At last, we got our unit off the bomb torn beach and away from the constant shelling," he wrote. "For the rest of the day there are only momentary recollections: Tough [sic] paratroopers wandering about, killing German snipers… The sniper (we later learned he was 75 yards [68.5 metres] from our command post) who shot at us all day without killing anyone. He was killed by a paratrooper who happened across him."

At Sword Beach, Major R.R. Reynolds kept the journal of the King's Shropshire Light Infantry. He wrote, "Ahead, X Coy. were meeting serious trouble from snipers in the north end of the village of Beuville. This consisted of strong stone buildings, interspersed with walled orchards – a paradise for determined marksmen fighting a delaying action. And delay us they did, so Major Slatter, impatient because X Coy. seemed held up, walked up the road to the centre of the bother. Here he fought a private battle with some snipers, and was seriously wounded in the arm. Nevertheless, he managed to give us a picture of the

ABOVE: General Charles de Gaulle braved sniper fire during the celebration following the liberation of Paris. (Public Domain)

ABOVE: General Charles de Gaulle strides down the Champs Elysees in Paris in August 1944. He was unconcerned when sniper fire broke out. (Public Domain)

THE MILITARY SNIPER

ABOVE: Citizens of Paris defend a strongpoint in a city street during the liberation of Paris. (Public Domain)

situation before he collapsed and was evacuated, protesting.

"Capt. Rylands took over, and went forward to Major Thornycroft for a palaver, which was joined by the C.O. Direct progress down the middle of the village looked like being a slow and costly affair; the civilians refused to evacuate themselves, and at that early stage we were too soft-hearted to shell their homes – a proceeding which might have facilitated our advance considerably.'"

Fighting in the bocage country amounted to sophisticated bushwhacking as the Germans fortified every ancient wall of earth that separated one farmer's field from the next and every country lane was in the field of fire of an enemy machine gun. In response to the slow grind, the US Army published frequent educational articles for those soldiers who might find a spare moment to read.

Under the collective title of Combat Lessons, these offered tips for survival, and one read, "The German soldiers had been given orders to stay in their positions… Some of their snipers stayed hidden for two to five days after a position had been taken and then 'popped up' suddenly…to take the shot for which they had been waiting. We found fire crackers with slow burning fuses left by snipers and AT (anti-tank) gun crews in their old positions when they moved. These exploded at irregular intervals, giving the impression that the position was still occupied by enemy forces. High losses among tank commanders have been caused by German snipers. Keep buttoned up, as the German rifleman concentrates on such profitable targets. After an action the turret of the commander's tank is usually well marked with rifle bullets."

Fighting their way across France, Allied soldiers were often subjected to the superior skills of the German sniper. Following the breakout from the Normandy beachhead, the sniper personified the tenacious resistance of the Wehrmacht. Allied officers were particular targets in the field, and one described the unsettling circumstance to author Adrian Gilbert in his book Sniper.

"At night snipers crept through the positions, to open fire…on parties coming up from the rear. Dozens of bloody little battles were fought behind the forward positions. The snipers were everywhere. Officers, their chosen prey, learned to conceal all distinguishing marks, to carry rifles like their own men instead of their accustomed pistols, not to carry maps or field glasses, to wear pips on their sleeves instead of conspicuously on their shoulders."

One platoon leader of the US 9th Infantry Division recalled the ordeal of a detachment of replacements who had not experienced combat previously. When they encountered a German sniper, paralysis ensued, with terrible consequences. "One of the fatal mistakes made by the infantry replacements is to hit the ground and freeze when fired upon," he remarked. "Once I ordered a squad to advance from one hedgerow to another. During the movement one man was shot by a sniper firing one round. The entire squad hit the ground and froze. They were picked off one by one, by the same sniper."

Captain Clifford Shore, author of the classic work With British Snipers to the Reich, remembered an officer's routine reconnaissance that turned sombre moments later. "I saw an officer leaving the assembly area in a Jeep, smiling broadly, driven by a harassed faced

ABOVE: American Private William Zukergrow sights a distant German sniper during counter-sniper operations in Aachen on October 19, 1944. (Public Domain)

ABOVE: Two British soldiers of the Glider Pilot Regiment search a Dutch school for German snipers in September 1944. (Public Domain)

ABOVE: In this photo from August 1944, American soldiers avoid becoming targets for German snipers as they advance out of a roadway. (Public Domain)

driver," he wrote. "A few minutes later the Jeep returned with the officer dead, a neat hole being drilled in the centre of his forehead. 'Sniper' muttered the driver hoarsely. I must admit that it gave me, and the others, a shock."

War correspondents came up close and became personally acquainted with the sniper as they experienced war and tried to impart its horrors through newspaper reports. Working for the Associated Press, Roger Greene found himself in the midst of raging battles between German snipers and detachments of Allied soldiers called up for counter-sniper operations. His audience in the United States caught a glimpse of a tension-filled ordeal in his subsequent column.

"As I write in the living room of a French chateau," Greene reported, "a stealthy manhunt is going on in the rose gardens and bushes immediately outside. A few minutes ago one of our soldiers came to the chateau door and then started back on the front path. A sniper's bullet kicked up dust around his feet and he fell prone in a shallow ditch. From a front window a British correspondent and I watched the soldier crawl down the path a scant dozen yards away with the sniper's shots trailing him until he reached the brick wall at the end of the path. Now scores of troops are combing the thick brush around the chateau and bullets are cracking like popcorn all around.

"Last evening…I crouched on a road between a brick wall and a Jeep for nearly two hours, while German snipers who had lain doggo all day sent tracer bullets crackling around us… One of the German snipers apparently lay hidden within whispering distance during the night, for he began his shooting from a nearby clump of bushes this morning… The manhunt is over. A stocky, bronzed sergeant strides into the room and points significantly to the woods opposite the chateau whence the sniper's bullets have been coming. 'Got him, the blighter,' he says, and then with a grin, 'well, what's cooking with you, Yank?'"

The most famous American correspondent of World War II was Ernie Pyle, working for the Scripps Howard news agency. Pyle became known for his coverage of the common soldier's experience – with death tugging at his elbow every day. He endeared himself both to the soldiers and to a vast readership in the US. In the summer of 1944, he wrote with the dateline "SOMEWHERE IN FRANCE." He was frank in his appraisal of the sniper's craft.

"Sniping, as far as I know, is recognized as a legitimate means of warfare. And yet there is something sneaky about it that outrages the American sense of fairness. I had never sensed this before we landed in France and began pushing the Germans back. We have had snipers before – in Bizerte and Cassino and lots of other places. But always on a small scale.

"Here in Normandy the Germans have gone in for sniping in a wholesale manner. There are snipers everywhere. There are snipers in trees, in buildings, in piles of wreckage, in the grass. But mainly they are in the high, bushy hedgerows that form the fences of all the Norman fields and line every roadside and lane. It is perfect sniping country.

"Every mile we advance there are dozens of snipers left behind us. They pick off our soldiers one by one as they walk down the

ABOVE: American soldiers pick their way through the rubble in the city of Prüm, Germany, as they search for Nazi snipers in February 1945. (Public Domain)

ABOVE: A British sniper applies camouflage face cream while training at the sniper school in Normandy in the autumn of 1944. (Public Domain)

THE MILITARY SNIPER

ABOVE: A German sniper peers through his telescopic sight in this posed photo on the Western front.
(Creative Commons Bundesarcchiv Bild via Wikipedia)

roads or across the fields. It isn't safe to move into a new bivouac area until the snipers have been cleaned out. The first bivouac I moved into had shots ringing through it for a full day before all the hidden gunmen were rounded up. It gives you the same spooky feeling that you get on moving into a place you suspect of being sown with mines.

"In the past our soldiers would talk about the occasional snipers with contempt and disgust. But here sniping has become important, and taking precautions against it is something we have had to learn and learn fast. One officer friend of mine said: 'Individual soldiers have become sniper-wise before, but now we're sniper-conscious as whole units.'

"Snipers kill as many Americans as they can, and then when their food an ammunition run out, they surrender. To an American, that isn't quite ethical. The average American soldier has little feeling against the average German soldier who has fought an open fight and lost. But his feelings about the sneaking snipers can't very well be put into print. He is learning how to kill the snipers before the time comes for them to surrender…."

Indeed, the sniper holds a somewhat unique place in the realm of chivalrous or unchivalrous combat. By his very essence, he gives not quarter. Therefore, should quarter be given to him? Many times, the retribution meted out to snipers captured alive – whether accomplished in the art and trained for their task or a mere German infantryman taking pot shots with a rifle – was swift.

The Allied juggernaut pushed into the Netherlands in late 1944 and across the great natural barrier of the River Rhine in the spring of 1945. All the while, the German sniper dogged the advance. At the same time, the American, British, and Canadian snipers gave as good as they got.

As World War II in Europe neared its end, one of its most poignant sequences of photography was recorded by the legendary Robert Capa. American troops were engaged in a fight for control of a bridge in the city of Leipzig, Germany, on April 18, 1945. Two soldiers of the US 2nd Infantry Division found a balcony with an unobstructed view of the bridge and set up their machine gun, loading and firing.

A few minutes later, one of the soldiers slipped inside the building, leaving the other to operate alone. Capa had climbed through a window to take up a position nearby, photographing the sequence as the two Americans went about their business.

The lone soldier was immediately engaged in reloading the machine gun when a single shot was heard. Private First Class Raymond J. Bowman, age 21, crumpled. He was dead before he reached the parquet floor. Three weeks later, Life Magazine ran the series of photos with the descriptive phrase, "The picture of the last man to die."

Life did not identify the two American soldiers, but Bowman's family in Rochester, New York, recognized him by a small pin he wore on his collar.

Two years later, Capa told a radio interviewer that Bowman "looked so clean-cut like it was the first day of the war and he was very earnest. So, I said, 'All right, this will be my last picture of the war.' And I put my camera up and took a portrait shot of him and while I shot my portrait of him he was killed by a sniper. It was a very clean and somehow a very beautiful death, and I think that's what I remember most from this war."

The Life article noted, "…Other members of the platoon [then] decided to find where the fatal shot had come from. Stealthily they single-filed on to the cobblestone street and surrounded Germans barricaded in several abandoned streetcars. They fired a few warning shots. Presently two Germans came out with their hands up shouting, 'Kamerad!' The Americans, feeling no elation, took them away."

In 2015, the people of Leipzig renamed the street before the apartment building where the young American soldier had died 70 years earlier "Bowmanstrasse."

ABOVE: Photographer Robert Capa looks through a motion picture camera. Capa took the photo sequence of the death of Raymond Bowman in Leipzig.

ABOVE: Dignitaries pose with the street sign honouring American Raymond Bowman during ceremonies in 2016.
(Creative Commons Caisare via Wikipedia)

EDGAR RABBETS

Following the German thrust into France on May 10, 1940, the troops of the British Expeditionary Force (BEF) and many of their French allies fought gamely during the retreat and rescue from the port of Dunkirk on the English Channel.

While the Germans were driving hard at the retreating BEF, one British sniper, Private Edgar Rabbets of the 5th Battalion, Northamptonshire Regiment, made the aggressive enemy pay dearly on several occasions. Contrary to standard procedure, Rabbets preferred to work alone. As he explained later, it caused considerably less concern than also having to worry about someone else. An expert in fieldcraft, he also utilized the standard .303-calibre Enfield rifle and was known to have crept as close to potential targets as possible.

Rabbets once explained that he preferred a head shot and was capable of completing the task from a distance of 100 yards (91 metres). "It was the best place to kill them," he said of his victims. "It's a nice white target and you know once you've hit him in the head he's dead. It's as good a target as any – you hit him just below the helmet in between his eye and ear."

During the retreat to Dunkirk, Rabbets was called upon several times to eliminate the threat of German snipers that often slowed the retrograde movement. He was ordered forward one day to fight an adversary in a small Belgian village.

"The sniper had got himself up in a roof and knocked a few slates away," said Rabbets. "He'd got a good field of fire if anyone walked into the square; he was roughly in the centre of one side of the square and his mate was in the corner. And they covered the whole square that way, the one effectively protecting the other."

A British officer entered the square and had to scurry to safety. It was just enough

ABOVE: Snipers wearing camouflage lead the way as British soldiers move out somewhere in France. (Public Domain)

ABOVE: British soldiers make their way through Dunkirk toward the beach and evacuation. Private Edgar Rabbets fought as a sniper and bought them time. (Public Domain)

ABOVE: A German sniper looks to acquire a target from his perch in a tree. (Creative Commons Bundesarchiv Bild via Wikipedia)

to give Rabbets the information he needed. He spotted "roughly where the flash had come from and went into a house opposite. The sniper was hanging out of the roof; I shot him from the bedroom window and he fell forward."

The snap of the other German's rifle was heard within seconds, but the fire was inaccurate because Rabbets had not given his position away while firing "deep from out of the bedroom window, and I wasn't exposed to view. He assumed wrongly that I was a lot nearer to the bedroom window than I was. And he gave himself away, so that was his lot."

Often given the freedom to roam in search of targets of opportunity, Private Rabbets recounted another story of sniper versus enemy. "One day I went out and found a German military policeman standing at a crossroads; the only reason they stand at a crossroads is to direct a unit into a new position. I wanted to know what he was doing, so I crawled to within 150 yards range. He gave himself away by continually looking up the road to where he expected the unit to come from, and because there was only one direction to our lines, I knew roughly where they were going to. I shot him and then bundled him out of the way so that when the enemy got to the crossroads they wouldn't know where they were going. Then I went back to my unit to give them this intelligence."

Later, Rabbets fell asleep in a ditch and was awakened by the commotion of German field artillery going into action. He raised his rifle and shot down the four-man crews of two enemy guns before slinking off into the forest.

Edgar Rabbets survived the war after further service in the Middle East and Burma. He died at age 87 in 2003.

HENRY SCHAUER

ABOVE: A German Mark VI Tiger tank and self-propelled gun pause near Cisterna, where Private First Class Henry Schauer earned the Medal of Honor. (Creative Commons Bundesarchiv Bild via Wikipedia)

In single combat, the edge would typically go to the sniper rather than the common soldier, given the training and experience of the former. There are, however, exceptions, and Private First Class (Pfc.) Henry Schauer of the 2nd Battalion, 15th Regiment, 3rd Infantry Division, proved just right man to take charge in a difficult situation on May 23, 1944.

Schauer, from Scoby, Montana, had joined the US Army in February 1941, one of 13 boys from the town to do so, months before the country entered World War II in December of that year. Schauer participated in Operation Torch, the Allied invasion of North Africa, in November 1942, and was seriously wounded during Operation Husky, the invasion of Sicily in July 1943. He spent four months in the hospital before he was well enough to rejoin his unit.

During the fighting in Italy, Schauer again was in the thick of it. As American troops were fighting their way out of the Anzio beachhead on May 23, 1944, he was with a patrol that became pinned down by enemy sniper fire near the town of Cisterna. German bullets plinked around the men from several directions to the rear of the patrol, as Schauer, armed with a Browning Automatic Rifle (BAR) displayed incredible courage.

Rising from the cover of a ditch, Schauer walked 30 yards and carried the battle to four enemy snipers, locating each one of them in turn and killing them with four accurate bursts from his BAR. Seconds later, he noticed a fifth German sniper taking up a position behind the chimney of a destroyed house. Another quick burst from the BAR took out this rifleman as well.

Even after facing five enemy snipers and living to tell the tale, Schauer was not finished. As German artillery shells began falling within 15 feet of his position, a pair of enemy machine guns began to chatter. After taking cover momentarily, he gathered his strength once more and sprinted into the open. A single burst from the BAR killed two Germans manning a machine gun just 60 yards away, and when two more enemy soldiers rose to take their places, he shot them dead.

Responding to threats as they emerged, Schauer was unaware that such heroism would earn him the Medal of Honor, his country's highest decoration for courage under fire. His citation reads: "Pfc. Schauer shifted his body weight to fire at the other weapon 500 yards distant and emptied his weapon into the enemy crew, killing all four Germans. Next morning, when shells from a German Mark VI tank and a machine gun only 100 yards distant again forced the patrol to seek cover, Pfc. Schauer crawled toward the enemy machine gun, [and] stood upright only 80 yards from the weapon as its bullets cut the surrounding ground, and four tank shells fired directly at him burst within 20 yards. Raising his BAR to his shoulder, Pfc. Schauer killed the four members of the machine gun crew with one burst of fire."

Few episodes of combat courage rise to the level displayed by Schauer, whose exploits accounted for 17 Germans. He had faced the snipers, soldier to soldier, and never flinched. A reporter tagged him with the nickname "Kraut-an-hour Schauer." Along with the prestigious Medal of Honor, Schauer was promoted to the rank of technical sergeant.

Sometime later, Schauer went out on a night patrol. In the darkness, he was hailed by a German lieutenant who was fluent in English. The officer said simply that he was tired of fighting and wanted to surrender along with his command. Schauer gave assurances that the Germans would be treated humanely if they surrendered. He returned to his unit with 23 prisoners.

Henry Schauer survived World War II and died in 1997 at the age of 78.

ABOVE: A German sniper looks through the telescopic sights of his Mauser rifle. Private First Class Henry Schauer dispatched five enemy snipers in battle at Cisterna, Italy. (Creative Commons Bundesarchiv Bild via Wikipedia)

ABOVE: British and American soldiers meet in the Anzio beachhead. This photo was taken in May 1944, just before Henry Schauer stared down the barrel of German snipers' rifles and killed five of them. (Creative Commons Fidodog14 via Wikipedia)

CAPTAIN CLIFFORD SHORE

One of the outstanding books on the topic of sniping to emerge in the years after World War II was Captain Clifford Shore's *With British Snipers to the Reich*, published originally in 1948. The book gives an eyewitness account of Captain Shores' experiences in the field from the Normandy campaign through the end of the war in Europe. It also provides in-depth discussion on British sniper tactics, equipment, and training, as well as those of the Germans.

Captain Shore became acquainted with the sniper's craft not as a soldier of the British army, but as an officer of the Royal Air Force. He served with the rank of flying officer with the RAF Regiment ground installations and forward airstrips and was appointed weapon training officer with 2834 Anti-Aircraft Squadron, RAF Regiment. The unit came ashore at Gold Beach on June 7, 1944, D-Day plus-1.

After the war, Shore was commissioned in the British army and served as an instructor in the field sniper school ion Holland, which had originally been organized in Normandy. He worked alongside fellow instructors of the famed Lovat Scouts, and they honoured him with the presentation of and the right to wear their distinctive bonnet.

Among his many wartime reminiscences, Captain Shore recalled an incident in Holland that remained fresh in his mind for the remainder of his life.

"The battalion were holding one bank of the Nederweet Canal in Holland with the Germans on the opposite bank," he wrote. "The distance between the combatants was only about twenty-five yards (22.8 metres) and it was possible for the snipers to hear the Germans speaking quite distinctly. There was a very high bank on each side of the canal and although the Battalion snipers waited patiently for hours on end Jerry was very careful, and remained in the safety of his own towering bank. But one afternoon

ABOVE: A British sniper camouflaged with steel wool takes aim with his Enfield rifle. (Public Domain)

the snipers' patience was amply rewarded, since for some reason or other the Germans decided to have a celebration, and proceeded to get really drunk.

"The first Hun to be accounted for had a bottle of wine to his lips and was in the act of taking a long draught. Perhaps that is as good a way to die as any! The shot caused a little consternation in Jerry's camp, but not much. The interpreter from the Battalion Intelligence section was alongside the sniper who had 'bumped-off' the imbibing one, and he was delighted to translate the resultant conversation for the edification of the snipers.

"Immediately after the shot had been fired and the German with the bottle killed, a wine-thickened voice bellowed, 'Who in the name of Venus fired that shot?' A reply in a similar voice was, 'I don't know, but who's the silly – who's been shot anyway?'

"That afternoon drinking party was very costly for the Hun for before nightfall the snipers had killed five. It was really too easy. One wonders what the German platoon commander thought about it all next morning when he awakened with probably a damned bad head and found that his platoon had indeed been sadly depleted in strength."

The sniper takes his toll on the unwary and on the vigilant. He is the consummate opportunist.

ABOVE: A British sniper takes aim at a distant target during the fighting in Normandy. (Public Domain)

ABOVE: At a sniper school in France, a British sniper demonstrates his camouflage in the summer of 1944. (Public Domain)

WORLD WAR II IN THE EAST

Adolf Hitler ordered Operation Barbarossa to commence on June 22, 1941, and the Nazi juggernaut plunged into the Soviet Union. The Führer had made no secret of his intent, even though there had been rapprochement between the ideological polar opposites, the Fascist Nazis and the committed Communist Soviets. He had written about such a venture in the pages of Mein Kampf in the 1920s, confident that greater Germany would expand into the East, gaining lebensraum, or living space.

However, Barbarossa became the greatest strategic blunder of World War II, and the conflict on the Eastern front one of the bloodiest epic struggles in history. Millions of men fought one another, but ironically the solitary sniper became an icon of the terrible trial. On the Russian steppes and in the rubble of the cities, the aura of the sniper grew to mythical proportions.

The Battle of Stalingrad was a turning point in the war, decided in a five-month siege as the Soviets steadily strangled the besieged German Sixth Army in the city on the great River Volga that bore Josef Stalin's name. The Red army sniper found a killing ground unsurpassed, as did his German adversary. And one of the enduring legends of Great Patriotic War, as the Soviets called it, came to be in the crucible of combat.

Senior Sergeant Vasili Zaitsev, born in the village of Elininski in the foothills of the Ural Mountains on March 23, 1915, became the stuff of legend as a key protagonist in the drama of sniper and counter-sniper. In single combat, he is said to have vanquished one of the finest snipers in the German army, who had been sent to rid the Wehrmacht of its Soviet scourge. However, theory and conjecture continue to shroud the story in mystery more than 80 years after it supposedly took place.

Zaitsev's opponent has been known to history as Colonel Erwin König, Colonel Heinz Thorwald, and simply Major Königs. He was believed to have been the commander of the SS sniper school at Zossen, outside Berlin. But there appears to be no hard evidence that their duel to the death actually occurred. The entire saga may have been an invention of the Soviet

ABOVE: German soldiers stream into the Soviet Union on June 22, 1941, heading toward an uncertain fate. (Public Domain)

ABOVE: German armoured vehicles mass for an attack somewhere in the countryside of Belarus. (Public Domain)

ABOVE: Famed Soviet sniper Vasili Zaitsev smiles while holding a tool of his trade, the Moisin Nagant rifle. (Creative Commons Ministry of Defence of the Russian Federation via Wikipedia)

ABOVE: A Red army sniper smiles and shoulders his rifle with telescopic sights in the spring of 1942. (Creative Commons Какой-то человек с Красной Армии via Wikipedia)

As a boy, Vasili's grandfather had told him, "The man of the forest is without fear." Now, the consummate sniper set out to prove that very fact. In the short span of four weeks, he killed 40 Germans, and by mid-December 1942, his tally had mushroomed to 225. Zaitsev swiftly became a national hero, and tales of his extraordinary marksmanship spread rapidly through the ranks of both the Soviet and German armies. He hunted, hid, stalked and killed with cold efficiency, his remarkable run halted only by wounds received in the blast of a mortar shell in January 1943 that temporarily took away his sight.

After the war, Zaitsev wrote a memoir of his combat experience, *Notes of a Russian Sniper*. He commented, "As a sniper I've killed more than a few Nazis. I have a passion for observing enemy behaviour. You watch a Nazi officer come out of a bunker, acting all high and mighty, ordering his soldiers every which way, and putting on an air of authority. The officer hasn't got the slightest idea that he only has seconds to live."

Zaitsev also told the story of his encounter with the German master sniper in the ruins of Stalingrad. He painted a graphic picture with great detail and pulsating insight. Could it possibly be pure fiction? If so, the story remains a compelling insight into the world of the sniper nevertheless.

"The arrival of the Nazi sniper set us a new task: we had to find him, study his habits and methods, and patiently await the moment for one, and only one, well-aimed shot.

"I knew the style of the Nazi snipers by their fire and camouflage. But the character of the head of the school was still a mystery for me. Our day-by-day observations told us nothing definite. It was difficult to decide in which sector he was operating. He presumably altered his position frequently and was looking for me as carefully as I for him.

propaganda machine at a time when the country needed heroes, but it is also possible that the events described were true and accurate.

Like the sniper himself, the real truth surrounding the most famous sniper versus sniper duel in history remains obscured, cloaked in a historical hide of its own.

Zaitsev grew up a shepherd. He protected his flock from prowling wolves and hunted game in the deep forest. When war broke out, he was serving with the Soviet navy at the far eastern port of Vladivostok, shuffling papers as a bookkeeper. He grew restless as his homeland was threatened and volunteered to serve with the army. Assigned to the 284th Rifle Division, he entered the cauldron of Stalingrad in September 1942, already having demonstrated proficiency with the 7.62mm (.30-calibre) Moisin Nagant Model 1891/30 rifle.

"Then something happened. My good friend Morozov was killed, and Sheikin wounded, by a rifle with telescopic sights. Morozov and Sheikin were considered experienced snipers; they had often emerged victorious from the most difficult skirmishes with the enemy. Now, there was doubt. They had come up against the Nazi 'super-sniper' I was looking for."

Two days passed, and the deadly game of cat and mouse proceeded. Zaitsev and the elusive German each sought the upper hand.

"On the third day, the political instructor, Danilov, also came with us to the ambush," Zaitsev continued. "The light increased and minute by minute the enemy's positions could be distinguished more clearly… 'There he is! I'll point him out to you!' suddenly said the political instructor, excitedly. He barely, literally for one second, but carelessly, raised himself above the parapet, but that was enough for the German to hit and wound him."

Scanning the battle-scarred landscape, Zaitsev spotted a point of interest as he sought the enemy's hiding place. "Between the tank and the pillbox… lay a sheet of iron and a small pile of broken bricks. It had been lying there a long time, and we had grown accustomed to it being there. I put myself in the enemy's position and thought – where better for a sniper? One had only to make a firing slit under the sheet of metal, and then creep up to it during the night…

"'There's our viper!' came the quiet voice of Nikolai Kulikov from his hide-out next to mine. Now came the question of luring even a part of his head into my sights… Time was needed…

"We worked by night, we were in position by dawn. The Germans were firing on the Volga ferries. It grew light quickly and with daybreak the battle developed with new intensity. But neither the rumble of the guns nor the bursting of shells and bombs nor

ABOVE: On the Volga front, Vasili Zaitsev receives information during a meeting in 1942. (Public Domain)

ABOVE: Camouflaged in a wooded area, a Soviet sniper scans the horizon for an unsuspecting German target. (Public Domain)

anything else could distract us from the job at hand.

"The sun rose. We had decided to spend the morning waiting, as we might have been given away by the sun on our telescopic sights. After lunch our rifles were in the shade and the sun was shining directly on the German's position. At the edge of the sheet of metal something was glittering: an odd bit of glass – or telescopic sights?

"Kulikov carefully, as only the most experienced can do, began to raise his helmet. The German fired. For a fraction of a second Kulikov rose and screamed. The German believed that he had finally got the Soviet sniper he had been hunting for four days, and half raised his head from beneath the sheet of metal. That was what I had been banking on.

"I took careful aim. The German's head fell back, and the telescopic sights of his rifle lay motionless glistening in the sun until night fell."

For two valid reasons, the Soviet Red Army had maintained the world's most dedicated sniper training program in the years between the world wars. First, its fighting men had gained experience during the Spanish Civil War, and second, the experience with the Finnish snipers of the Winter War had taught them a bitter lesson. Even before the Winter War, by 1938 the Soviets had boasted that six million military personnel had earned the Voroshilov Sharpshooter badge.

The Soviet concept of sniping differed somewhat from that of the Western nations, including requirements of fieldcraft, intelligence gathering, stalking capability and plenty of nerve, as well as general sharpshooting. Therefore, many of the millions to claim the badge may not have been actual snipers in the truest sense of the word. Still, the vast number provided a large pool of talent when it came to selecting the very best. The first Soviet sniper schools, in fact, came into being in 1924.

When the war began, two types of snipers existed in the Soviet army, those who were regular army personnel, and those who were designated reserves of the supreme high command, or RVGK. The RVGK snipers were regularly formed into separate brigades and assigned to fronts (army groups) or armies in numbers ranging from platoons to battalions. When World War II began, a single sniper squad was organic to an infantry division, but the number grew steadily as division sniper schools turned out graduates. By 1945, a standard infantry (rifle) battalion included 18 snipers, and each rifle platoon included two snipers.

While Soviet snipers primarily utilized the Moisin Nagant 1891/30, which was the standard issue rifle, they made it an extremely lethal killing tool with the attachment of Zeiss telescopic sights, available since the 1930s after the Soviet Union had purchased the famed precision optics company. Although semiautomatic Tokarev rifles were introduced to sniper formations in 1938 and 1940 in order to increase the sniper's rate of fire, both attempts were deemed unsuccessful and these were withdrawn. Some snipers carried a second firearm, the 7.62mm (.30-calibre) PPSh submachine gun, when they anticipated the possibility of close combat.

The Red army developed a detailed doctrine, which dictated that its snipers were to be deployed at the lowest tactical level and hunt in pairs. Their use became an integrated aspect of infantry operations, and junior officers were required to have some understanding of their proper use on the battlefield. The Red army sniper became a

ABOVE: Pictured in a Soviet publication in 1943, sniper Vladimir Vishchepanov was killed the following year. (Public Domain)

ABOVE: A German sniper of a Luftwaffe field division looks through his telescopic sight on the Eastern front. (Creative Commons Bundesarchiv Bild via Wikipedia)

www.keymilitary.com 55

WORLD WAR II IN THE EAST

ABOVE: German snipers, one with binoculars around his neck, work their way through a trench on the Eastern front. (Creative Commons Bundesarchiv Bild via Wikipedia)

ABOVE: Soviet sniper Lyudmila Pavlichenko creeps through a wooded area during a stalk. (Public Domain)

ABOVE: This Soviet award for sniper excellence was presented qualified personnel in World War II. (Public Domain)

ABOVE: Wearing camouflage snow suits, Soviet snipers move warily through a ruined building. (Creative Commons Russian National News Agency Novosti via Wikipedia)

said to have harassed a German panzer unit for five days. He was unseen, and the periodic report of his rifle systematically meant another German casualty. The sniper remained hidden until a wispy cloud was seen to emanate from the turret of the disabled T-34 tank one morning.

The Germans investigated the telltale smoke and discovered the Soviet sniper inside. He was taken prisoner, and his fate is unknown. But likely, he was summarily executed. Apparently, the sniper had lived inside the tank, among the bodies of the dead crew, eating their frozen rations and thawing their frozen water canteens with the warmth of his body.

The Soviet sniper was no doubt a continuing threat to the invaders, and the propaganda machine in Moscow did its mightiest to conjure the "cult of the sniper." Some experts are incredulous as to the number of kills that were reported, including the total claimed by Ivan Sidorenko of 500. Other master snipers menace to the German invaders, preying not only on them physically, but also exerting constant pressure on the psyche. Literally no German was safe, particularly in the confines of a static "battlescape" such as Stalingrad.

The effectiveness of the Soviet sniper comes into sharp focus when considering the ordeal of the German 465th Infantry Regiment, ordered to attack through a dense forest in September 1941. After action reports indicated that the regiment lost 75 killed and 25 men missing to a phenomenon described as "tree snipers." These elusive individuals were seldom seen and apparently not silenced by the Germans with any meaningful response. The resourceful Soviet sniper was relentless, and his exploits often amazed his adversaries. A single sniper is according to Soviet reports were Nikolai Ilyin with 496, Ivan Kulbertinov 487, Mikhail Budenkov 437, Fyodor Okhlopkov 429, and Fyodor Djachenko 425. Of course, there were more high scoring snipers in the Red army, but whether these phenomenal tallies are to be believed remains an open question.

Sidorenko was born at Smolensk in September 1919 and was drafted into the Red army in 1939, initially training as an officer at the Simferopol Military Infantry School. A junior lieutenant of a mortar company, he was said to have taught himself sniping skills during the fighting around the Soviet capital city of Moscow in 1941. His efforts gained notice among senior officers, and he was ordered to train others as well.

Transferring to the 1122nd Rifle Regiment, Sidorenko hunted the Germans with gusto, once destroying an enemy tank and three prime movers with incendiary bullets. He was wounded several times, and his last injury occurred in Estonia in 1944. It was serious enough to keep him from returning to combat for the remainder of the war, and his superiors forbade him to try. He achieved the rank of major, was named Hero of the Soviet Union, and had trained at least 250 others in the basics of sniper warfare by the time the conflict ended.

After the war, Sidorenko lived in Chelyabinsk in the Ural Mountains and worked as a coal miner. He died in 1994 at the age of 74 and held other awards including the Order of Lenin, Order of the Red Banner, and Order of the Red Star.

Ilyin was 21 years old by the time he made his last sniper kill. He was declared a Hero of the Soviet Union in February 1943, but was killed in action during the epic Battle of Kursk just six months later on August 4, 1943.

ABOVE: Red army sniper Aliya Moldagulova peers through a telescopic sight. She scored 91 sniper victories before she was killed in action. (Public Domain)

Little is known of Kulbertinov, although he earned the nickname of Siberian Midnight during his sniping career.

Okhlopkov was the son of a Siberian peasant family, born in 1908 in the town of Krest-Khaldzhay. When World War II broke out, he was 31 years old. However, when he was not working as a miner or machine operator on a collective farm, he had trained as a sharpshooter during the 1920s as part of a political defence organization. He earned the Voroshilov badge for his demonstrated talent but was drafted into the Red army in 1941 as a machine gunner with the 1243rd Infantry Regiment, 375th Division.

Within a year and after the death of his brother who had been serving in the same regiment, Fyodor was transferred to the 234th Infantry Regiment and given the role of sniper. He often engaged in long stalks and waited for hours for an enemy sniper to give away his location. A reputation for a single shot producing a dead German soldier swept through the ranks of his comrades. He was wounded several times and strangely denied the honour of Hero of the Soviet Union when it was first proposed in 1944. The reasons for the denial remain unclear.

Okhlopkov received the Order of the Red Banner instead and was seriously wounded in the chest within days of the award on June 23, 1944, while fighting in Belorussia. It was his 12th wound of the war and prevented his return to action before hostilities ceased. He marched in the Moscow Victory Day parade in June 1945 and was discharged from the Red army, serving in numerous political positions for the next 25 years, including head of the military department of the Tattinsky District Communist Party committee. He worked on a collective farm and finally in May 1965 received the long overdue award of Hero of the Soviet Union as well as the Order of Lenin. He died in 1968, the father of 10, and his wife, Anna, was named a Mother Heroine, for bearing the large number of children.

When Captain Clifford Shore addressed the issue of Soviet sniper scores in his book *With British Snipers to the Reich,* he downplayed the accuracy of such numbers. In fact, a chapter of his work was devoted to the topic and titled, Russian Sniping…and the Great Myth.

"Many fantastic stories have come out of the Slav mists," wrote Shore, "which envelop the U.S.S.R but none more grotesque than the extraordinary fables of Russian snipers and sniping.

"I do not think there was any subject about which there was so much balderdash printed and published during the course of World War II than Russian sniping. If we are to believe every report we read about the terrific casualties inflicted on the Germans by Russian snipers it was amazing there were so many Germans left to face the Americans and British in N.W. Europe!...

"I have met some Russians who had been Red Army men, and saw them shoot in the summer of 1945. If their shooting prowess be taken as a criterion I think that the printed Russian figures of sniper casualties should be divided by a hundred…

"The real sharpshooters of the Russian Army were much respected. But these were not the tommy-gun artisans so beloved of the war correspondents and the Russian information bureaus…."

While Captain Shore was not alone in his scepticism, it must be concluded that the Soviet sniper exerted significant influence on the course of the war in the East. And the Red army was an equal opportunity employer. Female snipers were regularly trained and deployed during the course of the conflict, and records indicate that as many as 2,000 women saw action.

Lidiya Gudovantseva volunteered for service at the age of 18 and was sent to the Central Women's Sniper Training School in Veshnyaki, outside Moscow. She vividly remembered her first contact with the Germans. "I was scared. We had no idea what our first engagement would be like, and could we fire at a living man. When I first saw a German in my scope, he was walking boldly. Afterward, I felt sorry for him. I signalled to Sasha, who fired and killed a second German who had come out to get his body."

BELOW: German sniper trainees wearing camouflage suits form up in front of an instructor. (Creative Commons Bundesarchiv Bild via Wikipedia)

WORLD WAR II IN THE EAST

ABOVE: German snipers move out toward their objectives during intense training.
(Creative Commons Bundesarchiv Bild via Wikipedia)

ABOVE: A German sniper looks across the space between his own lines and those of the Red army at Stalingrad.
(Creative Commons Bundesarchiv Bild via Wikipedia)

Among other female snipers of the Red army, Nina Petrova was credited with 122 kills, while Natalia Kovshova shot 167 Germans. The undisputed top scoring female Soviet sniper of the Great Patriotic War was Lyudmila Pavlichenko with 309 kills.

Though there may have been exaggerated reports of Soviet sniper scores during World War II, it may be safely concluded that the snipers played a significant role in winning the ultimate victory. Those who were credited with at least 40 kills were given the title "noble sniper" and decorated with a medal emblematic of their courage. Whether scores are inflated or not is somewhat immaterial to the value of the message delivered by Soviet propagandists, bolstering the people to fight on through dark days and then to victory as Red army tanks rolled through the streets of Berlin, vanquishing the black heart of Nazism.

In the meantime, the crack of the sniper's rifle, whether the shooter was male or female, meant sudden death or serious injury. German paratrooper (fallschirmjäger) Karl-Heinz Pollmann survived three years of combat on the Eastern front and was wounded twice. On August 21, 1944, he nearly lost his life to a sniper's bullet in a heart-pounding sequence. "I was lying prone behind my MG34, ready to reload," he reflected, "when an explosive bullet, fired by a Russian sniper, hit me in the left arm. Dazed with shock, I felt no pain and stared at the wound from which a bubbly trickle of blood was flowing. I swooned. When I came to, I was lying on a garden gate, which three of my comrades were using as a makeshift stretcher to take me to safety."

Pollmann probably considered himself lucky to be alive.

The great city of Leningrad endured a 900-day siege by German and Finnish

Gudovantseva became a skilled sniper, proving along with others over and over that women were capable and competent killers. She fought in numerous battles, and toward the end of her career was grievously wounded. However, she responded with cool precision, firing at the German shooter some distance away and hiding behind a tree. The single shot killed the enemy soldier, and Lidiya survived to receive the Order of the Red Star in recognition of her reported 76 kills.

With the outbreak of the war, Aliya Moldagulova, born in Bulak, Kazakhstan, in October 1925, was only 16 years old. She withdrew from the Rybinsk Aviatechnical School, enlisted in the Red army and trained at Veshnyaki. Assigned to the 54th Rifle Brigade, she was credited with 91 kills before her death in combat. Wounded by a mortar shell, she fought the Germans hand-to-hand until her body was riddled with bullets on January 14, 1944. She was posthumously declared a Hero of the Soviet Union and received the Order of Lenin.

ABOVE: Soviet soldiers climb through the rubble of a destroyed building in Stalingrad.
(Creative Commons Bundesarchiv Bild via Wikipedia)

ABOVE: German soldiers hole up in a Stalingrad building and look out for Soviet snipers at Stalingrad. (Creative Commons Ruffneck'88 via Wikipedia)

ABOVE: A pair of Soviet soldiers stay under the cover of a trenchline to avoid fire from German snipers at Leningrad. (Creative Commons Russian International News Agency Novosti via Wikipedia)

The book was rereleased in English three years later as Dance of Death.

Kern wrote of visiting German snipers ensconced near the Narva bridgehead, close to the embattled city of Leningrad. "We were lying hard up against the enemy, in places no more than forty yards (43.7 metres) from their lines. It was a sniper's war. Dead silence reigned in the narrow strip of shell-torn land between us and the Soviet sap. Occasionally a heavy shell rumbled across the lines, and occasionally we heard the swish of the 'Hitler Scythe,' as the Russians called our machine guns. Then silence, heavy and oppressive, dropped again over the spectral landscape. Rain fell in a steady monotony out of a pale grey sky. Water stood knee-high in the trenches and gurgled over the edge of our gumboots.

"Undeterred by the weather, men stood here and there in the trenches gazing motionless towards the Russian line, sometimes alone, sometimes in pairs, one with the periscope, and the other resting to save his strength for the strike.

"A boy's eyes gazed hard and cool towards the enemy trench. From the corner of his mouth came a whisper: 'Nothing doing

forces during the war, and at times the conditions the civilian population endured were unimaginable. Starvation, disease, and paralyzing cold stalked the citizens just as surely as the snipers, Soviet, German and Finnish, placed one another in their deadly crosshairs. In 1948, author Erich Kern, who had served with the 4th Battalion of the dreaded 1st SS Panzer Division Leibstandarte Adolf Hitler, released his book Der Grosse Rausch (The Big Rush).

ABOVE: Citizens of Leningrad abandon their homes after a German artillery bombardment during the 900-day siege. (Creative Commons Russian International News Agency Novosti via Wikipedia)

WORLD WAR II IN THE EAST

ABOVE: A German sniper lies in the snow as he creeps forward on the Eastern front. (Creative Commons Julius Jaaskalainen via Wikipedia)

ABOVE: Two female Soviet snipers search for targets from their dug-in position. Note the decoy helmet. (Creative Commons Cassoway Colorizations via Wikipedia)

here.' Two men who were walking bent and stooping, along the trench towards us, straightened a little as they passed and in the same moment a sharp report rent the sodden air like the crack of a whip. We ducked. Who wanted to die in the dreary grey of a wet morning?"

The German army and the Waffen SS both augmented their sniper ranks as World War II progressed, at least in part to counter the swarms of snipers the Soviets were committing to action. By 1943, sniper training was underway at multiple locations in Germany, Austria, Hungary, and Lithuania. Army and SS snipers often trained together, and the instructors were regularly combat veterans who had been wounded in action and were unable to return to the front.

In 1967, three of Germany's most accomplished snipers told their stories to Captain Hans Widhofer of the Austrian army, and their comments were published in the magazine Truppendienst. The three men, Matthias Hetzenauer with 345 kills, Sepp Allerberger with 257, and Helmut Wirnsberger with 64, had served with the 3rd Mountain Division and primarily fired the standard issue Mauser Karabiner 98K 7.92mm (.31-calibre) rifle equipped with telescopic sights. Allerberger also used a captured Soviet rifle for a while, and Hetzenauer and Wirnsberger had carried the semiautomatic Gewehr 43.

The three German veterans had been members of a battalion sniper unit that included as many as 22 members under the direct command of Wirnsberger. They explained that other soldiers in the battalion also carried the Karabiner 98K with telescopic sights, but these men were primarily functioning as ordinary infantrymen who occasionally received special orders to carry out a certain task.

The snipers always operated in pairs and used camouflage as necessary. Allerberger used a fan or umbrella with its canopy festooned with foliage to resemble uneven brush, and he remembered along with Hetzenauer the employment of dummies to draw Soviet fire. Some of these dummies actually were equipped with rifles that were discharged by pulling a remote wire to attract the attention of the enemy.

Hetzenauer was adamant that his marksmanship skills could bring down a standing target at a staggering distance of 800 metres (874 yards).

Priorities included the "Elimination of observers," the former snipers said, "of the enemy's heavy weapons and of commanders, or special order when all important or worthwhile targets were eliminated, for example, anti-tank gun positions, machine gun positions, and so on. Snipers followed closely the attacking units and whenever necessary eliminated enemies who operated heavy weapons and those who were dangerous to our advance."

Hetzenauer noted that he was sometimes ordered to work on the offensive. "In a few cases, I had to penetrate the enemy's main line of resistance at night before our own attack. When our own artillery had opened fire, I had to shoot at enemy commanders and gunners because our own forces would have been too weak in number and ammunition without this support."

Austrian by birth, Hetzenauer was the child of a farming family of the Tyrol in the town of Brixem, Thale. At age 17, he was drafted into Kufstein Mountain Rescue Battalion 140 in September 1942, briefly released from service, and then called back to duty in January 1943, to the military training centre at Seetaler Alpe, where he trained as a sniper and was subsequently assigned to the 7th Company, Mountaineer Regiment 144. A recipient of the Knight's Cross of the Iron Cross, he saw action against the Soviets in the Carpathian Mountains, Hungary, and Slovakia, and some sources aver that his entire tally of kills was recorded only in 10 months of action from August 1944 to May 1945, an astonishing average rate of at least one kill per day. He was only 20 years old.

Hetzenauer's longest confirmed kill was measured at 1,200 yards (1,100 metres), and the Karabiner 98K and Gewehr 43 he carried were equipped with ZF4 (4X) telescopic sights. On November 6, 1944, he was wounded in the head by artillery fire. He recovered and returned to service the following April but was captured by

ABOVE: After 59 kills, sniper Roza Shanina was killed in action in January 1945 at the age of 20. (Public Domain)

ABOVE: Sniper Natalya Kovshova of the Red army 528th Rifle Regiment, was killed in action near Novgorod in 1942. (Public Domain)

ABOVE: This Soviet postage stamp depicts the heroic deaths of sniper Natalya Kovshova and her spotter Mariya Polivanova. (Public Domain)

ABOVE: Now a museum piece, this Moisin Nagant sniper rifle once belonged to A.G. Shirnokleyev during World War II. (Creative Commons Franco Atirador via Wikipedia)

Red army soldiers a month later and held in prison in the Soviet Union for five years. He returned home in 1950, married, and worked as a carpenter. He died peacefully in 2004 at the age of 79.

Josef "Sepp" Allerberger was another young Austrian, born in 1924 in Steiermark, near Salzburg. He was first deployed as a machine gunner on the Eastern front in June 1943 and was slightly wounded at Stavropol. After recuperating, he made at least 27 kills before being sent to sniper training at Seetaler Alpe, some of them possibly with the Soviet Moisin Nagant rifle. Allerberger worked as a carpenter after the war and died in Walz-Siezenheim, Austria, at the age of 85 in 2010. Although there is no supporting documentation, Allerberger related that he had been awarded the Knight's Cross of the Iron Cross late in the war.

In 2005, author Albrecht Wacker published the book *Sniper on the Eastern Front: The Memoirs of Sepp Allerberger Knights Cross*. The work was based on extensive interviews the author had with the former sniper, and the description of the old veteran's experience paints an indelible image.

"'You got him, lad! A perfect hit. That swine is dead,' wrote Wacker of an encounter during Allerberger's first sniper deployment. "Sepp saw the muzzle flash of his opponent flicker from a pile of wood like a breath of wind…His counterpart stayed in his position and was waiting for a new target – a fatal mistake which he was about to pay for with his life…the Russian was lying only about 90m away, so he could aim the regular way using the fore and rear sights. Suddenly he became nervous. His comrades were expecting an absolute precise shot, and he abruptly realized he had the task of killing a man in calculated and pre-meditated cold blood for the first time in his life. Scruples gnawed at his conscience. His throat went dry, his heart was racing, and his hands trembled… 'Well, what now? Give him a wallop,' he heard a comrade saying… And suddenly the strain left him… He took the pressure point, breathed deeply in and out, held his breath and pulled the trigger…."

Years later, the misty memory of his sniper war came back to Sepp Allerberger in an electrifying flashback.

"A shining summer morning on the Eastern Front is just warming up," wrote Wacker. "The dampness of the night gives a spicy scent of earth and grass to the warming air. But he doesn't pay any attention to Nature; he cannot let it distract him now. All his senses are tensed. He resembles a predator searching for prey. Looking through the binoculars, he scans the approaches of the Russian front line again. Somewhere out there was his enemy's perfectly disguised position, the Russian sniper who'd killed nine comrades in the last few days. He had to be an expert, because Sepp had already been searching in vain for his position for two days. But when the marksman's bullet had hit the ninth rifleman in the early hours of the morning Sepp believed he'd been able to distinguish the approximate direction from which the shot had come.

"There, finally, a revealing sign. Tufts of grass standing somehow strangely below the edge of a bush. His gaze concentrated piercingly on the suspicious spot. Yes, that was exactly where he was. The adrenaline coursed through Sepp as he recognized shadowy parts of a telescopic sight, and the weapon's muzzle as it suddenly flashed. With a crashing bang he could see the projectile racing towards him. As if paralyzed, he lay there unable to escape. With a damp shock the missile hit the middle of his forehead and his head and thoughts exploded in a flash of light.

"At that very moment Sepp wakes up – from a deep dream…."

Indeed, the life of the sniper, even when his days in the field are complete and he has survived a spectacular ordeal, like no other wartime experience, the memory remains. It haunts his sleep and his waking moments for the rest of his days.

At Leningrad, Kern and company continued their hazardous walk down the German trenchline on that dreary morning, encountering snipers along the way. "We met more of them farther along the line, this time two boys from the Siebenburgen, Rudolf aged 19 and Michael aged 24. We talked to them about their homes, about the war, about everything. Rudolf's father was a huntsman, his brother a huntsman, and he had it in his blood. Put a gun in his hand and his eye looked for a target. Michael had seen his first hunt while still a boy. Now they were back at the butts,

ABOVE: SS troops await orders to move forward on the Eastern front. Sometimes snipers were ordered across enemy lines ahead of attacks. (Creative Commons Johannes Dorn via Wikipedia)

WORLD WAR II IN THE EAST

ABOVE: Estonian soldiers fighting with the Germans brave sniper fire to set up their machine gun at Narva, 1944. (Public Domain)

ABOVE: Caught briefly in the open, German soldiers scurry for cover before Soviet snipers open fire in Stalingrad. (Public Domain)

but this quarry fired back. 'We must only fire occasionally and we have to hit them when we do,' Rudolf said, his eyes alight, 'otherwise we give ourselves away…'

"A Red Army man showed himself in the opposite trench. A quick aim, then 'Crack!' and he fell forward. A hit? – or had he merely ducked for cover? More hours of waiting and then at last a target. Another shot. The man on the other side stopped and tilted backwards. A pencil mark on the stockade – that one counted. I asked what they thought about as they stood there crossing them off one after another. 'Only that there's one more gone; one less to hold a rifle,' they said.

"Sometimes the 'opposite number' across the way spotted one of our snipers. Where was he? Once the target was sighted, a duel developed in which every conceivable trick was used, every scrap of cunning. A whole magazine might be fired off from a feint position, then a quick dash back to the old stand to see if the enemy would reply. Once the position was located it was usually the end of the duel. Sometimes it was our man who lost. Then another took his place as the eyes of the forward line, behind whose vigilance the others could afford to relax."

Harry Mierlet, a German soldier on the Eastern front, was acutely aware of the sniper, and he knew well that the unguarded moment, no matter how fleeting, might be his last. He wrote a chilling letter home and described a fatal day for an officer of the German army.

"I stood immediately next to him [Captain O.], about 150 metres (164 yards) opposite an undergrowth in which Russian sharpshooters lay. He was hit, I had the luck instantly to have thrown myself down…as soon as I saw the fellow lying there before us. The captain reacted a fraction of a second later and was wounded."

The sniper was the purveyor of death not only for the enemy soldier. Tragically, particularly in the confines of urban warfare, civilians were often targeted when they ventured into the open. Whether the fatal shots were intentional, reactionary, or simply a mistake, lay only in the heart and mind of the man or woman who pulled the trigger. In 1973, author William Craig's book *Enemy At The Gates: The Battle For Stalingrad* was published. Craig recounts a tragic, heart rending occurrence.

"They ran into the street and fell into a zig-zag trench beside Russian soldiers and civilians. A little girl lay huddled up, her body punctured with shrapnel. She screamed and screamed: 'Find my mama before I die.' Mrs. Karmanova could not bear it. As she crouched under a hail of bullets and tried to block out the sounds of the dying child, she saw a family dart from shelter and run toward the river. At the same moment, a German sniper tracked them and quickly killed the son, the father, and then the mother. The sole survivor, a little girl, paused in bewilderment over her mother's body. In the trench, Russian soldiers cupped their hands and hollered, 'Run! Run!' Others took up the cry. The girl hesitated, then bolted from the corpses into the darkness. The German sniper did not fire again."

World War II on the Eastern front was the stage on which incredible brutality played out. Masses of humanity tore at one another in terrific carnage. And then, the sniper brought his silent, stealthy skill to bear like nowhere else in military history.

ABOVE: A determined German soldier rises to throw a hand grenade during Operation Barbarossa; however, soon enough such activity might find him in the sights of a Soviet sniper. (Public Domain)

GERMAN ARMY SNIPER SCHOOL

The German army gained tremendous respect for the Soviet snipers encountered during Operation Barbarossa, but at first its senior establishment determined to rely on heavy firepower and superior weaponry to overcome the delays the sniper presented at the tactical level of the offensive. Soon enough, though, it was determined that the Wehrmacht must fight sniper with sniper. Thus, by mid-1942 sniper schools had been established in several locations in Germany and in the conquered territories.

The duration of the sniper course was four weeks, and those chosen to participate were either combat veterans who had demonstrated talent with the Karabiner K98 rifle, draftees that had some experience in hunting or gamekeeping and displayed promise, and those already in the ranks who were perceived as sharpshooters. The senior sniper instructor, typically with the rank of sergeant major, was a combat veteran who was either specially assigned or had been wounded and lost medical clearance to return to a frontline unit.

The trainees were divided into groups of five, each handled by an instructor sergeant, and the newly arrived prospects were greeted with a welcome sign displayed in bold letters and reading in part: "The sniper is the hunter among soldiers!; His job is difficult and demands the dedication of body, soul and mind; Only a thoroughly convinced and steadfast soldier can become a sniper; It is only possible to destroy an enemy if one has learned to hate and persecute him with all the strength in one's soul!; A sniper is a man set apart from the common soldier; He fights unseen.

Sniper candidates were introduced to the various types of weapons available along with the multiple types of telescopic sights in use. The efficiency, strengths and weaknesses of each were explained in detail, and the weapons were fired on the practice range prior to a return to open firing with the 98K from a distance of 50 to 300 metres in standing, kneeling and prone positions. Hard lessons in tactical terrain assessment, camouflage, and digging foxholes, hides and trenches, followed.

The shooting garden was a challenge for the candidates. Made to resemble a small village, valley and approaching road, it was constructed on a small scale, and each rifleman was given a small-calibre sporting rifle. Then, dummy figures began to appear in windows and doorways; horse carts crossed the shooter's field of vision. Marksmanship scores were recorded, and the candidates visited the shooting garden often in the spirit of competition. The students received their 98K rifles and optics early in the second week and then calibrated them appropriately.

ABOVE: A German sniper and spotter team work together on the Eastern front at Voronezh in the Soviet Union. (Creative Commons Bundesarchiv Bild via Wikipedia)

ABOVE: Troops of the Waffen SS deploy with cover. SS snipers often trained with Wehrmacht personnel. (Public Domain)

Candidates were also shown a film titled Choice of, and Constructing Positions. Interestingly, the film was of Russian origin and made in 1935. German subtitles were supplied. The students were later put into real-time scenarios and introduced to offensive and defensive field tactics. During the final two weeks of the course, special emphasis was placed on the practical application of tactics and survival in the field.

Graduates of the sniper course received a certificate of completion, and its text included exhortations such as: "Fight fanatically! You are a people hunter!; Shoot calmly and deliberately, without haste: the hit rewards you!; The most deadly opponent is the enemy sniper! Always reckon with him and attempt to outfox him!; Never fire more than once from your position! Be a master of camouflage and the use of terrain!"

The trained German sniper then got down to deadly business.

ABOVE: A German sniper team is shown in action on the Eastern front in 1943. (Public Domain)

LYUDMILA PAVLICHENKO

Lyudmila Pavlichenko holds the distinction of being the highest scoring female sniper of World War II and probably of all time. Her total of 309 credited kills stands out among the Red Army elite, and though there is some question as to the accuracy of the number, there is no doubt that the Ukrainian born Hero of the Soviet Union made an unforgettable contribution to victory in the Great Patriotic War.

Pavlichenko was born on July 12, 1916, in the town of Bila Tserkva. Her family relocated to Kiev when she was 14 years old, and she grew up in an athletic environment, joining a local shooting club. While working as a grinder in the Kiev Arsenal Factory, she had developed her interest in firearms. She married and had a son, but after the union failed she enrolled in Kiev University in 1937, intent on becoming a teacher. She was in her fourth year of study when the Nazis invaded the Soviet Union on June 22, 1941.

Lyudmila volunteered for Red army service but declined to become a nurse, finally winning acceptance as a sniper with the 25th Rifle Division. She quickly completed training and was sent to the front, where she was not given a sniper rifle, but only a shotgun and a grenade. When she obtained a Moisin Nagant rifle from a wounded comrade, she put it to use immediately, shooting two German soldiers.

Soon afterward, she began a systematic campaign of destruction, killing 187 enemy soldiers during approximately 10 weeks at the siege of Odessa. She then fought during the siege of Sevastopol in Crimea and shot another 100 Germans while also training sniper candidates. By the spring of 1942, she had been promoted to senior sergeant and then lieutenant. In May of that year, her score had risen to 257 kills.

However, just a month later, Pavlichenko was seriously wounded by enemy mortar fire and evacuated from Sevastopol. After a month in the hospital, she returned to duty, but the high command refused to allow her to participate in further combat operations. She was a national hero, and her final score of 309 kills supposedly included 36 German snipers. Therefore, she was employed as a sniper instructor and participated in many events, making speeches and encouraging the Soviet people through the Red army's propaganda machine.

Pavlichenko travelled to Canada and the United States during the war and was received at the White House in Washington, D.C., by President Franklin D. Roosevelt and First Lady Eleanor Roosevelt. In November 1942, she visited Great Britain as well. Although she never returned to combat, her achievements were lauded as a Hero of the Soviet Union in 1943. She also received the Order of Lenin twice.

After the war, Lyudmila returned to Kiev University and completed her studies. She became a historian and research assistant to Soviet navy headquarters and participated in the Soviet Committee of Veterans of War. However, she was plagued by post-traumatic stress disorder and depression, having lost her second husband during the war. She died of a stroke on October 10, 1974, at the age of 58.

ABOVE: This photo of Lyudmila Pavlichenko in a trench with her rifle was taken in 1942. (Public Domain)

ABOVE: Lieutenant Lyudmila Pavlichenko posed for this portrait at the height of her career as a Soviet sniper. (Public Domain)

ABOVE: During a visit to Washington, D.C., in September 1942, Pavlichenko stands at centre with Supreme Court Justice Robert Jackson and First Lady Eleanor Roosevelt. (Public Domain)

ZAITSEV THE TEACHER

The service rendered by the snipers of the Red army during the siege of Stalingrad was so valuable that the training of replacements continued throughout the five-month campaign. The Lazur chemical plant was an immense structure, large enough to accommodate a firing range that included the use of distant targets shaped like a human torso, a head with the Nazi coal scuttle helmet, and firing embrasures where enemy machine gunners or riflemen might appear.

Vasili Zaitsev, the legendary sniper whose tally during the Battle of Stalingrad is believed to have been 225 or more, was also an instructor at the makeshift training centre throughout the pivotal struggle for control of the industrial city on the River Volga. One of his students was Tania Chernova, a Russian-American patriot who was believed by some to be Zaitsev's romantic interest.

Chernova was burning with hatred for the Nazis, who had murdered her grandparents, and she exacted her own brand of vengeance with 80 kills in only three months of fighting around Stalingrad. She earned the nickname of the "blond sniper" and only withdrew from the front when she was seriously wounded in the explosion of a land mine.

Although she gained fame in her own right, Chernova remembered vividly a series of events that presented a painful lesson and brought her face to face with a displeased Zaitsev. Tania referred to her victims as sticks and probably embarked on her daily forays in the vicinity of the Red October plant, which provided steel for the tractor factory in Stalingrad.

On one fateful day, Tania and several other sniper students ventured out. They found an upper floor of an abandoned building and settled in among scattered bricks and debris. Zaitsev had given them explicit instructions to wait for his order to open fire to avoid giving away their positions. And to Tania's consternation, the snipers waited – for hours – watching German soldiers pass nearby, but not pulling a trigger because of Zaitsev's prohibition.

Tania grew more and more impatient, waiting by a window. Then, when a large column of German troops came into view, she could stand it no longer. She shouted, "Fire!" and the entire upper floor erupted with the reports of sniper rifles. Tania poured fire into the enemy, and within minutes there were 17 bodies on the ground in front of her post. But some of the Germans had managed to evade the torrent of gunfire.

Even as the sniper students congratulated themselves, German artillery was zeroing in on the building where they were hidden. And then the crash of several large-calibre shells caused walls to crash down, killing and injuring several of them. Momentarily stunned, Tania gathered herself and rushed to tell Zaitsev what had happened.

When he heard her report, Zaitsev slapped her forcefully across the face. He told her frankly that she bore responsibility for the

ABOVE: The Tractor Factory in Stalingrad was the scene of heavy fighting and sniper activity.
(Creative Commons Bundesarchiv Bild via Wikipedia)

deaths of her comrades. For hours afterward, she was inconsolable.

After Tania was wounded, she lost contact with Zaitsev and believed that he had been killed in action. Nearly three decades after the war, she was surprised to learn that he had indeed survived. Chernova is believed to have married after the war and died sometime around 2015, aged possibly into her 90s.

Vasili Zaitsev recovered from wounds at Stalingrad that temporarily blinded him and returned to fight during the Red army drive on Berlin, finishing the war with at least 242 kills. He ended his military career with the rank of captain. After the war, he became the manager of a textile plant in Kiev. He died in the city at age 76 on December 15, 1991. Originally buried in Kiev, Zaitsev was reinterred in Stalingrad (now Volgograd) at the massive Mamayev Kurgan memorial.

ABOVE: Vasili Zaitsev and a pair of sniper comrades venture out clad in their camouflage snow suits.
(Creative Commons Ministry of Defence of the Russian Federation via Wikipedia)

ABOVE: Tania Chernova was known as the Blond Sniper.
(Creative Commons david bowie via Wikipedia)

BRUNO SUTKUS

On May 8, 1944, Bruno Sutkus, a sniper with the 196th Panzergrenadier Regiment, watched a Soviet sniper intently. "He wore a camouflage jacket and mask," the German wrote with clinical detachment in his post-war book *Sniper Ace: From the Eastern Front to Siberia*. "Some way to the right was a rise with some rubble where a house had probably stood. This location attracted me like a magnet, and I kept checking the position of the sun in relation to it.

"Around noon I noticed a flash and some movement. In the ruined cellar was a Russian artillery-spotter's post… I watched the Russians entering the cellar. At 500 metres two men – senior officers by their uniforms – came through the communication trench. I shot one down. The other reacted with shock and held his ground. I had already reloaded and shot him too.

"The Russian sniper I had detected earlier identified my position from these two rounds. He made a slight turn to fire at me and I hit him at the same instant as his bullet hissed past my head…."

On that day, Obergefreiter Sutkus began the journal entries that were required, describing each one of his kills. In turn, each entry was verified by an observer and his

ABOVE: Wearing camouflage, Bruno Sutkus sights his Mauser rifle. (Creative Commons Cassowary Colorizations via Wikipedia)

battalion commander. By the end of the war, there were 209 such entries.

Of Lithuanian and German ancestry, Sutkus was 19 years old, born in Tannenwalde, East Prussia, on May 14, 1924. He had joined the Hitler Youth in 1938 and then become a member of the SA (Sturmabteilung), or Storm Troopers, where his marksmanship prowess was noted, and he was given a rifle to continue sharpening his skills. He was drafted into the Germany army in July 1943 and then trained at the sniper school in the Lithuanian capital of Vilnius and posted to his regiment. He gained a reputation for deadly accuracy and was so successful that he was regularly summoned to deal with troublesome situations. In January 1945, Sutkus was wounded, and when he recovered sufficiently he was reassigned as an instructor, having given his sniper's journal to a friendly nurse.

After World War II ended, Sutkus was taken prisoner, tortured, and forced to join the Red army. He had been in possession of forged identity documents that declared him to be essentially without a country and having spent the war years as a farm labourer. He escaped and joined the anti-Soviet Lithuanian resistance but was captured once again.

Soviet authorities were suspicious of their prisoner's past, and Sutkus chose to join other prisoners in exile in Siberia rather than risk further investigation that might uncover his identity as a decorated Wehrmacht sniper. He endured forced labour for some time and was finally allowed to settle in Vilnius in 1971. Twenty years later, he visited Germany, and after the collapse of the Soviet Union he helped to train the newly created Lithuanian army. Miraculously, he received his journal from the nurse, who had kept it safe, and wrote his memoir, receiving German citizenship in 1994 and relocating to Germany three years later. He died on August 29, 2003, at the age of 79.

ABOVE: This photo of Bruno Sutkus was taken in the Carpathian Mountains in the autumn of 1944. (Creative Commons Sidas8888 via Wikipedia)

ABOVE: In full camouflage gear, Bruno Sutkus, one of the highest-scoring snipers of the German army, heads toward his hide. (Creative Commons Cassowary Colorizations via Wikipedia)

THE MILITARY SNIPER

WORLD WAR II IN THE PACIFIC

Only nine months after the Japanese attack on Pearl Harbor had plunged the United States into World War II, American Marines splashed ashore on an otherwise nondescript island in the South Pacific. The primary objective on Guadalcanal in the Solomons archipelago was control of an airstrip, construction begun by the Japanese but as yet unfinished, that would give the possessor potential air superiority at all points of the compass for hundreds of miles.

The American landing on Guadalcanal on August 7, 1942, was the first offensive combat land operation for the US military in World War II. With it came the first of many land battles with a tenacious foe. The Japanese defenders were dedicated to their emperor, Hirohito, pledged to die for the god-man who sat on the Chrysanthemum Throne in Tokyo and inculcated with the code of Bushido, which taught that giving one's life for the emperor was the highest virtue and surrender meant unthinkable shame.

Somehow, solitary combat seemed to suit the Japanese ethos, and the role of the sniper blended with it like a single rifleman hidden in the deep, death concealing jungle. Though the Japanese had trained snipers for their specific role, it must be acknowledged that in the Pacific, as in other theatres of war, individuals who were not formally trained did sometimes fit the broad definition of a sniper; that is, a rifleman who fires his weapon at a specific target as an individual and not within the context of a unit-scale action.

Trained snipers were instructed to seek high value targets, such as commissioned or non-commissioned officers and those who operated heavy weapons such as tanks and artillery, while often an untrained rifleman acting as a sniper might shoot at an available target regardless. Of course, the most telling difference between an ordinary infantry rifleman and a trained sniper is the trained sniper's intent to kill a specific target via the element of surprise, while an infantryman firing in concert with other infantrymen does not necessarily aim each shot carefully at a delineated target.

During the six-month ordeal on Guadalcanal, American forces finally wrested control of the island from the Japanese, but the introduction to jungle warfare was tough. Author Richard Tregaskis was there for much of the fighting, and from his experiences came his seminal book *Guadalcanal Diary*, published first in 1943 within months of the American victory.

ABOVE: US Marine Scout Sniper William Deane Hawkins received a posthumous Medal of Honor for heroism at Tarawa. (Public Domain)

Tregaskis encountered Japanese snipers on more than one occasion and wrote of the harrowing experiences for his audience at home in the US. "More Jap .25s (6.5mm rifles) opened up ahead; a storm of fire

ABOVE: A Marine of the 1st Division fires his M-1 carbine at Japanese along Wana Ridge, Okinawa, 1945. (Public Domain)

ABOVE: This photo was taken on the island of Makin during Operation Galvanic just as a Japanese sniper's rifle report was heard. The American soldiers are beginning to take cover. (Creative Commons National Museum of Health and Medicine via Wikipedia)

and allow American troops to pass by before opening fire from behind. At times, the movements of sizable formations were halted in their tracks while the sniper was hunted.

With incredible patience the Japanese sniper was believed to sometimes haul a small chair into the tree along with him, and he might even carry a light Nambu machine gun up as well. He might also dig a small spider hole, cover the entrance with leaves and debris, and then pop up without notice and fire. Contrary to the doctrine of most Western armies, the Japanese sniper usually worked alone, a thin veil of mesh or netting covering his face and wearing a cape adorned with palm fronds and camouflage to disguise his hiding place. He sometimes wore camouflage green makeup to conceal exposed

ABOVE: A US Marine fires at the Japanese troops occupying a pillbox on the islet of Betio during the assault on Tarawa, picking them off with his rifle. (Public Domain)

broke and filled the jungle. I dived for the nearest tree, which unfortunately stood somewhat alone and was not surrounded by deep foliage. When the firing continued and I could hear the occasional impact of a bullet hitting a nearby tree or snapping off a twig, I debated whether it would be wiser to stay in my exposed spot or to run for a better 'ole and risk being hit by a sniper en route.

"I was still debating the question when I heard a bullet whirr very close to my left shoulder, heard it thud into the ground and then heard the crack of the rifle which had fired it. That was bad. Two Marines on the ground ten or fifteen feet ahead of me turned and looked to see if I had been hit. They had evidently heard the bullet passing. That made up my mind. I jumped up and made for a big bush. I found it well populated with ants which crawled up my trouser legs, but such annoyances were secondary now.

"The sniper who had fired at me was still on my track. He had evidently spotted my field-glasses and taken me for a regular officer.

"I searched the nearby trees, but could see nothing moving, no smoke, no signs of any sniper. Then a .25 cracked again and I heard the bullet pass – fortunately not as close as before. I jumped for better cover, behind two close trees which were surrounded by ferns, small pineapple plants and saplings. Here I began to wish I had a rifle. I should like to find that sniper, I thought. I had made an ignominious retreat. My dignity had been offended."

Tregaskis was fortunate to have lost only his notional honour. The Japanese sniper was resolute, often armed with the 6.5mm (.25-calibre) Arisaka Type 38 rifle, the 6.5mm Type 97, or 7.7mm (.30-calibre) Type 99 with telescopic sights fitted. The sights were often of 4X magnification and fixed without the capability of adjustment for windage or other conditions. Equipped with spikes for his shoes that were specially made with a separate fitting for the big toe to assist in climbing trees, the Japanese sniper sometimes chose to perch in a tall palm, tie himself into his position above the thick jungle that might limit his visibility,

ABOVE: American soldiers of the 32nd Infantry Division, wary for snipers, inspect former Japanese positions in New Guinea (Public Domain)

THE MILITARY SNIPER

ABOVE: A Japanese soldier fires a Type 92 heavy machine gun in the jungle. American snipers took enemy machine-gunners out with well-placed single shots. (Public Domain)

ABOVE: Men of the 3rd Marine Regiment hit the beach on the island of Bougainville while under fire. (Public Domain)

body parts. Sometimes the trees were notched to make climbing speedier, and usually the sniper took provisions of food and water for an extended stay into the lofty post.

One again, on the advance at Guadalcanal, Tregaskis wrote of his charmed life. "Suddenly I saw the foliage move in a tree across the valley. I looked again and was astonished to see the figure of a man in the crotch of the tree. He seemed to be moving his arms and upper body. I was so amazed at seeing him so clearly that I might have sat there and reflected on the matter if my reflexes had not been functioning – which they fortunately were. I flopped flat on the ground just as I heard the sniper's gun go off and the bullet whirred over my head. I knew then that his movement had been the raising of his gun."

Although there were reports that Japanese snipers were frequently discovered in trees, US army historian John Miller, Jr., took a different perspective on the fighting at Guadalcanal in his official capacity. "One of the great bugaboos of the Guadalcanal campaign which slowed nearly all advances by the infantry was the belief, firmly held by nearly all troops, that Japanese 'snipers' operated from treetops. But this belief, which the Japanese curiously entertained about American snipers, was seldom supported by facts. The Japanese rifleman was not especially equipped for sniping, nor did he usually climb into trees to shoot."

Of course, considering the inherent instability of a treetop perch, a sniper might often have difficulty acquiring and effectively engaging a target from such a position. Nevertheless, there are many instances of American soldiers and Marines encountering Japanese snipers ensconced in trees, just as Tregaskis did.

The Japanese sniper fought through jungle, high mountains, and across desert islands from the frontier of India and Burma to China and the spits of land that dotted the Central and South Pacific. At times, the thickness of the jungle vegetation made accurate firing at considerable distance virtually impossible. Nevertheless, the sniper was still a deadly protagonist of warfare in the Pacific, even at closer range.

Soldiers of the US 41st Infantry Division slogged their way through the jungles of the island of New Guinea, fighting along the coastline of the large island beside their Australian allies. Wary of the deep jungle that hid the enemy sniper, they quickly became acquainted with his cunning.

"From a tree almost anywhere around our oval perimeter, a Jap sharpshooter could choose a Yank target who had to leave his water-soaked hole," read the division history. "The range could be all of 200-400 yards. The keen-eyed sniper could steady his precision killing tool on a branch and tighten the butt to his shoulder. He could take a clear sight picture and squeeze the trigger. All 1/Bn might hear is a Jap.25-caliber cartridge crack, like a Fourth of July cap sparked on a stone. Then a Yank cowering in a hole might hear the prolonged dying groan of a man in his next squad. Or long after a deadly silence, he might find his buddy a pale corpse with a deceptively small hole in his forehead."

The Japanese sniper was often so well concealed that his position was nearly impossible to pinpoint. Hidden in the thick jungle canopy, he was dislodged at times only by sweeping fire from a Marine's BAR, a .30-calibre machine gun brought up to spray the surrounding treetops and ground vegetation, or even an artillery barrage intended to saturate the area where a particularly troublesome series of shots had emanated from. The long barrel of the Arisaka rifle and the relatively small propellant charge in the 6.5mm cartridge allowed only for a brief report of the rifle and a wisp of telltale smoke, making the enemy sniper even more difficult to locate.

The Japanese were known to utilize their snipers in a limited offensive role, but the concept of fighting to the death naturally produced virtually no emphasis on the intelligence gathering aspect. When the 6th Infantry Division came ashore at Milne Bay on New Guinea, the Americans encountered an unusual adversary. In the division history, Thomas E. Price recounted the story.

ABOVE: A US Marine fires a Browning .30-calibre water-cooled machine gun in the thick jungle at Cape Gloucester, on the island of New Britain while his comrades cover against sniper fire. (Public Domain)

WORLD WAR II IN THE PACIFIC

ABOVE: Marines of the 4th Division search for a Japanese sniper position on the island of Saipan, 1944. (Public Domain)

ABOVE: The strain of intense combat and the harassing fire of Japanese snipers is apparent on the face of the Marine at Peleliu. (Public Domain)

"The Division set up camp near the Australian forces in a place that was a palm tree plantation owned by the Palmolive Palm Oil Company," Price related. "The men were told they would be fined if they cut down the trees. The first Japanese shot was wearing an American uniform. He was assumed to have been a scout or a spy. A 6th Division medic shot him. There were problems with Japanese snipers in the trees at Milne Bay. The trees came down, or their crowns were cropped and pruned with machine guns. There was no more talk of fines for trees."

One jungle fighting Australian soldier helped a comrade deal with a Japanese sniper in an unusual way. An artilleryman, Russell Braddon asked what the other fellow was up to when he saw the discharge of a Boys anti-tank rifle's 14mm (.545-calibre) shell. "'What the hell are you trying to do Harry?' I asked.

The response was a terse, 'Get that bloody sniper up the top of that bloody tree.'"

Braddon decided to lend a hand, the butt of the Boys resting on Harry's shoulder and the barrel on his own. "Harry took long aim, apparently quite undeterred by the bursts of bullets from all sides, which our stance attracted," wrote Braddon. "I was not in the least undeterred. In fact, as we stood there, our feet spread wide apart to take some of the shock, I was very deterred indeed. Then Harry fired and I was crushed to the ground and Harry was flung against a tree and the sniper toppled gracelessly out from behind his tree, thudding on to the earth below, and our job was done. I left Harry, still swearing volubly and rubbing his shoulder, and crept back to the line of men I now knew so well."

The anti-tank rifle was not the only "unconventional" weapon sometimes utilized against the Japanese sniper. Along with the BAR, the hand grenade, and even the bazooka, the Browning M2 .50-calibre (12.7mm) machine gun was available. Placed in its single-shot mode, the M2 was a deadly weapon at extreme distance when fired by a Marine with sniper experience. Such operation was a forerunner of the modern .50-calibre sniper rifles that are in use today, such as the M107 and the Barrett Light Fifty M82A1.

Some of the Australians discovered a real knack for sniper warfare, and a former kangaroo hunter was said to have shot 47 Japanese soldiers on the island of Timor. At the same time, the Australian and British troops that fought the Japanese in Southeast Asia, Burma, and India became adept at sniper and counter-sniper operations. One British sniper brigade, 48 strong, reported that it had accounted for 296 Japanese killed or wounded during the brief span of two weeks.

While neither the US Army nor the Marine Corps had invested much time or tactical evaluation in the sniper role, the experience in World War II did stir some necessary response to the proliferation of enemy snipers encountered. Further, the value of the sniper in intelligence gathering slowly but surely came to the fore as the conflict wore on.

By 1944, US Army Field Manual 21-75 titled Scouting, Patrolling, And Sniping, defined the sniper as "…an expert rifleman, well qualified in scouting, whose duty is to pick off enemy personnel who expose themselves. By eliminating enemy leaders and harassing the troops, sniping softens the enemy's resistance and weakens his morale."

Nevertheless, there were few dedicated snipers in the American military, as the army designated a single soldier per squad as a sniper – perhaps simply because he was the best shot in the unit. The designated sniper was usually armed with the proven Springfield Model 1903 A3 or A4 bolt action rifle equipped with the Weaver 2.5X 330 telescopic sight, a commercial product originally intended for deer hunting and named the M73B1 in military parlance, although the M-1 Garand semiautomatic rifle became standard issue for the infantry.

Despite the lack of commitment to sniper development, the US army did publish a general wartime doctrine in FM 21-75 that asserted, "Snipers may operate in pairs, in groups, or singly. Snipers may be employed by company commanders and platoon leaders in either the offense or defense. There are two types of snipers: mobile snipers and those who operate stationary observer-sniper posts."

Time and again the American experience in the Pacific demonstrated that a few well-placed Japanese snipers could disrupt or hold up the progress of an operation. In August 1942, the 2nd Marine Raider Battalion raided the Japanese installations on the island of Makin in the Gilberts archipelago. Nineteen Marines were killed in the raid, but the only officer to lose his life was shot by a sniper.

Regularly, after American forces landed on a Japanese-held island, they moved as rapidly as possible to their objectives. As they cleared the open expanse of the beach, they entered the thick jungle that was the domain of the enemy sniper.

The first trial by fire for the evolving Marine amphibious warfare doctrine was put

ABOVE: A war dog handler and his trusted canine partner rest on Peleliu. War dogs were used to flush Japanese snipers from cover. (Creative Commons USMC Archives via Wikipedia)

THE MILITARY SNIPER

ABOVE: Marine General William Rupertus was overconfident in his assessment of Japanese defences at Peleliu. (Public Domain)

ABOVE: US Marine Raiders, several of them sniper school graduates, pause at Cape Torokina on Bougainville. (Public Domain)

in motion on November 20, 1943, when the US 2nd Marine Division assaulted the beaches of Betio, an islet at Tarawa Atoll in the Gilberts, during Operation Galvanic. Betio was only 291 acres of land, about half the size of New York City's Central Park. But more than 3,100 Marines were killed or wounded in the four-day fight. Japanese Rear Admiral Keiji Shibasaki was so impressed with the defenses at Betio that he had boasted, "A million men cannot take Tarawa in a hundred years!" The Japanese garrison on Betio was destroyed as 4,690 were killed.

At Tarawa, the first Marines to land were the 34 men of the Scout Sniper Platoon attached to the 2nd Marine Division and led by 1st Lieutenant William Deane Hawkins. These Marines were not necessarily employed at Betio to scout or snipe. Their primary objective was the seizure of the long pier that jutted 500 yards into the lagoon formed by the atoll. The pier split the Marine landing beaches, and from it Japanese rifleman could pour flanking fire into the Americans as they came ashore. Although they were not fighting in the traditional role, Hawkins and his scout snipers burnished their reputation as highly trained Marines and some of the toughest combat troops in the Corps.

Hawkins and his men hit the beach five minutes ahead of the first full line of Marine amtrac and Higgins boat landing craft. They rousted the Japanese from positions on and around the pier with rifle, bayonet, grenade, and flamethrower. Hawkins stood in the well of an amtrac exhorting his men to advance. He was wounded early in the fighting but refused to retire, exclaiming, "I came here to kill Japs, not to be evacuated!"

Author Robert Leckie wrote in his book *Strong Men Armed*, "Like Hector in his chariot, Lieutenant Hawkins stood erect in his amtrac as it butted through barbed wire, climbed the seawall and clanked among the enemy spitting fire and grenades…He had often said, 'I think my thirty-four-man platoon can lick any two-hundred-man company in the world.' Now he was going on a company-size mission to prove it. His men moved methodically from gun to gun, while Hawkins crawled up to the pillbox gunports to fire point-blank inside or toss in grenades."

Hawkins personally took on several Japanese machine gun nests and pillboxes, silencing them one after another. As he fought on, a bullet caught him in the chest. He refused to stop. Then, the explosion of a mortar shell mortally wounded the 29-year-old officer. He died within minutes. Lieutenant Colonel Robert Shoup, operations officer of the 2nd Marine Division, was amazed at the young man's courage and remarked, "It is not often that you can credit a first lieutenant with winning a battle, but Hawkins came as near to it as any man could."

Lieutenant Hawkins received a posthumous Congressional Medal of Honor for his heroism at Tarawa. Although his platoon had been employed more as shock troops than scout snipers, its performance made the scout sniper concept one of lasting relevance in the Marine Corps.

Valuable lessons were learned at Tarawa, and the American methodology of amphibious assault, including preinvasion bombardment, tracked (amtrac) landing vehicles versus flat-bottomed Higgins boats that tended to get hung up on coral reefs, and air support, were modified accordingly. Still, the road to Tokyo was an arduous slog, and many lives were lost.

By the spring of 1944, the Americans were assaulting three key islands in the Marianas chain, Guam, Tinian, and Saipan. Guam had been an American possession prior to the war and its seizure by the Japanese. Control of the Marianas would place the home islands of Japan within range of US four-engine Boeing B-29 Stratofortress heavy bombers. These aircraft, often laden

ABOVE: American soldiers with the support of an M4 Sherman medium tank fire at distant Japanese snipers hidden in the jungle of Bougainville. (Public Domain)

WORLD WAR II IN THE PACIFIC

ABOVE: Exposed to Japanese sniper fire, Australian troops of the 42nd Battalion cross a stream on Bougainville. (Public Domain)

ABOVE: A Marine equipped with a flamethrower sprints across the black sand of Iwo Jima. (Public Domain)

with incendiaries, would soon lay waste to the industrial infrastructure and the cities of Japan, which were largely constructed of wood. The fire-bombing raids that devastated Tokyo and other population centres would come with vengeance, but first, the Marianas had to be taken.

The fighting at Saipan was protracted as the Japanese resisted on the beaches and the interior of the island. Marine snipers were brought forward on several occasions to eliminate stubborn enemy infantry concentrations or to place harassing fire on strongpoints that slowed the progress of larger units toward their inland objectives. One group of Marine scout snipers infiltrated behind Japanese lines and wreaked havoc, coming to be known as the 40 Thieves of Saipan.

"We were pinned down on the beach at Saipan by a machine-gun bunker," one Marine remembered in an interview with author Adrian Gilbert. "The pillbox commanded a sweeping view of the area, and there was just no way we could get at it. Plenty of our boys had died trying. Finally, one of our ninety-day wonders got on the horn and requested a sniper. A few minutes later, I saw two old gunnery sergeants sashaying towards us, wearing shooting jackets and campaign hats! As soon as I saw these Smokey Bears bobbing over to us, I figured this could be some show. And it was.

"These two old sergeants just skinnied up to the lieutenant and asked him to point out the bunker. Then, they unfolded two shooting mats, took off their Smokey Bears and settled down to business. One manned a spotter's scope while the other fired a 1903 Springfield with a telescopic sight rig.

"That bunker must have been 1,100 or 1,200 yards (1,006-1,097 metres) away, but in just a few minutes, with three or four spotting rounds, this old gunny on the Springfield slipped a round right into the bunker's firing slit. One dead machine-gunner. But their commander just stuck another man on that gun. Our sniper shot him, too. After the fourth man bit a slug, I think they got the idea. We moved up on their flank and destroyed the bunker while our snipers kept the machine gun silent. Then the two gunnys dusted themselves off, rolled up their mats and settled their Smokey Bears back on their heads. And just moseyed away."

A US navy medic on the island of Bougainville, Pharmacist's Mate 2nd Class Frank Viglas kept a diary of his experiences and wrote often about the presence of enemy snipers in and around the field hospital of the 3rd Medical Detachment with the 3rd Marine Regiment. Viglas related, "Nip snipers picking at us from the nearest island…No one got hurt. Finally, Raiders cleared off snipers and we unloaded supplies…can hear them cussing at snipers.

"Operations and plaster casts all morning…shock cases pouring in…one corpsman got himself two snipers with his automatic rifle. Couple of sniper victims came in this A.M. picked off just across the road from us. One is pretty bad… shot through the neck and chest… Party went out looking for those snipers that have been firing at us at the creek. They had no luck… Our serious sniper victim died on us tonight at about 2230."

The Marines on Bougainville paid grudging respect to the enemy sniper, and one of the Americans – who chose to remain anonymous – composed a short poem that ran in part, "Hear about the lady with the

ABOVE: While Marines raise a flag at Mount Suribachi on Iwo Jima, a comrade watches for enemy snipers with his M-1 carbine at the ready. (Public Domain)

ABOVE: Marine Lieutenant Colonel Lewis 'Chesty' Puller was wounded twice by Japanese snipers at Guadalcanal. (Public Domain)

ABOVE: A Marine atop Edson's Ridge at Guadalcanal scans the area where Japanese troops are concentrated through a telescopic sight. (Public Domain)

two gun style,/ Who shot 'em down dead for over a mile…" Although there had been rumours of female Japanese snipers since Guadalcanal, there was no credible evidence that any participated in combat in the Pacific War.

During their push toward the Philippines in the autumn of 1944, American Marines hit the beach at the island of Peleliu, about 500 miles east. Whether the operation was even necessary remains hotly debated today, and Major General William Rupertus, commander of the 1st Marine Division, was wildly over-optimistic when he announced that the conquest of the island would be "…rough but fast…We'll be through in three days. It might only take two."

The Marines and troops of the army's 81st Infantry Division fought for control of Peleliu from September 15 to November 27, 1944, and the Americans lost more than 10,000 killed, wounded, or missing while the Japanese garrison of over 12,000 troops was nearly annihilated. On October 3, a Japanese sniper killed Colonel Joseph Hankins, commander of the 1st Marine Division headquarters battalion. The death came at a familiar place on Peleliu, a rocky island marked by sheer cliffs, jumbles of boulders, caves, ridges, narrow valleys and draws, and tall palm trees that provided concealment for stubborn enemy snipers who took a considerable toll.

The area where Colonel Hankins lost his life was nicknamed Dead Man's Curve, and for two days prior to the incident Japanese snipers had worked their way into advantageous firing positions along high ground that commanded a lengthy section of the road. The sniper concentration was about 2,000 yards north of an airfield, and traffic along the road was regularly subjected to their fire.

On the morning of his death, Colonel Hankins had apparently become frustrated with the continual sniping from the mouths of caves and clifftops along the road. He had been a member of numerous Marine Corps rifle teams and was well-known for his prowess with the M-1 rifle. Taking a pair of binoculars and his M-1, Hankins decided to go hunting the Japanese. There were problems from the start. As Hankins reached the troubled stretch of road, he spotted an LVT amphibious landing vehicle and three trucks stopped and blocking the road ahead. The Japanese had halted their movement with heavy small-arms fire from cliff positions that were only about 50 yards

ABOVE: Lieutenant Colonel Evans F. Carlson welcomed trained snipers into his 2nd Marine Raider Battalion. (Public Domain)

distant. The occupants had bailed out and sought cover in the brush and ditches along the side of the road.

In a reckless display of bravado, Hankins shamed the crews back into their vehicles as bullets zipped around him. Just as he got the men back into their vehicles, a single bullet struck him in the chest, killing him. After the unfortunate incident, a company of Marines was ordered to root the enemy out. They were temporarily successful, but the Japanese still managed to infiltrate regularly. Finally, three M4 Sherman medium tanks were stationed at the troublesome curve. Buttoned up and impervious to the enemy sniper fire, they would blast the surrounding caves and cliffs with their 75mm guns until the snipers were – at least for a while – silent.

Lieutenant Colonel Edson A. Lyman remembered another approach to dealing with enemy snipers. Marine artillery "routed out a covey of Nips," he said. When a dozen Japanese soldiers were flushed into the open, they melted into the jungle and began firing again from about 75 yards distant. The artillerymen fired about 40 rounds, but one Marine was hit by a sniper, and by the next morning two more were shot through the head from across a wide canyon. Further artillery operations were suspended in the area.

The terrible fighting on Peleliu often devolved into individual acts of heroism in which Marines and soldiers put their lives on the line to save their buddies. Marine Private Russell Davis found himself taking cover beside a long causeway that led across a swamp in full view of Japanese snipers on the ridgeline beyond. He watched as another Marine dashed ahead and was shot.

The wounded man was just out of Davis's reach, and his hand opened and closed. But Davis did not know if this was a silent plea for help or a reflex as the last seconds of life

ABOVE: US Marines of the 22nd Regiment take cover from Japanese sniper fire at Eniwetok Atoll in the Pacific. (Public Domain)

ABOVE: Soldiers of the US 7th Infantry Division use a flamethrower to eliminate Japanese soldiers from a blockhouse at Kwajalein in the Pacific. (Public Domain)

ABOVE: Under sniper fire on the island of Okinawa, a Marine sprints for cover, 1945. (Public Domain)

approximately 50 yards, and a Marine shot him dead. The next day, a canine named Pardner flushed a sniper and chased the unfortunate enemy soldier for about 150 yards before he, too, was dispatched.

Still, there was more to come as American forces executed their island-hopping strategy, covering thousands of miles of ocean and inexorably approaching the Japanese home islands. While General MacArthur prosecuted the war in the south, along the coastline of New Guinea and into the Philippines, Fleet Admiral Chester W. Nimitz and the Fleet Marine Force moved forward through the Central Pacific.

Iwo Jima, a rocky, sulphurous, pork chop-shaped island just 760 miles (1,223 kilometres) from Tokyo, was essential in the American plan. Possession of its airstrips and runways would provide landing sites for crippled B-29 bombers that might otherwise not make it back to their bases in the Marianas, while it would also serve as a staging area for future amphibious operations. The fight for the island was brutal, lasting 34 days. When it ended, more than 6,000 Marines had been killed and nearly 20,000 wounded. The Japanese garrison numbered more than 20,000, and only 216 were captured alive.

On Iwo Jima, the Japanese sniper was a constant threat. One Marine wrote a gripping letter home to his family, and his stark description of an event surprisingly made it through the censors who filtered information regularly. Pharmacist's Mate 2nd Class Fred Brinkmann, a US navy medic attached to the Marines ashore, penned, "Just after noon things got hotter than ever before…Just behind us was a battered Jap pillbox which had been smashed in. But a Jap sniper poked his head out of a hole and opened up…Don Bowman was only a few feet away giving plasma to a wounded Marine. Don never knew what happened…He fell against me and knocked me down…Of course, the Nip didn't last long…I grabbed my carbine, and even though about ten other guys must have

ebbed away. Davis watched another Marine, unable to witness the suffering, climb to the edge of the causeway in an attempt to pull the wounded man to safety. A single shot knocked this second Marine backward, and he lay motionless on the ground. Next, a corpsman saw his duty and attempted to get to both wounded men. A third sniper shot found him as he sat on his knees beside the others. Then, finally, a Marine, imposing in size and reach, stretched across the edge of the causeway and managed to drag all three of the wounded men from harm's way.

On Peleliu, the Marines and army troops gained a renewed respect for the tenacious Japanese. They employed everything at their disposal to silence the resourceful enemy snipers. The 4th War Dog Platoon came ashore on the island, and its canine warriors went to work. One of the dogs sniffed out a Japanese sniper at a distance of

ABOVE: A Marine raises his Thompson submachine gun to fire at a Japanese sniper on Okinawa. (Public Domain)

ABOVE: In this interwar photo, an American soldier fires a Springfield Model 1903 sniper rifle equipped with telescopic sight. (Public Domain)

hit him first, I kept my finger on that trigger until my ammunition clip was empty. After we had ceased firing, I was so mad, I jammed the butt of my rifle into his face as hard as I could."

Another Marine, 19-year-old Charles Barnes of the 4th Division, vividly remembered the day when a machine gun went into action against the Japanese near Hill 382. "They started shooting at something across there. Directly, a sniper got the man on the machine gun. The next man took over and he was shot. Then the third man crawled up to the machine gun and the sniper got him. The sniper shot three of 'em. They hid everywhere. They would come up behind you, in front of you, it didn't seem to make any difference."

The last major battle of World War II began on April 1, 1945, a curious coincidence of Easter Sunday and April Fool's Day, when American forces landed on the island of Okinawa, just 330 miles (531 kilometres) from the Japanese mainland. Okinawa was intended as a close staging area for the expected invasion of Japan, and the defenders fought like tigers during the battle. After more than 80 days of combat, Okinawa was declared secure, but more than 7,000 Marines and soldiers of the US army were killed ashore with more than 31,000 wounded while the US navy lost nearly 5,000 dead or missing. Of the 100,000 Japanese on the island, only 11,000 were taken prisoner.

Perhaps the greatest feat of marksmanship in World War II was accomplished by Marine Private Daniel W. Cass at Okinawa. He remembered, "Carter cast a glance at me as he slung his 20X spotting scope on a strap across his back and gave his Thompson .45 a quick check to make sure it wasn't plugged with mud. I stuck a .38 revolver in my pocket and led the way forward with my '03. Panting from exertion, we found our way to the top of a ridge overlooking the valley, all the time listening to the intermittent chatter of the Nambu as it grew louder the closer we got…At least 1,200 yards (1,092 metres) of valley separated us from the machine gun nests. Fog made for such poor visibility that I could not tell where the firing came from.

"Desperately, I used my rifle scope to search for gun smoke or some movements to give the Japs away. Carter used his spotting scope. I saw caves and coral ledges and ragged stumps. Down in the valley a Marine jumped up to improve his position. An invisible finger fell out of the air and seemed to flip off his head. The body went tumbling and flopping.

"Carter spoke first: 'I found them.'"

Cass followed Carter's prompt to spot a coral ledge that fronted a series of caves. A tiny wisp of dark smoke curled above the well-camouflaged Japanese machine-gun nest. The weapon chattered, and the sniper team considered the situation.

"'I estimate twelve or thirteen hundred yards (1,097 to 1,189 metres),' Carter said…A whole lot of variables entered into shooting at a range of even one thousand yards, the longest shot I had ever tried. Wind and heat waves and, in this case, fog distorted the scope picture…Deep breath, Let half out. Cross-hair, cross-hair, squeeze…Carter grunted. 'All right,' he said when my first round plunged into the enemy's barricade…

"I worked the bolt with a feeling of elation. My hands and breathing were surprisingly steady. I fired and worked the bolt, fired and worked the bolt, pouring accurate fire into the Japanese defences, cross-hairing handkerchief-sized targets momentarily exposed more than half a mile away. Even through his spotting scope, Carter couldn't tell when I scored because the targets were so fleeting they disappeared whether I made a hit or not, but he was all grins. The machine gun fire ceased."

The sniper team on embattled Okinawa had done its job.

With the end of World War II, the concept of the sniper had become ingrained in the combat philosophies of military establishments around the globe. In the years that followed, the sniper's tactics, weapons, and equipment were continually refined, and his presence on the battlefield was pervasive.

ABOVE: Marine Corps riflemen practice firing on the rifle range. Some of these men may have been selected for scout sniper training. (Public Domain)

ABOVE: British snipers in training meet the Queen and Princess Elizabeth. British and Commonwealth snipers performed admirably in the China-Burma-India theatre. (Public Domain)

LEE-ENFIELD SNIPER RIFLE

ABOVE: An Indian soldier fires his SMLE in the desert. The SMLE was used in the sniper role in both world wars. (Public Domain)

From 1895 through 1957, the 7.7mm (.303-calibre) Lee-Enfield rifle was the primary shoulder arm of the British and Commonwealth armies. Named for its principal designer, James Paris Lee, and for the Royal Arms Factory at Enfield, where it was initially produced, the bolt action rifle was rugged and dependable and fed with a 10-round box magazine that loaded from the top with five-round chargers. Lee's most innovative contribution to the design was the outstanding smooth operation of its bolt, which allowed the rifleman to maintain his sight picture between chambering of rounds, providing a more stable platform and performance than contemporaries, including the German Mauser.

The earliest Lee-Enfield, developed from the black powder Lee-Metford, was known as the Magazine Lee-Enfield (MLE), and by World War I the famed Rifle No. 1 Mk III, the Short Magazine Lee-Enfield (SMLE), a shorter and lighter version of the MLE, was standard issue. The experienced user of the SMLE, introduced in 1907, was capable of a sustained rate of fire of 15 rounds per minute, but during heavy combat the British infantryman sometimes experienced the "mad minute" in which the SMLE fired an amazing 30 rounds. The concentration of such firepower made a lasting impression on German soldiers who faced it.

When World War II broke out, the standard British infantry platoon included roughly 30 men divided into three rifle sections of eight soldiers along with headquarters personnel. Each rifle section included seven riflemen and a lance corporal or corporal in charge, all armed with the SMLE. During the course of both world wars, the No. 1 Mk III was used in the sniper role.

Although the No. 4 Mk I was not formally adopted by the British army until 1941, a few of them trickled into service as early as 1939. The Mk I included improvements that eased mass production, and it was easily distinguished from the SMLE because its barrel extended beyond the end of the stock. The newer variant was also somewhat heavier due to a heftier barrel. By 1942, factories in Canada and the United States were also producing the Mk I with the addition of an indented bolt track that simplified the more heavily engineered bolt release catch in the earlier model.

In tandem with the introduction of the No. 4 Mk I came the rifle's purpose-built sniper variant, the No. 4 Mk I (T). While the standard SMLE and No. 4 Mk I were highly accurate in themselves, the No. 4 Mk I (T) was built to accommodate a sniper sight, the 3.5X No. 32, and incorporated a wooden cheek rest. The sniper variant was primarily manufactured in Britain by the respected gunsmithing firm of Holland and Holland, though some standard rifles were retooled to the sniper configuration in Canada.

With the sniper enhancements, the No. 4 Mk I (T) was even more lethal at the rifle's effective range of 1,000 metres (3,280 feet), and its weight of nine pounds was only slightly greater than that of the SMLE at slightly over eight and one-half pounds. While the family of Lee-Enfield rifles proved its worth over more than half a century, the SMLE remained in production into the 1950s, and the No. 4 Mk I has remained in service around the world. The sniper No. 4 MK I (T) was retained in service with the British army through the 1960s. Beginning in 1970, many examples of the No. 4 MK I (T) were converted to accept the NATO 7.62mm round and designated the L42A1, which remained the standard British army sniper rifle into the 1990s.

Altogether some 17 million examples of the Lee-Enfield rifles were produced in roughly 40 variants, including a shorter and lighter jungle carbine.

ABOVE: The Lee-Enfield No. 4 Mk I was the basis for the British army sniper rifle widely used in World War II, The No. 4 Mk I (T). (Public Domain)

ABOVE: Sergeant H.A. Marshall of Canada's Calgary Highlanders poses for a sniper's photo. (Public Domain)

MARINE CORPS SNIPER SCHOOLS

Although neither the US Army nor the Marine Corps had placed significant emphasis on the sniper role prior to World War II, its influence prompted some action as the conflict expanded and American ground troops engaged the Axis enemy.

Prior to the outbreak of the war, the Marine Corps had maintained a competitive marksmanship program during the 1930s, but its scope did not include the other attributes of the sniper's craft. It did, however, provide a basis for further training. The Marine Corps command establishment generally assumed that every Marine was capable of performing in something of a sniper role, with or without a formal sniper school or training program. The existing marksmanship program was, therefore, considered capable of supplying the Marine riflemen in the field to perform such duties, and they were to be equipped with the appropriate rifles and other kit.

A brief army course at Camp Perry provided marksmanship instruction but almost no field training.

In the spring of 1940 as war with Japan was contemplated, the 8th Marine Regiment

ABOVE: Marine Henry 'Jim' Crowe headed the Marine sniper school established in 1940. He rose to the rank of lieutenant colonel and was a combat veteran. (Public Domain)

was activated to organize a scout sniper school under the command of Chief Marine Gunner Henry "Jim" Crowe, a champion marksman, at Mission Valley, California's Kearny Mesa, the present-day site of Miramar Naval Air Station. Graduates of Crowe's program were often earmarked for the Marine Raider battalions then forming.

When a volunteer stepped up to join a Raider battalion, he was asked why he thought he could handle the rigors of such an elite unit. When the response came that the volunteer had completed Jim Crowe's sniper course, he was automatically accepted as a Raider. Lieutenant Colonel Merritt A. "Red Mike" Edson and Lieutenant Colonel Evans F. Carlson, commanders of the two Raider battalions, believed that anyone who could complete Crowe's regimen could cut it in the Raiders. Crowe's alumni were described as being "leaner, harder and had a haunted look. But they were also more confident and certainly more competent Marines."

By 1942, the Marines had begun to develop a basic sniper program with the opening of schools at Camp Lejeune, North Carolina, near the city of Jacksonville and Camp Elliott, California, near San Diego. Plans for Camp Elliott had been approved in the autumn of 1939, and the sniper school was one of three subsidiary camps constructed on the sprawling 19,000-acre complex. Green's Farm, as the sniper school was known, was located five miles northeast of the main camp in some of the most rugged country of southern California. Activated in January 1943 under the command of Lieutenant Claude N. Harris, the purpose of the Marine school was to introduce jungle warfare to the participants while providing them with basic instruction in the sniper craft, scouting, and combat initiative.

Harris, a US national rifle champion in 1935, put classes of 15 Marines through a five-week course that supported the Marine concept of reconnaissance in the sniper role, and the name "scout sniper" probably originated early in the school's history. From January to August 1943, a total of 275 Marines graduated from the school at Green's Farm. When the course was completed, the graduates would be allocated to field units. Three scout snipers were assigned to an individual company, with two of these functioning as the active team while

ABOVE: A Marine patrol moves across a waterway on Guadalcanal. A Marine sniper school was started on the island in 1942. (Public Domain)

MARINE CORPS SNIPER SCHOOLS

ABOVE: US Marines rest in a jungle clearing on Guadalcanal. Japanese snipers were a continual threat that was countered by Marine sniper training on the island. (Public Domain)

the third man was in reserve in case of an injury or sickness in a combat zone.

In September 1942, a month after the landings at Guadalcanal, the Marines established a scout sniper school on the island itself with the intention of training two such individuals for each rifle company plus a separate detachment at higher level for the 1st Marine Division.

Colonel William J. "Wild Bill" Whaling, an experienced marksman, hunter, and jungle fighter, was given command of the Guadalcanal sniper school. Whaling had been in command of the Marine Corps Rifle and Pistol Team based at Quantico, Virginia, during the 1930s. He proposed to Colonel Gerald C. Thomas, chief of staff of the 1st Marine Division, that a group of Marines, 100 strong, might be further trained in sniper and scouting activities while actually on Guadalcanal and near the combat zone. The idea was brought up with Major General Alexander Vandegrift, the division commander, and approved. By April 1943, the Marines authorised a 43-man scout sniper platoon for each infantry regiment.

Whaling's scout snipers made a direct contribution to the American victory at Guadalcanal, which took a gruelling six months to achieve. In the hours preceding a major clash on the island, scout snipers reported observing numerous campfires rising from a concentration of enemy troops close to Marine lines on Edson's Ridge. The intelligence assisted in repelling the enemy with heavy losses when the Japanese mounted a nocturnal attack. During other operations, Colonel Whaling employed his trained scout snipers as the spearhead of attacking Marine forces and in screening and flank coverage.

While fighting at the Matanikau River in early October, the scout snipers were combined with the 3rd Battalion, 2nd Marines in a task force called the "Whaling Group." Executing an encircling movement against the Japanese 4th Infantry Regiment and other units, the Whaling Group inflicted heavy casualties on the enemy, killing at least 750. After regrouping, the scout snipers then participated in the annihilation of the remnants of the 4th Infantry Regiment. Whaling later received the Legion of Merit and a Presidential Unit Citation for the scout sniper achievements on Guadalcanal. He went on to earn the Navy Cross during the fighting at Okinawa three years later. He retired in 1954 with the rank of brigadier general after 37 years of service and died at the age of 95 in November 1989.

ABOVE: Major General Alexander Vandegrift, commander of the 1st Marine Division, authorized the formation of a scout sniper school on Guadalcanal. (Public Domain)

As one group of handpicked Marines finished its training at Whaling's school, another rotated in for the intense program. One Marine observed, "When selecting men to be trained as snipers, care must be taken to choose soldiers capable of acting on their own. This means steady nerves, physical strength, agility and patience. They must have good eyesight and be natural marksmen."

Those who had completed the course were returned to their original units, while Whaling regularly had a contingent under his command that was available for special assignments. During Guadalcanal operations, the scout snipers discovered that the thick jungle and inhospitable terrain were sometimes obstacles to efficiency and asked for armoured reinforcement. With tanks assigned in a supporting role, the scout sniper reconnaissance function took on a new dimension. Often the Marines would ride aboard the tanks during scouting forays and dismount quickly when opposition was encountered. They would gather intelligence as they were able and retire, bringing the information back for disposition.

ABOVE: Sitting on the ground, Lieutenant Colonel William 'Wild Bill' Whaling discusses operations on Guadalcanal. (Public Domain)

ABOVE: William 'Wild Bill' Whaling, shown here with the rank of brigadier general, ran the scout sniper school on Guadalcanal. (Public Domain)

THE MILITARY SNIPER

KOREAN CONFLICT AND THE COLD WAR

With the end of World War II, half a century of ideological turmoil ensued. Rather than fostering a lasting peace, the greatest conflict in human history had led to the emergence of new rivalries between the polarized super powers. The cooperation between the United States and Great Britain and their wartime Soviet allies quickly evaporated. East and West, democratic and communist, clashed in proxy wars while nationalistic and revolutionary movements flourished across the globe. Against the backdrop of the nuclear age, these conflicts flared while the partners who had vanquished Axis aggression jockeyed for geopolitical hegemony.

The first major post-World War II hotspot erupted in the summer of 1950 when communist North Korean forces crossed the 38th parallel and invaded democratic South Korea. The ensuing Korean Conflict remains unresolved, although the shooting war was paused with the 1953 Panmunjom armistice. However, only five years after the end of World War II, the armies of the US and its allies mobilized under the banner of the United Nations, and they rediscovered the value of the trained sniper to counter their effective use by the North Korean and Chinese militaries.

Called up once again from an immediate shelving by the American and British

ABOVE: A Dutch soldier serving with United Nations forces in Korea prepares to return enemy fire with his sniper rifle. (Public Domain)

military establishments, the snipers serving with the UN forces in Korea rendered valuable service. And surely, after decades of controversy, the sniper might gain acceptance as an integral component of armed forces in the field rather than an afterthought or even a non-chivalrous and less than ethical tactical tool.

The practical situation, however, had changed. In the midst of the Korean Conflict, the US Marine Corps issued a 1951 study that stated, "The Marine Corps no longer trains snipers, nor are such personnel designated in TOEs (Tables of Organization). The identification of Marine snipers was to become the "prerogative of commanders." Likewise, the US army provided no standards for selection, training or tactics with regard to snipers.

All that changed in the field. As American involvement increased, the first ad hoc sniper schools were organized in Korea. The 2nd Battalion, 5th Marines put together a school in April 1951, distributing the 18 scoped rifles allocated to the battalion and training that many candidates. Because of the exigencies of combat, the course was only one week in duration. But other battalions caught on with dramatic results. By early 1952, the army's 2nd and 25th Infantry Divisions were also training snipers in Korea.

The need was met.

The fighting in Korea was just the beginning. During the latter half of the 20th century, the military sniper often came to symbolize the most highly trained and

ABOVE: This display of US Marine sniper kit includes an M3 infrared scope matched with an M-1 carbine. (Creative Commons Curiosandrelics via Wikipedia)

www.keymilitary.com 79

ABOVE: Clad in white suits a group of prisoners identified as North Korean snipers is readied by UN soldiers for transport to a prison camp. (Public Domain)

commander came to test their efficiency. Where only a week before men had hardly dared to stick up their heads, the two-star general strode the entire length of Item company's MLR armed with nothing but his walking stick."

During the Korean Conflict, the UN snipers, primarily American and British, were armed with their venerable Springfield Model 1903 and Enfield No. 4 Mk I (T) rifles or even the older No. 3 Mk I, also known as the P14. The Americans also deployed the C or D variant of the M-1 Garand semiautomatic rifle. The Browning M2 .50-calibre machine gun set in single shot mode was a long-distance partner, while the Browning Automatic Rifle (BAR) was capable of concentrated .30-calibre firepower from a 20-round clip at the squad level, often substantial enough to silence and enemy sniper. American troops did not receive the updated M-14 rifle until 1957, four years after the Korean fighting ended.

skilful of land combatants. He fought amid inhospitable extremes of climate and often against long odds.

Ever committed to the sniper concept, the Soviet military provided weapons and training for its North Korean understudies and their Chinese cohorts. The Moisin Nagant Model 1891/30 with telescopic sights was common in the field. It was the UN awakening to the menace that again prodded the Western armies to action.

On one crisp morning, the recently arrived commander of the US 3rd Battalion, 1st Marine Regiment looked through his binoculars at distant positions where he was sure the enemy had come up in strength. As the sun rose, the gleam of his field glass lenses no doubt caught the attention of a distant communist sniper. A split second later, a bullet creased the officer's hand and blood began to drip to the ground. The binoculars, shattered, fell in pieces.

Although he was only slightly wounded, the battalion commander realized the distinct disadvantage he faced if unable to survey the front line without fear of being shot by an enemy sniper. Author Adrian Gilbert related, "Right then and there he decided that something had to be done about the enemy sniper. Now was the time to bring in the pin-wheel boys – the Marines who could keep every shot within the V ring at five hundred yards…

"…The colonel learned that within the supply section there was an adequate number of rifles and telescopic sights. The colonel next sent for an experienced gunnery sergeant who had spent considerable time firing with rifle teams. He told the gunny what he wanted: he then sat back and waited. His expectations were completely fulfilled."

The gunnery sergeant went to work, visiting individual companies to find candidates for an ad hoc three-week sniper school. He chose six two-man teams per company and prepared a rifle range for qualification, all the while stressing that the successful sniper candidate was one who was not only accurate but patient – not just an experienced rifleman but a man of certain character and perspective.

"At the time the snipers finished their special training, enemy artillery and mortars were daily peppering both the MLR (main line of resistance) and the outposts," wrote Gilbert. "Enemy snipers seemed to be in control. Then the Marine sniper teams were sent out to the various outposts. To spur them on, a case of cold beer was awarded to the men of each outpost that got 12 kills within a week…" The colonel later recalled, "'In nothing flat there was no more sniping on our positions.'"

Gilbert concluded, "Only a week after the sniper teams went into action, the division

ABOVE: Located at a position known as Sniper Ridge, a bunker formerly occupied by Chinese snipers is shown after its capture. (Public Domain)

ABOVE: Private Chris Bell-Chambers, a sniper with the 3rd Battalion, Royal Australian Regiment, greets Korean children, his sniper rifle slung across his shoulder. (No Restrictions Australian War Memorial Collection)

ABOVE: Chinese soldiers move along a rocky cliffside somewhere in Korea. (Public Domain)

ABOVE: This example of the sniper C variant of the M-1 rifle is now a museum piece. (Creative Commons Joe Mabel via Wikipedia)

Nevertheless, the North Korean and Chinese snipers exhibited great competence and skill. One soldier of the US 7th Infantry Division told a newspaper reporter of a gut wrenching experience that occurred during the epic UN defence of the Chosin Reservoir in the autumn of 1950. "That's where my buddy got killed," the soldier sniffled. "We were bringing up the rear. There was a road that cut into the mountains. He darted across and hit the ditch. I darted right behind him. A sniper got him. He was lying dead in the ditch. I was left by myself."

Another soldier recounted the experience of watching a friend shot dead by a communist sniper. He then saw a second soldier move out to recover the body, and that soldier was also shot. That day, the observer made the decision to become a sniper himself and avenge the losses he had witnessed.

Gunnery Sergeant Francis H. Killeen told of his experiences on both the giving and receiving ends of the sniper experience in Korea at an otherwise inconsequential place called Su Dong Ni. Moving into a ditch along a roadway, he calculated a range of roughly 400 yards to a line where he could see the "fuzz" of enemy bullets as opposing snipers squeezed off their rounds. He delivered the information to his unit's 60mm mortar squad, and in a few moments the enemy fire was suppressed.

"This was the first time I found my sniper gun to be more effective than my M-1 rifle," Killeen explained, "I chose a rock on the far ridge and got my lieutenant to spot my strikes with his binoculars. In that way, I made sure my rifle was still shooting where I aimed…In the late afternoon, columns of enemy began moving into position for evening festivities. I got off a couple of rounds, but without a spotter I could not tell if I was making hits. I got a BAR man to register his rifle on the same rock I had used for zeroing. When he had his sights right, we tried some team shooting…The technique was instantly popular, and I soon had a big light machine gun and two more BARs creating the biggest beaten zone I ever saw. My lieutenant got more riflemen into the fray, and we had the enemy falling all along their wood line."

Killeen had his own close call, just as his mind wandered a bit. "In the heat of the action and with the obvious success we were enjoying, I forgot about the 'hit and run' rule. We have to remember that the other guys also have people who can shoot. A bullet about one click low reminded me, and I cleared out just as a few more came into where I had just been."

Other incidents in the Korean War included the harassment of a US army graves registration detail. Every day after dark, approaching vehicles would be subjected to one or two rifle shots from a hidden assailant. The ricochets were unnerving, said the veteran who told the story. The solution to the perilous distraction lay with the M2 Browning. Loaded with a belt of shells, the Jeep-mounted weapon was driven to the graves registration post one night. When the sniper squeezed off a shot, the response was a stream of .50-calibre fire from the Browning. There were no more sniper incidents at the location. A former US Army warrant officer remembered a .50-calibre story told by his platoon sergeant. A company commander in Korea was said to have ventured to the front line every evening when he knew it was dinnertime for the Chinese along the opposite line. A single soldier would carry a bucket of rice down the same path at the

ABOVE: An American machine gunner pauses with a belt of .50-calibre ammunition around his neck somewhere in Korea. (Public Domain)

ABOVE: Bundled against the cold, an American sniper team returns from an extended deployment in Korea. (Public Domain)

same time. Setting his Browning to single shot, the company commander dispatched numerous delivery men evening after evening.

Snipers in the intelligence gathering role often made a significant contribution in breaking up enemy attacks. Lieutenant Allan Limburg served as a platoon commander with the 3rd Royal Australian Regiment, and he remembered one incident that brought a rain of artillery down precisely where it was needed.

"Two battalion snipers were allocated to my platoon. They kept the enemy's head down during the day. One day, while firing at them, they were amused to see Charlie waving a shovel from side to side, signalling a 'washout,' 'you've missed me.' A prime aim of both sides in defence is to stop the enemy getting supplies to their forward troops. Charlie could not replenish his forward positions during the day as we overlooked them. He did this at night. Instead of using the difficult route forward, in his trenches, he preferred to take the easy way, above ground. From under our camouflage-netted fire pit, using binoculars, our snipers and I often observed heavily laden parties of twenty or more Chinese moving forward just on dusk.

"Why not have a go at the buggers, Skip?" they asked. To be successful all fire

ABOVE: Marines use scaling ladders as they come ashore at Inchon during the Korean Conflict. (Public Domain)

would have to land simultaneously before they dived into their trenches. I planned a codeword to call our fire down. When used over the radio the Kiwi guns opened up first. It took about 24 seconds for their shells to land. When the Centurion tank crew heard the artillery shells overhead, they commenced firing. Their shot took about six seconds. When we heard the shells my two .50-calibre machine guns opened up. We used it several times to great effect."

This tactical victory, though small, had come about through the observation of snipers and the intelligence they had been able to gather.

One of the enduring combat sagas of the Korean Conflict was the battle for control of Pork Chop Hill. When US army troops were called on to make a frontal assault against entrenched Chinese positions, Corporal Chet Hamilton was brought forward to provide some covering fire.

The attack ran into trouble from the beginning, but sniper Hamilton did what he could and made the Chinese pay measure for measure as they inflicted heavy casualties on the Americans. "I felt helpless watching from the sandbagged trenches," he remembered, "until I noticed something. It was only about 400 yards across the valley from the Chinese lines. My position put me on almost the same level with the chink defenders on the other hill. In order for the Chicoms to see our troops and fire at them down through their wire as the GIs charged up the hill, they had to lean up and out over their trenches, exposing wide patches of their quilted hides. That was all I needed.

"It had become a clear morning in spite of the smoke and dust boiling above the Chinese hill. The four-power magnification of my scope made the chinks leap right into my face. All I had to do was go down the trench line, settle the post-and-horizontal-line reticle on one target right after the other, and squeeze the trigger. It was a lot like going to a carnival and shooting those little toy crows off the fence. Bap! The crow disappeared and you moved over to the next crow. By the time you got to the end of the fence, you came back to the beginning and the crows were all lined up again ready for you to start over. I don't know who the Chinese first sergeant was over there, but he kept throwing up another crow for me every

ABOVE: A British centurion tank takes up a firing position in support of snipers somewhere in Korea. (Public Domain)

minute or two. And I kept knocking them off the fence. The fight for the hill lasted about two hours. The other guys came to watch, point out targets, and cheer when I zapped one."

Hamilton estimated that he killed at least 40 Chinese soldiers during the fight at Pork Chop Hill that day. The experience had been somewhat surreal. At the same time it was a competition, a detached contest of marksmanship, endurance, and – heaven forbid – sport. Nevertheless, the spectacle of such destruction wrought by his hand alone must have had a profound impact on his perspective of death and the assumed value and sanctity of life.

Still, such is the career of the sniper. An expert dealer in death, his experience of sighting and pulling the trigger is an intensely personal method of warfare while it remains oddly detached and distant at the same time. The target is just that, not necessarily more or less. Human yes, but that is secondary to the performance of the mission.

ABOVE: An American soldier takes aim to return fire during street fighting in the South Korean capital of Seoul.
(Public Domain)

At lonely dots on the Korean map called Outpost Yorke and outpost Bruce near Panmunjom, platoon sergeant John E. Boitnott and his spotter, PFC Henry Friday of the 3rd Battalion, 5th Marine Regiment, were scanning their surroundings one day when the situation got lively in an instant. Boitnott recalled the events that produced some risky moments, making Friday a somewhat willing target.

"Our position… was about two miles forward of our front line and due north of the place where the peace talks were taking place. We were on the northern parapet of our hill, watching the valley for hostile movement. Friday suggested it was his turn for breakfast and asked permission to go through the centre trench to the reverse slope for chow. The centre trench ran sort of perpendicular to the front and had to be rushed through before an enemy took a crack at you.

"I was lying along the forward parapet and when Friday ran through someone took a shot at him. I thought I saw movement on a hill mass across the valley. The area was about 670 yards (613 metres)

ABOVE: Royal Marines board a ship following an extended deployment during the Korean Conflict.
(Public Domain)

away. I called to Friday and told him to come to me. As Friday cleared the trench the enemy sniper rose again to fire, and this time I saw him clearly. One shot, one dead North Korean sniper. Lt. Johnson verified the kill and reported it to the company commander.

"Friday and I teamed up, with him running the trench and me shooting the enemy for two more kills, which seemed to entertain about everybody on our side. Shortly thereafter word of our 'operation' reached someone less imaginative and we had to knock it off. Over a two-day span, I made nine confirmed kills in nine shots from 670 to 1,250 yards."

The 5th Marines 1953 staff journal validated Boitnott's exploits with entries such as, "July 15 – S/Sgt. Boitnott on Outpost Bruce expended eight rounds of rifle ammunition in killing four enemy," and "July 17 – This morning S/Sgt. Boitnott on Outpost Bruce killed on enemy at long range with a rifle and four hours later killed another."

Boitnott is believed to be the highest scoring American sniper in Korea with 70 confirmed kills.

During the late 1940s, Korea was not the only area of unrest around the world. In Palestine on the eve of the founding of the state of Israel, British forces were executing a withdrawal from the region. As this occurred, Royal Marine No. 40 Commando drew responsibility for maintaining a tenuous separation of the antagonistic Arab and Jewish militia and armed citizens in the port of Haifa, where ships were embarking with civilian and military personnel.

The intelligence section of No. 40 Commando described the circumstances. "As it happened, the evacuation was completed without incident but when it was decided that 40 Commando would be the last British unit to leave Palestine, the situation was tense and a peaceful withdrawal seemed very uncertain."

Indeed, the situation escalated as 40 Commando tried to exit. "Shortly before 1000 hrs, the Jews opened fire on the Arab village outside No. 1 Gate, and battles commenced in various areas," reported the intelligence section, and a British armoured car came under fire as well. "An hour later one of our Staghounds became involved in an exchange of fire in Bank Street. Two British policemen had been shot and the Staghound gave covering fire while they were being evacuated. The sniper was located and three direct hits with 37mm shells from the Staghound silenced him forever."

Snipers, untrained as military personnel but dangerous nevertheless, opened up repeatedly on the British forces, sometimes with automatic weapons. A report of one

ABOVE: Westland Whirlwind helicopters lift off with men of No. 45 Royal Marine Commando in the Middle East.
(Public Domain)

action read, "In the afternoon a Jewish Bren gun sniper was causing considerable confusion firing at traffic along Kingsway. His position behind an armoured plated window was impervious to Bren fire, which was returned from our positions. Three PIAT (projector infantry anti-tank) bombs, however, effectively silenced the offending sniper. A little later a Jewish Bren gunner wounded Lt. A.H.W. Seed, RM, in the back of the head with a deliberate burst of fire at one of our forward positions. Lt. Seed was evacuated to the British Military Hospital. A patrol of one corporal and two Marines immediately went out, located the sniper, and eliminated him. At approximately the same time, our position on the British Sailors' Society's club by No. 3 Gate silenced three snipers firing on the gate."

The Middle East remains a tinder box of military conflict to this day, and the Arab-Israeli Six-Day War of 1967 and the Yom

ABOVE: Israeli paratroopers like these fought pitched battles with Jordanian snipers in Jerusalem during the Six-Day War. (Public Domain)

ABOVE: British soldiers patrol a street in Aden during the emergency in 1967. (Public Domain)

Kippur War of 1973 were fertile ground for encounters between opposing snipers. Israeli airborne troops of Battalion 66 battled the Jordanians of the al-Hussein Battalion for control of Jerusalem during the Six-Day War and came upon a heavily fortified position at Antenna House on the summit of Ammunition Hill.

As the Israelis moved from street to street, Jordanian snipers occupied the upper floors of Antenna House and fired on them relentlessly. While clearing reinforced bunkers and trying to suppress the deadly rain of sniper rounds, the Israelis lost 24 killed and 90 wounded. Before the fighting was over, 71 Jordanian soldiers were dead and heavy explosives and tanks were required to silence their positions. Meanwhile, snipers from surrounding rooftops in the Sheikh Jarra neighbourhood harassed the Israeli drive toward St. John's Hospital, requiring that each hide be reduced one at a time, house to house and room to room.

Seven years later, Israeli paratroopers dropped into a beehive of sniper fire as they assisted ground troops already engaged with Arab forces during the Yom Kippur War. "Snipers were shooting at the soldiers as they descended," Rabbi Mordechai Katz said in telling the fortunate story of one paratrooper. "So, the paratroopers had to travel very lightly. The paratrooper assembled his backpack with great care. He then came upon his Tefillin (these were Jewish laws carried in two small black boxes); he was about to leave them behind on the plane, when he reconsidered. 'These Tefillin have been with me wherever I've gone,' he thought to himself. 'Perhaps having the words of Hashem with me when I jump will bring me good fortune.'

After placing the Tefillin in his backpack, he hit the silk. Under heavy sniper fire when he landed, the paratrooper reached safety, only later to discover a fortunate circumstance. "Immediately, he noticed a bullet hole in his Tefillin and the bullet

ABOVE: Violence erupts in the streets of Aden as British forces attempt to restore order. (Public Domain)

ABOVE: Under fire from Jordanian army snipers, Israeli soldiers scurry forward during the fight for Ammunition Hill. (Public Domain)

lodged in the siddur which had been in his Tefillin bag! 'It's a good thing I decided to take my Tefillin bag along,' said the soldier. 'If I hadn't, that bullet would have gone through my bag and into my body.'"

British army sniper training did not take on much of a new character for decades after World War II, actually the formalized training was dropped in the years immediately afterward. However, the military was intermittently engaged in numerous actions during the Cold War years as the cohesion of the empire was challenged. Almost on an "as needed" basis the army revived sniper use, while the Royal Marines, which took over Commando operations, were the sole arm of service to maintain consistent sniper development.

The Royal Marines trained snipers from around the world, including the US and other NATO countries, and the British army sent snipers to train under Royal Marine instructors at Lympstone in Devon beginning in 1970. Sometime afterward, the army developed its own sniper training at the School of Infantry, Warminster. The Royal Marine curriculum earned a reputation for its rigor, including six weeks of training followed by the Sniper Badge Test, which included the marksmanship, camouflage, stalking, observation, judging distance, map reading and aerial photograph interpretation, and sniper knowledge standards. Each sniper graduate was required to repeat the demanding test on an annual basis to maintain the skill set necessary in each man who wears the coveted badge.

Meanwhile, a bitter struggle took place in the early 1960s for control of the city of Aden, now in the country of Yemen, and environs on the Arabian Peninsula. As various factions fought one another, British forces were inevitably drawn into the conflict. At times, the outcome was decidedly in doubt. On April 30, 1964, when Royal Marine No. 45 Commando was inserted to secure high ground at Dhanaba Basin, a coordinated operation involving B Company, 3rd Battalion, the Parachute Regiment ran into trouble.

Although the effort to secure a hill called Cap Badge was eventually successful, it involved a brisk 10-hour firefight. Major Peter Walter, commanding B Company, assaulted the village at Wadi Taym, driving most of the insurgents out and killing several. But a small group managed to work its way behind the paras and launched an attack, only to be set upon by the follow-up element of paras under Captain Barry Jewkes. The entire insurgent group was killed, but snipers opened on the paras from the surrounding high ground, and several went down wounded.

The snipers had chosen their hides well, out of view or access by the Royal Marines occupying the hill above them and requiring Hawker Hunter fighter bombers to make ground attack runs. In spite of the air superiority, Captain Jewkes was killed by sniper fire along with another para, while six more were wounded in the melee.

ABOVE: British soldiers examine the damage after a bomb blast in Haifa during the fighting in Palestine. (Public Domain)

ABOVE: Israeli soldiers look for hidden enemy snipers as they cross a railroad track at Ismailia during the Yom Kippur War. (Public Domain)

Frustrating and costly as that fighting had been, the British adventure in Aden was still destined for hard struggles in an area called the Crater. When a battalion of the Argyll and Sutherland Highlanders with No. 45 Commando in support were ordered to clear the Crater, a labyrinth of buildings and streets actually constructed inside the dome of an extinct volcano, much of the fighting was close quarter.

The snipers of No. 45 Commando, however, found advantageous positions among the clefts and crags that surrounded the Crater and scanned the city for targets. As the Argyll and Sutherland Highlanders proceeded, the snipers began to squeeze off rounds that repeatedly found their marks. A pair of Commandos showed remarkable economy, only 25 rounds of ammunition, in exchange for the killing of 11 Arab fighters and the wounding of five more for a hit rate of 64 percent.

Lieutenant Colonel Colin "Mad Mitch" Mitchell led the Argyll and Sutherland Highlanders in clearing the Crater, and one sniper of No. 45 Commando took a bit of umbrage when Mitchell's command received the lion's share of credit for the success. "The Argylls under Mad Mitch made all the news when they retook the Crater," he groused,

ABOVE: A British soldier mans a roadblock during the Jewish Insurrection in Palestine. (Public Domain)

ABOVE: In this rare photo, an Israeli sniper poses with his rifle in 1954. (Public Domain)

ABOVE: A British soldier guards suspected insurgents on a street in Aden, 1967. (Public Domain)

"but without us they'd never have done it without taking a lot of casualties. It was us who wore the Arabs down and made them realize they couldn't have it all their own way. We were right up above the town and I could look through my telescopic sight and see them moving about. We waited for hours. The heat was incredible, bouncing off the rocks and burning you to a turn. But it was worth it when I saw an Arab coming out of a mosque carrying a rifle.

"I knew he was a terrorist; we'd found out that they used mosques as meeting places. As he walked up this alleyway towards me I took aim. He couldn't see me, of course. And then I squeezed the trigger, and he fell backwards, dropping his rifle. I'd definitely got him. Everyone else around him ran off in panic, leaving him lying there until nightfall."

While the proven Enfield No. 4 Mk I (T) remained the prevalent British sniper rifle into the 1960s, the L1A1 rifle, which fired the 7.62mm (.30-calibre) NATO cartridge, replaced the venerable Enfield rifle as standard issue for infantry units. The new rifle failed to win favour with snipers, though. As a result, they got a weapon better suited for their craft, the L42A1, fitted with a heavier and more durable barrel still with the capability of accepting the NATO 7.62mm cartridge. The purpose-built Parker Hale Model 82, a military version of the 1200TX target rifle, was distributed to many Australian and Canadian snipers during the 1950s.

Royal Marine sniper Mick Harrison, a reformed poacher, spent four days in action near Aden and shot eight Arab fighters while expending 18 rounds of ammunition. In 1968, he received a special commendation for gallantry, and the Defence Ministry press release that accompanied the award read, "…He was in a position overlooking [the] Crater under sporadic small-arms fire and was the target of a blindside (anti-tank missiles and grenades) attack. Over a period of four days, working with another sniper position, he systematically eliminated terrorist snipers opposing him so that all terrorist fire ceased during daylight hours."

Admiral Sir Michael Le Fanu, formerly Commander-in-Chief, Middle East and then First Sea Lord, commented, "Marine Harrison showed a standard of professional skill and devotion to duty of the highest order and made the greatest single contribution to the successful control of terrorism in successive company areas."

In a contemporary interview, Harrison recalled, "The terrorists in Aden had been shooting up the Argylls or the Northumberland Fusiliers and they wanted a sniper, so I was called for. I got in the back of a Land Rover, and they had got my kit, my rifle, and scope. I checked my ammunition – Vickers .303 7Z rounds. They told me to go up the mountain, and for 14 hours a day, for four days, I made my base in an old, ruined Turkish fort. Each morning I hauled myself up with a rope while it was still dark, around 5:30 or 6:00. When I got up there I hid. The important thing wasn't to go popping off at anything. I saw I was all right for water before I went up, and in that climate you needed plenty. It was just a question of using training. just a matter, so to speak, of giving the other man enough rope to hang himself.

"I had to make the terrorists show themselves. What I did was to expose myself to them deliberately. I'd kill one, then I'd move to a new position. They were about 400 to 500 yards away. I'd get up and wave to them to draw their attention. It was the old idea of bringing your quarry to you. They thought they were good and I let them come to me. The first person I shot came out all dressed in black, and I remember I shot him in the throat. They wanted to go to Allah's garden, and I just paved the way for them."

ABOVE: Soldiers of the Queen's Dragoon Guards man their Saladin armoured cars in Aden. Armoured cars were sometimes called in to deal with troublesome snipers. (Creative Commons Brian Harrington Spier via Wikipedia)

ZHANG TAOFANG

According to Chinese sources, the most prolific sniper among the ranks of the Volunteers who fought in support of the communist North Koreans was Zhang Taofang. Born in Xinghua City, Jiangsu Province, he joined the army at the age of 19 in March 1951. Zhang was reported to have killed 214 United Nations soldiers during only 32 days of action on the front at Triangle Hill.

In January 1953, he was assigned to the 8th Company, 214th Regiment, 24th Corps, and later that month, armed with the Soviet-made Mosin Nagant Model 1891/30 rifle, he moved to the front lines. His first encounter with the enemy nearly cost Zhang his life. Spotting a target, he immediately opened fire. Expending 12 rounds, he missed each time, and then the heavy incoming response nearly ended his brief sniping career before it began.

Zhang realized he had to improve his marksmanship and adjusted his target acquisition and firing technique. In mid-February, he was again on the line. This time, when he fired his Mosin Nagant, the target crumpled to the ground. Remarkably, Zhang is said to have fired only over his rifle's basic iron sights without the use of any telescoping enhancement equipment. He quickly established himself as a deadly sniper, once scoring seven hits in a series while firing only nine rounds of ammunition.

Word of Zhang's exploits worked their way up through the army's chain of command, and when one senior officer got wind of his results, an aide was sent to the front with explicit instructions. The aide carried with him a pair of expensively lined leather boots and was told that if he personally witnessed Zhang dispatch three enemy soldiers to present them to the master sniper as a reward. If, on the other hand, these stories of sniper prowess turned out to be false, severe punishment was to be meted out to officers at company, regimental and corps level.

Zhang is said to have proficiently scored three kills in the presence of the aide and was deeply honoured to receive the expensive boots. However, he did not wear them and kept them as a trophy for his service.

Another vignette of Zhang's sniping skill relates that he went one on one against the top-scoring American sniper of the Korean Conflict, the so-called Colonel Ike. The story goes that Zhang killed Colonel Ike with a well-placed head shot just as Ike's bullet passed near his own. This tale, however, may well be the product of the Chinese propaganda machine. It is quite similar to the Soviet account of the duel between Vasili Zaitsev and Major König. As in the case of König, there is

ABOVE: Their ammunition depleted, Chinese soldiers throw rocks at attacking United Nations troops on Triangle Hill. (Public Domain)

little or no mention of the alleged Colonel Ike in Western histories of the war.

Zhang supposedly kept the spent shells when he made confirmed kills and collected them in one of the prized leather boots. He explained this to a visiting officer, and at the time he had 211 casings. The officer wanted him withdrawn from the fighting and allowed him to score three more kills for a total of 214 to match the number of his regiment. Afterward, Zhang's sniper career ended. He had spent just over three months in the combat zone, and his commanding officer once noted that he would not exchange Zhang for "10 mortars."

In 1954, Zhang transferred to the People's Liberation Army Air Force. He became a pilot and flew the famous MiG-15 fighter. After holding a number of instructor and command positions, he retired from the military in 1985. He died at age 77 in Shandong Province on October 29, 2007.

ABOVE: Chinese soldiers' firing positions, one of them with a machine gun, on the slope of Triangle Hill. (Public Domain)

ABOVE: Zhang Taofang creeps forward with his Moisin Nagant rifle in this 1953 photo. (Public Domain)

IAN ROBERTSON

ABOVE: Ian Robertson took this photo of Australian soldiers in action at the Battle of Yongju in October 1950. (Public Domain)

ABOVE: Sergeant Ian Robertson reaches into his bag while standing with Corporal Mick Hatton adjacent to a wounded North Korean soldier captured during the Battle of the Apple Orchard, October 1950. (Public Domain)

Australian Private Ian Robertson remembered many occurrences during his tour of duty in Korea. They remained with him for the rest of his life.

A soldier of the 3rd Battalion, Royal Australian Regiment, Robertson recalled bitter combat against the North Koreans in an area designated "Hill 614." He spent a week on the windswept line at high altitude and took many shots with his SMLE sniper rifle at the enemy from a distance he estimated at roughly 600 yards.

"I would say I had hit after hit there," he told an interviewer years later, "…When I saw these blokes suddenly drop or fling themselves away or something like that, I thought that, most of the time, it would be a near miss. They were flinging themselves out of the way to give the impression that I'd hit them or something like that. I was able to do it time after time – every time I fired, the figure would disappear. I had the idea that they must have had a huge bunker, because so many people were going down there.

"I nutted it out that when they passed a particular point, if I fired then, they would run into the bullet. They had to come down at the same speed because of the rough ground they were moving on. I tried an experimental shot low down and saw the blast of the bullet just above that bloke, so I made another guess and fired another shot, and this bloke disappeared. It seemed to confirm what I thought. Then I got the measure of them coming uphill as well.

"Once in a while, one of them would come uphill," he concluded. "A lot of them were going down, though. What seemed to happen was that one or two might have made it, and then they were eventually coming back and being replaced by others. But they weren't getting down there, because I was knocking them off as they went."

Robertson never tried to keep track of the number of enemy soldiers he killed with his sniper rifle. "I never did the arithmetic. I still don't want to," he remarked. Nevertheless, Robertson remains one of the most successful United Nations snipers of the Korean Conflict. When his unit claimed the high ground that once belonged to the North Koreans, he investigated the area where the bunker was located and found approximately 30 bodies, each of them killed with a single shot. His work.

During the course of the war, Robertson also made other shots – as an accomplished photographer. His studies provide insight into the experience of war in Korea, some of them haunting reminders of the inherent human suffering. When his talent for photography was discovered, he had been given the responsibility of battalion photographer while also serving as member of its sniper section. He killed as a sniper and took photos of fellow soldiers of the 3rd Battalion, some of whom later lost their lives in combat. His is a lasting and somewhat unique legacy. He served in Vietnam, married, and took up ballroom dancing to help cope with the memories of war. He died in Greensborough, Victoria, in 2014 at the age of 87.

ABOVE: Robertson captured this image of the 3rd Battalion, Royal Australian Regiment, moving out at Hill 614 in March 1951. (Public Domain)

THE MILITARY SNIPER IN FILM

Hollywood is always in search of the storyline that delivers drama, suspense, and perhaps an unexpected conflict resolution. And the concept of the military sniper, a player in many feature films through the decades, comes through on all counts.

No plot line, vignette, or dramatic sequence provides a more compelling visual experience than the sniper drawing a bead, his target framed in the reticle or crosshairs of his rifle. No cinematic moment is more intense than the second the sniper squeezes the trigger and the weapon's report cracks the stillness.

In cinema, the sniper is a creative vehicle to convey emotion and the immediacy of death on the battlefield or in the throes of urban combat. One would be hard pressed to find more substantial support for post-World War I pacifism than in the Oscar winning 1930 classic All Quiet on the Western Front starring Lew Ayres, the 1979 remake starring Richard Thomas in which Paul Bäumer is killed by a sniper's bullet while reaching for a butterfly, or the 2022 screen interpretation of the novel by Erich Maria Remarque with Felix Kammerer as Bäumer.

In the 1968 film Anzio, Robert Mitchum portrays war correspondent Dick Ennis, who becomes trapped behind German lines with six American soldiers. As the group attempts to reach safety, they come under fire from several enemy snipers, who kill and wound with great accuracy. Ennis is forced

ABOVE: This poster advertised the 1930 feature film All Quiet on the Western Front. (Public Domain)

ABOVE: The sniper rifle and personal belongings of Vasili Zaitsev are on display at the Stalingrad Panorama Museum. (Creative Commons Mark F. Levisay via Wikipedia)

to defend himself, becoming a soldier who must confront the sniper menace head-on.

As the film concludes, one of the Germans asks out loud, "Wo bist du, Amerikaner?" Ennis, carrying the weapon of a sniper victim, has worked his way to the rear of the enemy and responds, "Right here, German!" prior to firing a death dealing burst.

The 1993 film Sniper, starring Tom Berenger as US Marine Gunnery Sergeant Thomas Beckett, spins the yarn of a sniper team sent to assassinate a general in the Central American country of Panama and spawned a series that includes at least eight more movies centred on the Beckett sniper thread.

The 2014 film American Sniper tells the story of US navy SEAL sniper Chris Kyle and his four tours of duty during the Iraq War. Bradley Cooper portrays Kyle, and sequences are heart pounding. Jake Gyllenhaal and Jamie Fox star in the 2005 film Jarhead, the true story of Marine sniper Anthony Swafford as he progresses from boot camp through sniper training and finally to the front lines during the Gulf War of 1991. In 2017, John Cena and Aaron Taylor-Johnson starred

THE MILITARY SNIPER IN FILM

ABOVE: Richard Thomas portrays Paul Bäumer in the 1979 version of All Quiet on the Western Front. (Creative Commons Peabody Awards via Wikipedia)

ABOVE: Barry Pepper turns in a gritty performance as Jackson in Saving Private Ryan. (Public Domain)

ABOVE: Chris Kyle, shown signing a copy of his book at Camp Pendleton, is the subject of the film American Sniper. (Public Domain)

in The Wall, a dramatic account of two American soldiers facing an Iraqi sniper with only a small wall for protection. In 2022, a Chinese film production with a budget of $95 million premiered, telling the story of Zhang Taofang, the celebrated sniper of the Korean Conflict.

The sniper experience during World War II in the West came home to many film goers with the 1998 motion picture Saving Private Ryan. In one pulsating sequence, actor Barry Pepper, portraying sniper Jackson, warns his comrades not to venture into the open before a German sniper's hide, relating that this guy's "got talent." One of their own already lies fatally wounded, prostrate in a gravel road that winds through a devastated French village with a steady rain pelting down, but Jackson is calm and calculating. He eyes the German in the upper floor of a distant building through his scope just as the opponent sees him as well. Jackson pulls the trigger first, and with a flash sends a bullet through the German's telescopic sight. For some, the image on screen is simply unnerving – all too real.

During another heart stopping sequence, Jackson acts as a scout, perched in the steeple of a ruined church in another French town. He warns his commanding officer, Captain John Miller portrayed by Tom Hanks, of approaching enemy tanks and infantry using hand signals in a display of the sniper's ability to perform reconnaissance tasks. Once the Germans are in the streets and harrowing close quarter fighting breaks out, Jackson returns to his primary task, working his bolt action rifle and repeatedly choosing German soldiers to eliminate. He hits more moving targets than he misses but loses his life when a large calibre German shell impacts his towering hide.

Saving Private Ryan introduces the viewer to combat sequences that are as realistic as anything ever screened. The first 20 minutes, depicting the horrific ordeal of the American landings at Omaha Beach on D-Day, are only the beginning. While viewer discretion is advised, those who seek a glimpse of real war cannot do more than screen this epic adventure.

The story of the great sniper confrontation perhaps in history between Vasili Zaitsev and Major König is the basis for the 2001 World War II thriller Enemy at the Gate. Jude Law stars as Zaitsev, the hunter and shepherd from the foothills of the Ural Mountains in central Russia, while Ed Harris portrays Major König, the enigmatic German master sniper who is supposedly the commandant of the sniper school at Zossen, although there is little evidence to support whether there actually was a sniper school at Zossen during World War II. The film provides riveting sequences of snipers in action and is acknowledged as a fictionalized account of the life of Zaitsev and the events depicted, but there are elements of intrigue, including a love triangle involving an officer of the Soviet military propaganda engine and the so-called Blond Sniper, Tania Chernova.

Without doubt, the sniper scenes are suspenseful as the film is punctuated with heavy action, moments of sniper versus sniper and sniper versus unwary victim. The showdown between the protagonists is entertaining and insightful, perhaps as close as a filmgoer can come to being in the sniper moment. Then, considering that the personal aspect plays out against the backdrop of the epic battle of Stalingrad and is filled with stunning battle scenes, the package is complete.

The motion picture industry has given viewers ample opportunity to evaluate the sniper through more than a century of conflict. Whether true to history or fictionalized, each storyline offers its own perspective on the life and times of the sniper, a solitary figure who shatters the relative calm with one shot, one kill.

ABOVE: An American sniper sights his .50-calibre rifle in the Middle East; The film American Sniper portrays the service of Navy SEAL Chris Kyle. (Public Domain)

THE VIETNAM WAR

The conflict in Vietnam, a tumult of ideological and nationalistic fervour that finally prevailed against the effort to "contain" the spread of communism in Southeast Asia, ended in 1975. Sometimes called the 10,000 Day War, the fighting had dragged on for more than 30 years from the end of World War II and the demise of French colonialism.

During the lengthy war in Vietnam, jungle fighting was the order of the day, and the skilled sniper often flourished amid the dense underbrush and the canopy of foliage sometimes so thick that it shut out the light of the sun. American and allied forces fought an elusive foe, dedicated and experienced in the hit-and-run ambush tactics that precluded a major, decisive battle. For the communist insurgent Viet Cong in the south and their partners, the well led and equipped North Vietnamese army, a war of attrition was to their advantage.

And the sniper played a key role in inflicting casualties on the Americans. Unlike the US armed forces, whose commitment to the sniper ebbed and flowed, the North Vietnamese fielded sniper units in company strength. These volunteers completed a two-month intensive course in sniping and then infiltrated to the south along the Ho Chi Minh Trail. In turn, they passed along their knowledge to Viet Cong snipers who were armed with the World War II era Soviet-made Mosin Nagant Model 1891/30 rifle equipped with telescopic sights.

ABOVE: A US Marine sniper peers through his rifle's telescopic sight across open country in Vietnam.
(Creative Commons USMC Archives via Wikipedia)

The communist snipers earned the grudging respect of the Americans and their South Vietnamese understudies. Meanwhile, the US army lagged in sniper development after the Korean Conflict as snipers were officially "optional," although some research into the use of telescopic sights and sniper rifles continued. By 1967, ACTIV (Army Concept Team in Vietnam) was conducting evaluations of army sniper operations and equipment. The army had adopted the M-14 rifle as its primary sniper weapon, upgraded with the M84 telescopic sight and sometimes the starlight night vision scope that could assist in nocturnal target acquisition up to 400 metres (437 yards) range, while the M-21, a national match grade variant of the M-14, was also issued to army snipers trained in country at the division level beginning in 1968.

Captain (later Major General) Julian Ewell was the leading sniper advocate in the army during the Vietnam era. He put together a formal sniper protocol for his 9th Infantry Division and requested resources to make the sniper program effective against a real concern – the prowess of the communist snipers his men faced with regularity. Ewell allocated six trained snipers to each infantry battalion and a pair at each brigade headquarters level. The fact that the army command structure limited the deployment of snipers to operations at the unit level hindered the progress, but in time army snipers made their presence known in the jungle fight.

The US Marine Corps differed in its approach to sniper tactics, allowing scout

ABOVE: A sniper team of 3rd Battalion, 7th Marines operates in South Vietnam. Note the sniper is manning a Browning .50-calibre machine gun. (Creative Commons USMC Archives via Wikipedia)

THE VIETNAM WAR

ABOVE: Marines evacuate a wounded buddy, Operation DeSoto, January 1967. (Public Domain)

snipers to deploy forward – ahead of larger units – regularly in company with a spotter and sometimes with the nearby support of a fire team or squad when the situation became hot and the sniper needed to pull out. After Korea, two Marines, Captain Jim Land and Captain Robert A. Russell had been responsible for maintaining some emphasis on sniper operations in the Corps.

Russell put together the first Marine sniper training school in Vietnam in the spring of 1965. His first pupils were "grunts" of the 3rd Division. Land had established a sniper school in Hawaii five years earlier specifically for Marines of the 1st Division. Both officers continually evaluated their programs and improved the curricula. In Vietnam, the course was two weeks in duration and included specific counter-sniping techniques to combat the proficient communists.

While the Springfield Model 1903 was still available in its sniper variants, the Marines looked to a new generation of sniper rifle, equipping the Remington 700 with the M84 telescopic sight and designating the combination the M40. Variants and upgrades of the 7.62mm M40 were standard issue sniper rifles with the Marines until 2018 when the Corps announced the replacement of the latest M40 with the .30-calibre Mk 13 Mod 7, incorporating the Accuracy International Chassis system with the Remington 700 receiver.

The Marine choice of the M40 in Vietnam followed extensive testing of the M-14 and the Winchester Model 70, which was chambered for the .30-06 round rather than the NATO 7.62mm cartridge. Another innovation rose from the availability of the lightweight M-16 standard issue assault rifle that was ubiquitous with the Marines and army troops. While the M-16 fired the smaller 5.56mm (.22-calibre) cartridge, it was not engineered for sniping, but some Marines and soldiers asked armourers to affix telescopic sights. One officer of the 25th Infantry Division had tremendous success with the modified M-16, scoring 50 kills by late 1966.

Land established his sniper school near Dong Ha on a promontory called Hill 55 and became one of the first prominent sniper proponents to demonstrate the worth of his craft in Southeast Asia. General Herman Nickerson, Jr., commander of the 1st Marine Division, made his sniper expectations abundantly clear to Land. "I want mine to be the best in the Marine Corps," he growled. "I want them killing VC, and I don't care how they do it – even if you have to go out and do it yourself."

With Nickerson's admonition ringing in his ears, Land faced an early test. Hill 55 was a commanding height, highly visible, and from it emanated five ridges like fingers from a hand. Just as the school was getting established, a single Viet Cong sniper had also set up shop on the ridge designated as Finger One. Land later commented, "Just in the past two weeks he had killed two Marines and wounded two others. The grunts had been unable to locate his hide and eliminate him. Marines on the finger darted about like mice afraid to show themselves to a cat whose taloned paws were capable of swatting them at will."

Land and his spotter, Sergeant Don Reinke, accepted the challenge of

ABOVE: A machine gun team from Marine Company L, 3rd Battalion, 7th Marine Regiment fires on a Viet Cong sniper south of Da Nang.
(Creative Commons USMC photo Staff Sergeant Bob Bowen Wikipedia)

ABOVE: A Marine rifleman sits in a destroyed church steeple after a Viet Cong sniper has been dislodged, 1967.
(Creative Commons Defense Department photo Lance Corporal Worden via Wikipedia)

ABOVE: A Viet Cong insurgent crouches with his Soviet-made rifle, 1968. (Public Domain)

ABOVE: Soldiers of the North Vietnamese Army mount an attack in the south with Soviet-made rifles. (Public Domain)

eliminating the menace at Finger One. They collected intelligence on the sniper's previous shots, the angle of the bullet, the location of the incident, the direction of the round. They also realized that birds going about their business had purposely stayed away from a particular section along the ridge. They crept forward on a reconnaissance foray and determined that the sniper was using a tunnel and had approached his hide from several different directions on various days.

Land continued, "Reinke and I worked our way back…careful to leave behind as few signs of our visit as possible. I had a plan."

Consulting with the platoon leader on Hill 55, Land pointed out an area where a pile of brush and tall grass didn't quite look the same as the surroundings. He asked the officer to order an anti-tank 106mm recoilless rifle to register the spot for a quick response when the sniper returned to squeeze off his next round. A Marine did as instructed, and then the only thing to do was wait. Some days later, the afternoon sun was setting. The Viet Cong sniper fired a shot, which missed its target and slammed into a sandbag.

It was enough. The recoilless gunner hit the trigger, and the target erupted in smoke and flame. The sniper was obliterated.

As the Americans awakened to sniper operations in Vietnam, the communist adversary was indeed plying his craft with dexterity. Marine sniper Joseph T. Ward remembered a single tenacious enemy sniper who stymied the movement of a Marine company. Pinned down by the sniper's accurate fire, the company commander called for air support, but cloud cover prevented the trio of F-4 Phantom fighter bombers from swooping in for more than two hours. Meanwhile, so much as a twitch from a Marine drew the sniper's unwanted attention. When the F-4s at last came overhead and dropped napalm, the sniper somehow survived and continued to fire. Just as a second airstrike rolled in, the sniper slipped away, but only after wounding another Marine.

Ward said, "While we cleaned our rifles, I thought what a day's worth one of Uncle Ho's best had given. One enemy sniper had killed three grunts, wounded four, tied up two companies and six fighter-bombers a good part of the day, and we hadn't seen any sign of him."

Michael Belis arrived in Vietnam in August 1970 and was assigned to Company C, 1st Battalion, 22nd Infantry Regiment, 4th Infantry Division. He recalled an enemy sniper's disruption while supplies were being unloaded at a jungle position between An Khe and Kontum, which his unit had occupied for four months. The supplies were carried from helicopters and the landing zones to the base, and as the Marines began unloading they became prime targets.

"About 20 minutes to half an hour later we heard the brush breaking in the jungle at our end of the LZ halfway to the sniper's treeline," said Belis, "then a whole lot of shouted curses. It was the unmistakable voice of Livingston, our squad leader for the first squad… Livingston had led the rest of the squad around the LZ to go get the sniper, but had run into growth so thick they couldn't get through it… After things quieted down the sniper popped off another round, just to let us know he was still there. Half an hour or so after that, the guys yelled out to us to get ready to run toward our side of the LZ. They were calling in artillery on the opposite tree line, and would lay down cover fire with M-60s for us…Not but a few seconds later the artillery began impacting on the far side of the LZ. Sometime after it finished…a patrol…found neither hide nor hair of the sniper."

In October 1966, the 5th Battalion, Royal Australian Regiment fought the Viet Cong for nine days straight. Captain Robert O'Neill reported for the regimental association later, "…A shot rang out and Corporal Womal fell, yelling that he had been hit. A bullet had passed through his neck…"

When a Sioux helicopter was called in to evacuate the Diggers, the pilot had to brave fire directed at the chopper and maintain a steady hand as well. "…The snipers knew where Womal lay and could shoot anyone moving to his assistance…Despite orders to the contrary, the Platoon stretcher bearer, Private Fraser, began to crawl forward to Womal, under fire. He reached Womal and proceeded to dress his wound, placing his own body between Womal and the enemy in order to shield Womal from further fire. The snipers opened up again, missing Fraser by inches…By this time, the enemy had learned to recognize the voice of Deak as that of the leader. Each time he shouted orders bullets flew overhead from the snipers… However, the extraction was successful and the stretcher party struggled back to the cover of the rocks."

The US Marine sniper program "in country" was operating by the autumn of 1965, but it took three years before the Corps made the sniper an official component of its organization. That decision was based, at least in part, on the success of the snipers in Vietnam. In June 1968, sniper platoons were organized in the headquarters

ABOVE: US Army sniper Adelbert Waldron, top scoring sniper of the Vietnam War, made numerous kills from a Brown Water Navy swift boat such as this. (Public Domain)

THE VIETNAM WAR

ABOVE: Women of a South Vietnamese militia force march through the jungle. (Public Domain)

and service companies at the reconnaissance battalion level, as well as in the regimental headquarters companies. The Marine infantry regiment contained a sniper platoon of three squads with five two-man teams and a squad leader, senior non-commissioned officer, officer, and armourer. Its total strength was 35 Marines. Four squads of three two-man teams were assigned to the reconnaissance battalion along with a squad leader, NCO, officer and armourer, a complement of 31 Marines.

To fill their available sniper school slots, Land and Russell went recruiting, and one of Land's first takers was Gunnery Sergeant Carlos Hathcock, an MP who had become disenchanted with the role while stationed at Chu Lai. Hathcock was already well known in the Marines for his marksmanship. Weighing just 140 pounds, he was small in stature, but his record was impressive. While stationed at Cherry Point, North Carolina, Hathcock had won the Marine Corps interservice and national shooting championships and captured the 1965 Wimbledon Cup, besting 2,600 other military and civilian marksmen to claim the coveted prize. He also won the US 1,000-Yard High Power Rifle championship that year.

Hathcock would become legendary in the annals of sniping history during his two tours of duty in Vietnam. Twice the communists placed bounties on his head, and one of those was levied after he and another Marine sniper had teamed to pin down a company of North Vietnamese soldiers in a rice paddy, paralyzing the enemy unit for three days. The North Vietnamese sent special sniper detachments to hunt Hathcock and gave him the respectful nickname of "Long Tra'ng," or White Feather, in reference to the small adornment he had slipped into the band of his camouflage bush hat. By the end of his first tour, he had logged 86 kills, and he kept a record of his activities in a dog-eared pocket notebook that he carried.

Hathcock ended his combat service with 93 confirmed sniper kills although his score is likely to have been considerably higher. Some of his victims were never located due to heavy artillery fire in the area or the evacuation of the bodies by the enemy. His second tour was abruptly cut short when the armoured vehicle he was riding on struck a mine in September 1969, blowing him 40 feet into the air. Severely burned, he rescued six injured Marines from the flames before collapsing. He spent six months in hospital recovering, joined the Marine Rifle Team at Quantico in 1970, and retired due to disability in 1979. He died of multiple sclerosis 20 years later.

Leaving a legendary record of one shot – one kill, Carlos Hathcock was pragmatic in his assessment. "I have no guilt," he told an interviewer. "It was a job, my job. Just like an artillery man has his job – except he didn't look people in the face when he shot 'em." Possessed of steely nerves, Hathcock told a reporter once that he preferred the single combat of the sniper to larger infantry fighting. Still, he was never overconfident.

ABOVE: Marine Gunnery Sergeant Carlos Hathcock emerged as a legendary sniper of the Vietnam War. (Public Domain)

ABOVE: A US Marine sniper team operates under pressure in the Khe Sanh Valley. (Public Domain)

"I always had butterflies," he told the interviewer. "I was scared to death all the time. Anybody tells you different, stay away from him. He's a fool."

Among his numerous exploits, Hathcock set a record for distance sniping when he shot a Viet Cong weapons carrier with a .50-calibre round fired from an M2 Browning machine gun in single shot mode. The distance was 2,500 yards (2,286 metres). He also told the story of an encounter with a North Vietnamese master sniper known as the Cobra, one of a dozen snipers sent specifically to neutralize Long Tr'ang.

As the afternoon shadows lengthened and the sun sank lower in the west, Hathcock and his spotter, Lance Corporal John Burke, watched the crest of a hill and the wide grassy slope that led to a nearby ditch. Through his binoculars, Carlos saw a fleeting glimmer, a flash of light perhaps reflected off the binoculars of his worthy opponent. He whispered to Burke, "I'm gonna gamble a shot."

Seconds later, his breath steadied and his scope framing the spot where the light had been seen, Hathcock squeezed the trigger. The crackle shattered the stillness, and then the Cobra lay dead. The two Marines moved to the scene, and as Burke congratulated his partner, Hathcock came to

ABOVE: South Vietnamese rangers armed with M-16 rifles await orders during the Tet Offensive. (Public Domain)

THE MILITARY SNIPER

ABOVE: A sniper of Marine D Company, 1st Battalion, 5th Marines takes aim during the Battle of Hue. (Public Domain)

ABOVE: Specialist 4 Richard Champion, US Army, shouts to his squad after a Viet Cong sniper has opened fire. (Public Domain)

a startling conclusion. His .30-06 round had penetrated the Cobra's scope, passed through his eye, and out the back of his head. The only way for such a shot to happen was for the Cobra to have eyed Hathcock at the same moment. The sliver of time – the difference between life and death – had been Hathcock's earlier squeeze of the trigger.

Another hazardous mission involved Hathcock's stalk of a North Vietnamese general. The assignment was specific, and he was airlifted to the Laotian frontier, where the officer's headquarters was supposedly located. Staying hidden from enemy patrols, some of them so close he could hear their conversations, Hathcock crept forward, sometimes covering only a few inches over several hours. Ants crawled up his pant legs, while insects bit and stung incessantly. He endured, and on the fourth day found his quarry.

The sound of an engine was soon followed by the appearance of a white automobile, which proceeded up a dirt road and stopped in front of the complex of bunkers and buildings that Hathcock had patiently kept under surveillance. When the general stepped through the doorway, the sniper picked up his form, but just as he readied to shoot, an aide stepped in front of the senior officer.

Momentarily frustrated, Hathcock resumed his wait and watched intently. When the sight picture was clear once again, he adjusted for the heat and wind conditions that might affect the flight of the bullet as it flew faster than the speed of sound toward the general's chest. An attending group of officers had stepped away, and the aide had taken his place to the general's left. The time had come. An instant later, the old general was down, blood spattering his uniform, and his eyes yawing open and sightless.

With 109 confirmed kills, army Staff Sergeant Adelbert Waldron of the 9th Infantry Division was the highest scoring American sniper of the Vietnam War. Waldron had served 12 years in the US navy prior to becoming an infantryman. He amassed such a tally in just eight months of combat and was later assigned as a marksmanship instructor at Fort Benning, Georgia.

While serving in Vietnam, Waldron was once aboard a small riverine boat of the American "Brown Water Navy," which patrolled the Mekong River and its delta. He spotted a Viet Cong sniper in the top of a coconut tree some 823 yards (900 metres) distant and killed the man with a single shot. Then, in February 1969, Waldron was working with a spotter in a night ambush position at the edge of a rice paddy while supporting the 3rd Battalion, 60th Infantry Regiment south of Ben Tre.

When he spotted a group of five Viet Cong moving from the cover of a wooded area, Waldron shot the first guerrilla. The others immediately hit the dirt, lying motionless for some time. When they started to move out, he quickly shot all four in succession. Just before midnight during the same support mission, Waldron spotted four more Viet Cong moving into the rice paddy from left to right. Quickly, these four fell under his match-grade M-14 rifle equipped with the starlight night vision scope.

During those few hours, Waldron had dispatched nine Viet Cong in the darkness at an average distance of 437 yards (400 metres). He was a two-time recipient of the Distinguished Service Cross and also received the Silver Star along with several awards of the Bronze Star during his tenure.

The highest scoring US Marine sniper in Vietnam was Sergeant Chuck Mawhinney with 103 confirmed kills and another 216 probables. As a young man Mawhinney hunted deer in the forests surrounding his Oregon home, and after graduating from high school in June 1967, he followed his father's lead and enlisted in the Corps. After graduating from sniper school at Camp Pendleton in April 1968, he was deployed

ABOVE: M40 sniper rifles such as these were prevalent among US Marines in Vietnam. (Creative Commons Curiosandrelics via Wikipedia)

www.keymilitary.com 95

ABOVE: A pair of US Army snipers pose with their weapons of war in South Vietnam. (Public Domain)

ABOVE: A US Marine sniper team prepares to sight a target in South Vietnam, December 1967. (Creative Commons USMC Archives via Wikipedia)

ABOVE: A sniper of Company I, 3rd Battalion, 3rd Marine Regiment walks along a jungle trail in Vietnam. (Creative Commons USMC photo Corporal Larry White via Wikipedia)

ABOVE: US Marine sniper Sergeant Howard Greene stands with his rifle during Operation Prairie II. (Creative Commons USMC Archives via Wikipedia)

ABOVE: A Marine scout sniper enjoys a holiday meal somewhere in South Vietnam. (Creative Commons USMC Archives via Wikipedia)

to Southeast Asia with the 1st Battalion, 5th Marine Regiment, 1st Marine Division.

Mawhinney served with his regimental headquarters scout sniper platoon and numerous other companies throughout the division, scoring most of his kills with Company D, 1st Battalion while using the M40 standard USMC sniper rifle of the period.

Another high scoring US Marine sniper of the Vietnam War was Master Sergeant Eric England, who joined the Corps in 1950 at the age of 17. Two years after enlisting, England claimed a US national shooting championship, and he was both a member and coach of Marine rifle team for 24 years. He recorded 98 kills as a scout sniper in Vietnam while serving with the 3rd Division and was the subject of the book Eric England: The Phantom of Phu Bai, written by Dr. Joseph B. Turner.

The author tells of England's gruelling stalk of a North Vietnamese colonel, which lasted well over six hours as he sat watching a curve in a dirt road 800 yards distant and the only clear space in the jungle for miles. He had been inserted by helicopter and then crawled a quarter mile until he found the position that he wanted, entering what he described as his "bubble." Then, when the time was right, England would squeeze the trigger. During the months he was near the Phu Bai combat base south of the city of Hue in 1967-68, England is believed to have killed approximately 50 officers of the North Vietnamese army and the Viet Cong.

Carlos Hathcock said of England, "Eric is a great man, a great shooter, and a great Marine." Along with Hathcock, he also had a price on his head only to emerge safely in the United States in the autumn of 1968 to train new scout snipers. He continued to win shooting competitions and retired from active duty in 1974. A statue of England was dedicated in 2006 at the Union County courthouse in Blairsville, Georgia, his hometown. He died in 2018 at the age of 84.

On January 6, 1967, Marine scout sniper Vaughn Nickell was stationed at Phu Loc halfway between the provincial capital of Hue and the bustling coastal port at Da Nang. Ron Willoughby was paired with Nickell on that unforgettable day and later wrote of the incident in which Nickell scored the longest confirmed kill with the elderly M-1D sniper rifle at a distance of just over 1,200 yards (1,097 metres).

"The outpost was manned by a Company from 2nd Battalion, 5th Marines," recalled Willoughby, "and the Company Commander's concern was that he had started to hear that some of the Marines were teasing Charlie and challenging him to shoot. The unfortunate thing was they didn't know where he was going to show up. And the unfortunate thing for 6 o'clock Charlie was that after slightly wounding a teasing Marine in the back side, the Marines at Phu Loc 6 got their own sniper team."

In addition to their other responsibilities, Nickell and Willoughby began hunting for the troublesome Viet Cong sniper around 6 o'clock each evening. They moved from one

ABOVE: A female Viet Cong guerrilla fires her weapon during an attack in South Vietnam. (Public Domain)

location to another and had no luck until that afternoon in January when Willoughby was pulled away from the hunt for a while and left Nickell with the M-1D. Just after Willoughby departed, a call came in from a nearby hillside as Marines thought they had spotted their assailant.

When Nickell arrived on the scene, he peered through his 4X scope and indeed found 6 o'clock Charlie moving into a concealed position for his nightly engagement. After summoning a nearby Marine to act as his spotter, Nickell settled in and took aim. At that distance, a hit with a single shot was unlikely, and the first round missed by about three feet, just short of the human target. A puff of dirt flew into the air when the second shot landed just beside the enemy sniper, who then realised that someone was hot on his trail.

Willoughby reported later, "…Charlie started to make his move to get out of harm's way when the third shot rang out dropping Charlie in his tracks. It was an excellent 1,100 metre shot on a cold rainy day by Vaughn Nickell at Phu Loc 6 using the M1D. Time of Charlie's death – 6 o'clock. Body and weapon recovered."

Whether the fighting took place in Vietnam or in some other locale before or since, one aspect of the sniper experience is timeless. Whether the sniper feels remorse is a personal emotional response, but the first kill remains with the individual for the rest of their life.

ABOVE: US Navy SEALs lead a Viet Cong prisoner into captivity at My Tho in 1969. (Public Domain)

Corporal Jerry Clifford was a scout sniper with the 1st Battalion, 1st Marine Regiment, and he was haunted by the spectre of his sniper baptism. "I guess a first kill is always an unforgettable experience," he reflected. "I certainly will never forget mine. 'She' was about eighteen and was carrying an M1 carbine. At the time I did not know that he was a 'she,' and, of course, I did not know she was pregnant. The shot was overlooking a free-fire zone (which was a slightly elevated plateau) outside a deserted villa. A small VC patrol broke from the tree line and was re-entering it when I took out 'tail-end Charlie.' The shot was about 600 yards (549 metres), through the lower back and out the front. The body and rifle were recovered, the kill confirmed. The grunts gave me credit for 'two with one shot.' I took solace in staring at the sun."

Such is the lot of the military sniper.

By the end of the Vietnam War, the sniper had become ingrained in the psyche of military establishments around the world. Loved or loathed, hailed or shunned, the sniper had prepared his place for future conflicts. As Hathcock said, it was a job. And it could be measured with cold efficiency.

Experts estimated that every Viet Cong guerrilla or North Vietnamese soldier killed or wounded in Vietnam required the expenditure of 50,000 rounds of small arms ammunition in general combat conditions, and the monetary cost of a round was roughly 20 cents. The ratio, however, was quite different for the sniper – economical if you will. Proficient army and Marine Corps snipers, it was said, killed or wounded and enemy combatant with an average of every 1.3 rounds fired.

ABOVE: Australian soldiers return to base after an extended mission in the Vietnamese jungle, 1966. (Public Domain)

ABOVE: US Army rangers train South Vietnamese soldiers during early operations in Vietnam. (Public Domain)

APACHE

Carlos Hathcock said the story was true. It remains one of the most intriguing questions of the Vietnam War. Did the Viet Cong sniper, a female about 30 years old and trained in the craft of intelligence gathering as well, actually exist? Further, did she lead a platoon of snipers into action – possibly in search of Hathcock – after she had inflicted misery, pain and death on Marines near Hill 55?

She was nicknamed Apache, and the story goes that she was a skilled interrogator, torturing any prisoner she was able to question and conducting her sadistic ritual at times within earshot of Marines on the line. Her mystique was powerful, and she was known as deadly accurate with her Moisin Nagant rifle and its 3.5X PU telescopic sight.

According to author Charles Henderson in his biography of Gunnery Sergeant Hathcock titled *Marine Sniper 93 Confirmed Kills*, when Hathcock was informed of Apache's methods, he responded, "Sir, I reckon we ought to put this Apache right at the top of our list." Henderson's narrative relates a burning desire that builds to a crescendo within Hathcock after he hears for himself the terrible sounds of a suffering captive at the hands of Apache. "I want her," the Marine sniper murmured.

In the late afternoon of November 13, 1966, Hathcock sat still watching the crest of a hill, while his commanding officer, Captain Jim Land, acting as spotter, sat nearby. Daylight was fading, and Land whispered that it was time to pack up. Hathcock asked for 10 more minutes while the sun retreated. An instant later, the Marine sniper saw several figures clad in black spill across the top of the hill, heading down a dusty trail toward their hidden position. Land confirmed the identity of the onrushing group.

"They're VC," he confirmed. "Check out the one that just squatted off to the left, just below the rise from the others." He was certain, matching her features to photos, that this was a woman. She had to be the dreaded Apache. Land asserted that the best opportunity to wipe out the guerrilla sniper contingent was with a quick artillery barrage. He called in coordinates, and shells began to fall. The Viet Cong took casualties and began to run.

Three enemy insurgents lay dead after the first artillery shell burst. Two others began running away down the trail as more shells crashed. Apache hit the ground but then rose up. She mistakenly ran toward the two Marines who were waiting. Another Viet Cong who had momentarily taken cover saw his leader running the wrong way and called to her.

Apache turned and looked back. Hathcock was ready. His bullet struck between the shoulder blades, and Apache fell to the ground. A second rifle shot passed through her chest. Apache died in the open. Within seconds, Hathcock acquired another the other Viet Cong target and killed his second guerrilla of the afternoon. Hathcock smiled as Land embraced him with a congratulatory, "You got her Carlos! You did it!"

Years later, Hathcock affirmed the encounter with Apache and admitted that her death had been the only one of the Vietnam War that pleased him. "I really wanted that woman," he grumbled. "She was an animal. That was a good day."

ABOVE: Female members of the Viet Cong gather. Apache was a supposed Viet Cong sniper and interrogator. (Public Domain)

ABOVE: A Viet Cong guerrilla stands below his flag and holds an AK-47 assault rifle. Apache was supposedly a notorious Viet Cong sniper. (Public Domain)

ABOVE: This 1968 photo depicts female Viet Cong fighters during communist indoctrination activities. (Public Domain)

THE MILITARY SNIPER

CHUCK MAWHINNEY

After his discharge from the Marine Corps as its top scoring sniper of the Vietnam War and in Corps history with 103 confirmed kills, Chuck Mawhinney went to work for the US Forest Service. He has since retired from that job and lives quietly in Baker City, Oregon, now in his mid-70s. Through the years since his Vietnam experience, Mawhinney has spoken to many gatherings, including classes at the US Army Mountain Warfare School at Fort Carson, Colorado, and the Marine sniper school at Camp Pendleton, California, but he has never really sought the limelight.

However, in the year 2000, three decades after his 1969 discharge from the Marines, Mawhinney sat down with Tony Perry, a reporter for the Los Angeles Times, and talked about his life on the edge while "in country." He discussed the attitude and the perspective of the sniper with candour.

"When you fire," he said, "your senses start going into overtime: eyes, ears, smell, everything. Your vision widens out so you see everything, and you can smell things like you can't at other times. My rules of engagement were simple: if they had a weapon, they were going down. Except for an NVA (North Vietnamese Army) paymaster I hit at 900 yards, everyone I killed had a weapon."

One incredible experience secured Chuck Mawhinney's place in the annals of sniper history. In February 1969, he accomplished an extraordinary feat.

"Near the An Hoa base outside Da Nang," Perry wrote, "he caught a platoon of North Vietnamese army regulars crossing a stream. He hit 16 with head shots with an M-14, which he often carried in addition to his bolt action (a Remington Model 700). The 16 were listed only as probable kills because no officer was there to see the lifeless bodies float by and there was no chance to search the bodies."

Regardless, Mawhinney had done his duty with clinical precision and detachment. He explained, "I never looked in their eyes. I never stopped to think about whether the guy had a wife or kids."

Perry noted, "…As a sniper, Mawhinney had an uncanny ability to gauge distance, moisture, weather and terrain – factors that determine how much a bullet will rise or drop during flight. He had the patience to wait for hours for the right shot. He was scared but exhilarated. 'Normally I would shoot and run, but if I had them at a distance, I wasn't worried. I would shoot and then lay there and wait and wait and wait and pretty soon somebody else would start moving toward the body. Then I would shoot again.'"

ABOVE: Viet Cong guerrillas cross a river. Chuck Mawhinney killed 16 insurgents in a river crossing engagement. (Public Domain)

ABOVE: This view through a sniper rifle's telescopic sight was taken in Vietnam in 1968. Such a view was familiar to Sergeant Chuck Mawhinney. (Creative Commons USMC Archives via Wikipedia)

Years after his combat life was over, Mawhinney was wistful over one encounter. He regretted missing a single Viet Cong guerrilla that eluded him one day. He had been on leave from Vietnam, and upon his return asked an armorer if he had done as requested and refrained from altering his rifle's sights. The armorer assured Mawhinney that he had not touched the weapon.

Subsequently, Mawhinney was in the field and spotted the enemy insurgent only 300 yards away, well within range of the expert sniper. Mawhinney fired… and missed. He fired again and again. The result was the same. Obviously, the rifle had been altered, and the enemy slipped away.

"I can't help thinking about how many people that he may have killed later," Mawhinney mused, "…he deserved to die. That still bothers me."

ABOVE: The sniper rifle belonging to Chuck Mawhinney resides in the National Museum of the Marine Corps, Quantico, Virginia. (Creative Commons Mark Pellegrin via Wikipedia)

THE FALKLANDS WAR

In the spring of 1982, the military junta that governed Argentina took action, launching amphibious and airborne landings on "Islas Malvinas," to forcibly seize territory it declared to be its own. The Falkland Islands, however, were British, and the 74-day war that followed the temporary Argentine occupation of these windswept spits of land in the South Atlantic resulted in violent clashes of arms.

Sniper activity was constant during the fighting that occurred across the Falklands until British forces secured the capital of Stanley and the war ended on June 14. Fierce clashes, some hand-to-hand, occurred at locales such as Goose Green, Darwin, Mount Tumbledown, Wireless Ridge, Mount Longdon, Two Sisters, and Mount Harriet.

The opposing forces were both well equipped, the Argentine snipers fielding a variety of weapons from the US-made M-14 to their license-built version of the German Mauser K98K with telescopic sights, and the sniper variant of the French 7.62mm FAL. British snipers were often armed with the venerable L42A1. Both sides utilized night vision equipment as well.

During the short conflict, the Argentines also briefly seized the island of South Georgia, 900 miles west of Stanley. However, before they took temporary possession they had a fight on their hands. In one of the most unusual encounters in sniper history, Command Sergeant Major Peter Leach, a 19-year veteran of the Royal Marines and a trained sniper, took on the Argentine navy corvette Guerrico, firing gamely at the figures on the bridge, shattering windows, and hastening the Argentine warship's withdrawal to a safer distance.

Heavy fighting broke out as the 2nd Battalion, the Parachute Regiment, or 2 Para, attacked Argentine positions at Goose Green on May 27-28. Before the Argentines surrendered, Lieutenant Colonel Herbert "H" Jones was killed, possibly by Corporal Osvaldo Olmos, a sniper of the Argentine army special forces. Jones received a posthumous Victoria Cross for his gallantry.

ABOVE: Argentine soldiers await British landings in the Falklands. Snipers played an active role in the brief 1982 war. (Public Domain)

ABOVE: A memorial honours three teenage British soldiers killed in action in the Falklands in 1982. (Creative Commons TenthEagle via Wikipedia)

In early June, the Reconnaissance Troop of No. 42 Commando reached Mount Wall, southwest of Two Sisters and Mount Harriet, and ran into elements of the Argentine 4th Monte Caseros Regiment. When the Commandos opened fire, two Argentine soldiers were killed immediately, and the non-commissioned officer leading the riflemen was incapacitated by the concussion of a British sniper round that pierced his helmet.

Elsewhere, the battle at Mount Longdon, fought June 11-12, was a bare-knuckle brawl. Seventeen-year-old Private Jason Burt of 3 Para was killed by a sniper. He was one of three men there aged 18 or younger who lost their lives. At Mount Tumbledown two days later, Lieutenant Robert Lawrence of the Scots Guards was shot in the head by an Argentine sniper, the bullet passing through his skull an exiting above his right eye. Although he suffered from paralysis and the loss of 42 percent of his brain, Lawrence miraculously survived, authoring the book, *When the Fighting is Over: A Personal Story of the Battle for Tumbledown Mountain and Its Aftermath*.

Reverend David Cooper, who served as the 2 Para chaplain and was also a champion marksman, is said to have worked with British snipers during their long sea voyage to the Falklands. He remembered, "The snipers tried to help out where the companies were being held up. On one occasion we had to move quickly when we came under antiaircraft fire. Then it was suppressing fire while the companies or platoons moved. That amounted to putting down harassing fire into Argentine bunkers.

"In one incident when I called the wind," Cooper added, "the sniper fired and a white flag appeared out of the bunker, which was a good 600-700 metres (656-766 yards) away. On the shooting range the signal for a miss is a white and red flag, and the sniper made the comment that they were signalling a wash-out. Clearly, the Argentines were unhappy about the rounds going through the slots in their bunkers, but there was not a lot we could do when someone 700 yards away wants to surrender."

BELOW: Command Sergeant Major Peter Leach, a qualified sniper, fired multiple shots at the bridge of the Argentine corvette Guerrico during action at the island of South Georgia. (Creative Commons Martin Otero via Wikipedia)

THE MILITARY SNIPER

THE GULF WAR AND HOTSPOTS

"I request permission to take shots. The men are perfect targets. The CO tells me, Negative, Sierra Tango One – break. Negative on permission to shoot – break. If their buddies next to them – break – start taking rounds in the head – break – they won't surrender, copy. I reply, Roger, roger."

So ran the exchange remembered by US Marine scout sniper Anthony Swofford in his 2003 memoir *Jarhead: A Marine's Chronicle Of The Gulf War*. Swofford was frustrated and added, "I can't help but assume that they don't want to use us because they know that two snipers with two of the finest rifles in the world and a few hundred rounds between them will in a short time inflict severe and debilitating havoc, causing the entire airfield to surrender. The captains want some war, and they must know that the possibilities are dwindling… In a few more hours, the assault is over and I've remained a spectator."

Perhaps there was a grain of truth in Swofford's assessment, but in the event, the world had stepped up to stop the naked aggression of Saddam Hussein's Iraq, his army having stormed into neighbouring Kuwait on August 2, 1990. After a build-up of men and women and military hardware that took months, the ground phase of the Gulf War, or Operation Desert Storm,

ABOVE: A British soldier of the Queen's Dragoon Guards fires an M40A1 sniper rifle while training with US Marines during the buildup for Desert Storm. (Public Domain)

lasted only 100 hours as Coalition forces decimated the Iraqi invaders.

Nevertheless, there was an appreciation of the sniper's capabilities during the brief Gulf War. General Salah Aboud Mahmoud, who sent Iraqi forces to occupy the town of Khafji just across the Kuwaiti frontier with Saudi Arabia, commented, "…I emphasized how the snipers should be accurate and effective against the helicopters of the enemy." Iraqi snipers were also active against Coalition ground personnel, and in one confrontation took the life of a US army sergeant.

The historian of the 1st Brigade (Tiger), 2nd Armored Division described the scene in a town that had been cleared. "The fighting here had to be done room by room; when it was over, 40 Iraqis had been killed or made prisoner…While assisting in positioning the command post, the battalion's master gunner, Sergeant First Class Harold R. Witzke, was shot by a sniper and died while awaiting evacuation."

ABOVE: Members of the US Army ODA 525 team pause before infiltrating Iraqi positions in Desert Storm. Note the soldier with the sniper rifle, scope attached, at lower left. (Public Domain)

ABOVE: A United Nations armoured vehicle patrols 'Sniper Alley' in war-torn Sarajevo. (Creative Commons Paalso via Wikimedia)

www.keymilitary.com 101

THE GULF WAR AND HOTSPOTS

ABOVE: A soldier from Kazakhstan aims his Russian-made Dragunov SVD sniper rifle. (Public Domain)

As they retreated, the Iraqis carved a path of destruction, setting fire to oil facilities, laying mines as they could, and attempting to reach weapons caches. US Marines of Company K, 3rd Battalion, 5th Marines were in action amid the smoke and flames. Author Mark Welch described their activity. "The Al Wafrah oil fields were not too far away. The minefields had been under the watchful eyes of Marine snipers throughout the night. Every now and then the snipers would fire a round and take out an enemy soldier in one of the many bunkers…."

The Gulf War was by far the largest conflict of the 1990s, but also during that time various incidents of sniper warfare broke out during United Nations peacekeeping efforts and other operations. Paramilitary or guerrilla snipers were common, but the trained military sniper was a force with which to be reckoned. The rifle he carried continued to evolve. US Marine snipers were often armed with the M-40A3, still based on the proven Remington Model 700, as the older M40A1 was phased out beginning in 1996. Among other weapons, US army snipers carried the .30-calibre (7.62mm) M-24, another Remington Model 700 modification. These rifles were fitted with 10X sights and bipods to assist with steady firing.

In the mid-1990s, British army and Royal Marine snipers were regularly issued the 8.59mm (.338-calibre) L115A1 Long Range Accuracy International sniper rifle along with the 7.62mm L96A1, which had been adopted in 1980s. These were two of several Accuracy International variants to eventually see service and were regularly outfitted with Schmidt & Bender telescopic sights. The reliable L42A1 was being phased out by 1990.

During the Blackhawk Down incident in Mogadishu in war-torn Somalia, US Delta Force snipers Master Sergeant Gary Gordon and Sergeant First Class Randy Shughart bravely roped down to defend the stricken crew of one of the two Blackhawk helicopters shot down on October 3, 1993. The two heroes pulled wounded men to temporary safety and proceeded to kill or wound approximately 100 marauding Somali guerrillas before they were overwhelmed. Both men received the Medal of Honor posthumously.

Hostilities flared in the Balkans as Serbs and Bosnians fought for preeminence during the period as well. The city of Sarajevo became a battleground often dominated by snipers. French forces took steps to quell indiscriminate sniper activity, putting together an anti-sniping team that spent a week monitoring an area known to be frequented by snipers. Fighting erupted later in the southern Serbian province of Kosovo, and one correspondent for the Armed Forces Press Service related, "Rogue elements targeted US service members during two violent acts in Kosovo…In the most serious incident, Serb snipers opened fire on Marines manning a roadblock in the village of Zegra…Marines killed one sniper and wounded another."

Russian forces fought rebels in the breakaway republic of Chechnya, but their doctrine, which call for sniper action in a combined arms mode, left them often unprepared for the sniper activity that occurred amid the rubble of ruined buildings

ABOVE: US Army snipers Randy Shughart (left) and Gary Gordon received the Medal of Honor posthumously for heroism in Somalia in 1993. (Public Domain)

and from street to street. Both the Chechens and the Russians employed the 7.62mm Dragunov SVD sniper rifle, but a single Chechen sniper, according to US intelligence reports, often pinned down substantial Russian units.

Authors Lester W. Grau and Charles Q. Cutshaw wrote an assessment of the Russian response to the Chechen sniper threat for Infantry magazine. "The Chechens met the Russians in urban combat in Grozny and soon Chechen snipers took a toll on Russian forces."

But the Russians adapted.

"…The war in Chechnya saw the return of the elite sniper who was part of the government special reserves and hunted Chechens," added Grau and Cutshaw. "These men avoid carrying their weapons in public since they do not want the locals to identify them as part of the sniper elite force. The sniper works as part of a team – two snipers plus a five-man security element armed with Kalashnikov assault rifles." The Russian sniper pair covered an ambush area of about 300 metres (328 yards) distant with the security team in position for support.

At any given time, American forces were deployed in several hotspots around the world during the 1990s, and one officer was asked about such involvement. He related that troops often found themselves threatened by hostile civilian populations or paramilitary forces. These situations, he said, cried out for a skilled sniper with the capability to execute a surgical shot when needed. Relating a personal incident he witnessed, the officer added that while serving in Sierra Leone he watched a rebel leader brandish an automatic weapon.

The civilians had been warned to stay some distance away from the Americans, but this guerrilla got too close. A single shot from an American sniper neutralized the threat and sent a clear message to the rest of the crowd that had gathered.

ABOVE: A French sniper takes up a position atop a hotel in Sarajevo during unrest in the Balkans. (Public Domain)

BARRETT M82 LIGHT FIFTY

ABOVE: Norwegian soldiers of the Telemark Battalion engage Taliban fighters in combat in Afghanistan. The soldier in the foreground is firing an M82 .50-calibre sniper rifle. (Creative Commons P via Wikipedia)

Tracing its origin back more than 40 years, the Barrett M82 Light Fifty series of semiautomatic rifles has been proven in combat around the world in the anti-material and sniper roles. American Ronnie Barrett founded his Barrett Firearms Manufacturing Company in 1982 with the intent of producing semiautomatic rifles capable of chambering the .50-calibre (12.7mm) NATO cartridge that was originally made compatible with the venerable Browning M2 machine gun.

The Barrett Light Fifty, as it is commonly called, weighs 12.9 kilograms (28.3 pounds), and its maximum effective range with telescopic sights is estimated at 1,800 metres (1,969 yards). Such a heavy weapon would inherently present issues with recoil when operated by a single soldier; however, the M82 series was engineered to absorb much of the shock of firing with a barrel assembly that absorbs energy along with a large muzzle brake that also curtails the recoil effect.

In the anti-material role, the Barrett M82 is effective against caches of weapons, ammunition, fuel, and other supplies, communications apparatus, even bunkers or pillboxes and other targets that might otherwise require the use of artillery or rockets to destroy. As a sniper rifle, it has been configured with rails to accommodate a variety of telescopic sights and manufactured as a shoulder-fired weapon that minimizes recoil.

An improved version of the early M82 became available in 1986 and was designated the M82A1. Fed from a 10-round detachable magazine, the first of these rifles were sold to Sweden in 1989, and the following year the US Marine Corps purchased 125 M82A1 rifles, semiautomatic and equipped with the picatinny rail atop the receiver for scope mounting. The version adopted by the Marines was designated the M82A1M. The US army and air force followed with their own procurement, and the M82A1M is today classified as the Special Applications Scoped Rifle (SASR). In 2002, the US army adopted a modified M82A1 as its long-range sniper rifle and designated it the M107.

In the sniper role, the M82 presents a distinct advantage with its extended effective range and the capability of its powerful

ABOVE: A US Marine scout sniper fires down range with the Barrett M82A3. Note the spent shell casings. (Public Domain)

ABOVE: A US Navy sniper stands on the tarmac at Kandahar, Afghanistan, holding his Barrett M82A1 sniper rifle. (Public Domain)

.50-calibre round, which has been known to penetrate stone, brick or concrete walls of varying thickness. Its mere presence on the battlefield is demoralizing to adversaries who at times have virtually no place to hide. Although there are other sniper rifles with longer effective range, in combination with its penetrating power the M82 is a formidable opponent.

In 2004, US Marine Staff Sergeant Steve Reichert scored a kill in Iraq with the M82A3 from a distance of one mile (1,614 metres), while Sergeant Brian Kremer of the army's 75th Ranger Regiment was accurate at 1.43 miles (2,300 metres). In 2008, US army Specialist Nicholas Ranstad recorded a kill in Afghanistan at 1.3 miles (2,092 metres). In 2012, an unidentified sniper of Australian No. 2 Commando struck his target from 1.75 miles (2,815 metres) with the M82A1.

The Barrett Light Fifty is in service today with the armed forces of more than 50 countries, and it has seen action in numerous conflicts, including the Troubles in Northern Ireland, the Soviet war in Afghanistan in the 1980s, the Gulf War, Kosovo War, the conflicts in Iraq and Afghanistan, and the Russian invasion of Ukraine in 2022.

IRAQ AND AFGHANISTAN

For the United States, the war in Afghanistan was the longest in its history. While its steadfast allies remained in support, the struggle against the Taliban regime ended in withdrawal in the summer of 2021. For much of that time, the allies had also been fighting in Iraq, intent on regime change and the deposing of ruthless Ba'athist dictator Saddam Hussein. That conflict devolved into a lengthy counter-insurgency effort before the withdrawal of American and other forces.

In the meantime, both conflicts, spurred by the horrific terrorist attack by Al Qaeda on the World Trade Center in New York on September 11, 2001, and the subsequently erroneous contention that Iraq harboured an arsenal of weapons of mass destruction, became killing grounds for snipers. By the turn of the 21st century, technology had placed weapons of unprecedented capability in the hands of the military sniper, and warfare in desert, mountainous country, or in the urban settings of villages and even of downtown Baghdad made the lives and times of military personnel challenging.

Within days of the World Trade Center tragedy, American and allied troops were on the ground in Afghanistan, hunting Al Qaeda and engaging in military operations against their militant Taliban hosts.

ABOVE: A sniper of the US Army's 4th Infantry Division keeps watch above Kandahar, Afghanistan. (Public Domain)

Canadian snipers were among the first in action, and their impact was immediate.

The afternoon sun shone brilliantly on the position of Corporal Rob Furlong whose hands clutched his .50-calibre Macmillan Tac-50 bolt action sniper rifle. The wind blew steadily as his comrade, Master Corporal Tim McMeekin, crouched close at hand. Both men picked up a distant sight, three enemy fighters apparently moving into position with a machine gun. Operation

ABOVE: A sniper of the Afghan National Army peers through the scope of his M-24 weapon system. (Creative Commons NATO Training Mission-Afghanistan via Wikipedia)

Anaconda was in full swing, and the Shahikot Valley of eastern Afghanistan was a hotbed of sharp small-arms clashes.

Using Vector laser ranging equipment, McMeekin estimated the distance at 2,430 metres, just over 1.5 miles. The immediate threat was the centre fighter carrying the machine gun, and quickly the pair made the decision to engage. Of course, the likelihood of a hit was complicated with every metre of distance, but Furlong's training kicked in. The first shot missed, and the second was closer, striking the pack on the fighter's back.

Furlong remembered in an interview in 2006, "They had no fear. They didn't run. I guess they've just been engaged so many times."

ABOVE: A US Army sniper team looks to acquire a target in the Dur Baba region of Afghanistan, 2006. (Public Domain)

The third shot was deadly, and the Taliban fighter was dead when he hit the ground. The flight of the bullet had been accomplished in just four seconds. Furlong had adjusted for wind and heat conditions that would no doubt affect its path over such a distance, and the long-range kill was a record that stood for some time.

Furlong and McMeekin were members of the two three-man sniper teams, Alpha and Bravo Detachments, that belonged to the Canadian army's 3rd Battalion, Princess Patricia's Light Infantry, a storied unit. The Canadians were attached to the scout platoon of the US army's 187th "Rakkasan" Brigade for three weeks, and these professionals displayed incredible skill. In fact, Furlong's remarkable shot had just broken another distance record, set by Master Corporal Arron Perry at the head of one of the teams.

Days earlier, Perry had killed a Taliban forward observer with a shot fired from 2,310 metres, or 1.44 miles. Perry's shot eclipsed a distance record set 30 years earlier in the jungles of Vietnam by US Marine legend Gunnery Sergeant Carlos Hathcock. At age 30, Perry was a weightlifter, a man of physical strength who also worked as a bouncer in a downtown bar in Edmonton, Alberta.

ABOVE: A sniper provides cover with his L96A1 rifle as a patrol of British paras crosses a road in the Sangin Valley of Afghanistan. (Open Government License Sgt Anthony Boocock via Wikipedia)

ABOVE: A sniper of the US 3rd Battalion, 6th Marines participates in counter-sniper operations in Afghanistan. (Public Domain)

After their insertion buy Chinook helicopter, the two sniper parties had set about their business. Perry remembered, "Anyone who says they are not scared is crazy, but it was great." They came in under fire, and Perry was noted for taking shots during the first hour of combat, some as distant as 1,500 metres, or nearly a mile away. For the next nine days, they were regularly engaged, recording numerous kills and providing cover for American troops on the move. An American Sergeant Major of the 101st Airborne Division said of Perry, "His shots were incredible. One shot, one kill." The captain commanding a US army scout platoon added, "These guys, regardless of what country they were from, what flag they fought under, they were just excellent military professionals. We didn't want to give them up. I would have brought them home with me if I could."

Furlong, Perry, McMeekin and two other Canadian snipers received the US Bronze Star medal for their service in Afghanistan.

Seven years later, Corporal of Horse Craig Harrison of the British army's Household Cavalry, Blues and Royals Regiment, spotted two Taliban fighters manning a machine gun south of Musa Qala in Afghanistan's Helmand Province. In November 2009, Harrison was in command of three Jackal armoured cars that departed their base at 4 a.m. to provide cover for a British and Afghan army patrol clearing a village in the valley several hundred feet below their intended sniper perch.

For much of its mission the patrol was in a gulley and unable to see much of the surrounding hills and countryside. "The area was crawling with Taliban and as soon as the sun came up they started their attack," Harrison wrote in his memoir *The Longest Kill: The Story of Maverick 41, One of the World's Greatest Snipers*. "For three hours I'd provided oversight, acquired and taken out Taliban targets…I watched as a vehicle-borne patrol from my regiment was dispatched to help the foot patrol…They were dangerously exposed and fighting for their lives. From my vantage point I could see the enemy machine gun that was pouring fire down at them. I'd witnessed too many casualties being loaded on the back of a Chinook in this war. I had to take out the machine-gun crew."

Harrison gathered himself and took stock of the situation. No doubt, it would be a long shot. But he knew he had to give it his best effort. He was standing, bracing himself against a wall as he strained to capture the sight picture.

"All the evidence said that it couldn't be done; that this shot was impossible," wrote Harrison. "It was far outside the recognized range of the rifle, I was out of adjustment in my scope and my position was appalling. Every time the rifle recoiled a little chunk of wall broke away and I had to hold the bipod with my left hand just to stop it falling off. Once the hammer falls, the 16.2-gram bullet will leave the barrel at a speed of around 3,000 feet per second. I calculated that the bullet would take almost six seconds to reach the Taliban machine-gun crew."

Harrison knew the factors involved in an accurate shot, wind, temperature,

ABOVE: A sniper of the British Army's 2nd Battalion, The Royal Anglian Regiment takes aim with his L115A3 rifle. (Open Government License Cpl Daniel Wiepen via Wikipedia)

IRAQ AND AFGHANISTAN

ABOVE: A US Marine sniper of 3rd Platoon, Bravo Company, 1st Recon Battalion engages the enemy in a firefight in Northern Trek Nawa, Afghanistan. (Public Domain)

ABOVE: Soldiers of the Princess Patricia's Canadian Light Infantry provide covering fire. Snipers of the fame regiment rendered outstanding performance in Afghanistan. (Public Domain)

ranging equipment more powerful than the sniper's telescopic sights to acquire targets and assist in judging distance and other conditions. It is not uncommon for snipers and spotters to switch roles after several hours to avoid fatigue in the field.

Brandon Webb served as a US navy SEAL in Afghanistan and reflected later on the mindset of the sniper in action. "The cold morning air hung thick in the Afghan valley," he commented. "Each warm exhalation would briefly fog the outside corner of my rifle scope. But I held steady and maintained a clear view of the middle-aged man. He wore a traditional Afghan dress and had a crook in his step, perhaps a story from the Soviet or Taliban conflict. The intense training I'd received years earlier in the Navy SEAL sniper course had taught me to be patient, wait for a perfect shot, make sure this is a bad guy, control my breathing, and then go over my mental checklist… breathe, focus, squeeze. I reflected internally. I alone at this moment held this man's life in my hands. And he had no idea I was aiming center mass with my 300 Win Mag."

The "Win Mag." used by Webb is a Navy SEAL variant of the 7.62mm M24 sniper system chambered for the .300 Winchester Magnum cartridge. Along with the Win Mag., numerous other sniper rifles were used in Afghanistan and Iraq. Thousands of M-14s were placed in service with telescopic sights by both the US Marines and army. These were dubbed Designated Marksman rifles according to army Major John Plaster, who wrote of the sniper war in Afghanistan. US Special Operations Command adopted the Stoner SR-25 semiautomatic sniper rifle in 2000. The 7.62mm SR-25 offered a detachable magazine of 10 or 20 rounds, and its semiautomatic action appealed to the Special Ops community in the event of a volume fire situation. The US army issues the SR-25 today as the M110 semi-automatic sniper system.

In 2011, Plaster said, "American sniper teams go wherever the US infantrymen go, operating primarily in support of their fellow soldiers and Marines, usually from overwatch positions or scouting to the front or flanks. They typically engage enemy forces at 600 to 750 metres, where the Taliban like

humidity, and even the rotation of the earth. Then, there were his comrades in a desperate battle – everything converged in a moment of supreme tension. He pulled the trigger, and seconds later his spotter assessed, "Miss."

But the sniper was determined. "I cursed before getting a grip of myself. I cycled the bolt, chambering a fresh round, and started my firing sequence all over again. I got control of my breathing, took up the slack in the trigger and got my aiming point back on the target. I know I can make this shot…I have to make this shot…."

Harrison used a bracketing technique to range the target and then fired at one of the machine gunners. The kill shot travelled a distance of 2,475 metres, 1.54 miles. A second round from his L115A3 long-range rifle, chambered and fired, accounted for another Taliban fighter. The distance was later verified by an Apache helicopter using laser range-finding equipment.

Since that time, three longer sniper kills have been reported. An unidentified sniper of Joint Task Force 2, Canadian special forces, killed an enemy insurgent in Iraq at 3,540 metres, 2.2 miles, firing a Macmillan Tac-50 in May 2017, while an Australian sniper, name withheld, of No. 2 Commando fired a kill shot in Afghanistan at 2,815 metres, 1.75 miles, with a Barrett M82A1 in April 2012. Then, in November 2022, a member of the Ukrainian National Guard is said to have shot a Russian target from 2,710 metres, 1.68 miles, with an XADO 14.5mm (.57-calibre) Snipex Alligator bolt-action rifle.

Distance is always a factor in sniper operations, and the cool head and steady hand are complemented by the spotter, also a qualified sniper, in company and utilizing

ABOVE: New Zealand army snipers pause with their rifles at Camp Taji, Iraq. (Public Domain)

ABOVE: An American sniper with a .50-calibre rifle watches civilians cross the River Euphrates in Iraq. (Creative Commons James McCauley via Wikipedia)

to hover, just beyond the range of 5.56mm rifles. These sniper teams also sometimes operate independently, whether lying in wait for terrorists planting improvised explosive devices (IEDs), searching for targets of opportunity, or acting on intelligence to intercept and ambush Taliban fighters."

In his narrative, the retired major also described one of several sniper incidents of importance. "Such was the case for Sgt. Holmes, an 82nd Airborne Division sniper. Eyeing several Taliban peering from a distant wadi, Holmes discerned which was in command and fired a single shot, dropping him at more than 700 yards. Intelligence later determined he had eliminated an enemy battalion commander and IED cell chief, for which Holmes was awarded the Army Commendation Medal."

The Taliban had their own snipers, some of whom were well-trained and deadly. One of these, the so-called Sangin Sniper, worked in the town of Sangin in Helmand Province, Afghanistan. Probably one of several snipers, he is thought to have been behind the scope when two US Marines were killed and a 20-year-old British army combat engineer, while two other Marines were wounded in one terrible day. Another Marine was wounded, and a fourth lived to tell the tale when a ricochet was stopped by the Kevlar lining of his helmet.

In August 2010, the Wall Street Journal reported, "one or two snipers, who have shown good marksmanship, have tormented the men of Lima Company, Third Battalion, Seventh Marines and British troops." US News added a comment from a veteran Marine sergeant, "He's hitting people – that's very disruptive. But it's not interfering with what we're trying to do here."

Regardless, something had to be done to quell the unnerving sniper fire. So, both the British and American special forces in the area deployed their own counter-sniper teams and gathered intelligence from the local populace revealing that six snipers, probably foreign trained mercenaries, were operating in the Sangin area. The intelligence gathering skill of the counter-snipers paid off when the location of six enemy marksmen was confirmed and US Air Force F-16 Fighting Falcon fighter-bombers were called in to deliver a death-dealing strike that put paid the problem.

Sergeant Nicholas Irving of the US 3rd Ranger Battalion is remembered with the coldly efficient nickname of "the Reaper." Serving in both Afghanistan and Iraq, Irving carried a MK 11, a modified version of the SR-25 rifle nicknamed "Dirty Diana." Irving was quite proficient with his Mk 11, with 33 kills in four months in Afghanistan, while his total including unconfirmed kills may actually be more than 100.

Irving worked in film and television after his discharge and has coped successfully with the scourge of Post-Traumatic Stress Disorder (PTSD), a common affliction among combat veterans, including recurring nightmares of his first kill – with a .50-calibre rifle. In 2015, Irving wrote of his combat experiences with co-author Gary Brozek in the New York Times bestseller *The Reaper: Autobiography of One of the Deadliest Special Ops Snipers*.

The sniper has the ability to control the scene of confrontation, and then to destroy the illusion of safety or respite from immediate danger. His patience and purpose serve to not only deliver a direct blow to the opponent but also to shatter his psyche. One such occurrence took place for Kacy Tellessen, who described the drama of his unit's awakening to danger in the New York Times in 2019.

"We had all been dodging bullets and shrapnel like young matadors, twisting and gyrating our hips, whipping our flak jackets to the side like capes as the superheated shards of metal chased us," Tellessen remembered. "It was our brief age of innocence during 2nd Battalion, Third Marines' deployment to Iraq in 2006. We had been largely unscathed by the true essence of war…"

All that changed one day when the 2nd Battalion lost one of its own to an unseen assailant, an Iraqi sniper that was obviously adept at his work. "The sound of a rifle shot bounced off the beige buildings

ABOVE: Soldiers of the Iraqi Security Forces sight their sniper rifles. The soldier on the right is handling a Russian-made Dragunov rifle. (Public Domain)

that made up the town of Haqlaniyah, but most of us didn't think much of it," noted Tellessen. "The city was a constant echo chamber of M16 and Kalashnikov percussion, a violent symphony of rage…

"One shot from the marksman came from a window or rooftop that we would never find and travelled through the city, over the heads of butchers and mechanics, mothers and their children, maybe even over the heads of Marines on patrol looking for exactly that kind of window or rooftop. The bullet flew closer to our base, closer to the post with our Marine on it…He was doing everything right, but the bullet didn't care. It found the tiny void in the glass and passed through it, then it cleared the plate and slid into the flak jacket just above the life-saving armour, easily cutting through the Kevlar, which is only rated to stop pistol rounds… He fell to the ground where he stood…."

One elusive sniper, perhaps a hired gun fighting on behalf of the Taliban, cultivated a sense of dread among American personnel. While the existence of a single sniper or several is debated, the persona of Juba was haunting. Videos were posted purporting to show Juba's sniper handiwork, and his propaganda value soared. One American soldier said, "He's good. Every time we dismount I'm sure everyone has got him in

ABOVE: US Army snipers scan the horizon for the enemy at the ruins of the ancient city of Nineveh, Mosul, Iraq. (Public Domain)

IRAQ AND AFGHANISTAN

ABOVE: A soldier of the 505th Parachute Infantry Regiment, 82nd Airborne Division, aims his M-14 sniper rifle in Fallujah, Iraq. (Public Domain)

ABOVE: An Australian instructor works with an Iraqi sniper trainee on a firing range at Camp Taji, Iraq. (Public Domain)

It was a detached death.

The sniper's quarry had tried to hide from the helicopters overhead, but when the order to engage was heard, the trigger was squeezed, firing two .50-calibre rounds from nearly 1,250 yards away. "When you are bred to kill, you know. You just know," the sniper related.

The most famous sniper to emerge from the war in Iraq was undoubtedly Navy SEAL Chris Kyle, who completed four tours of duty and was officially credited with more than 150 kills. Kyle's biography, *American Sniper*, was released in early 2012 and spent 37 weeks on the New York Times bestseller list. The 2014 film adaptation produced by Clint Eastwood and starring Bradley Cooper was a box office smash, grossing $547 million worldwide.

Kyle earned the nickname "Devil of Ramadi" and performed his duty as ordered. His first kill saved a group of Marines from a woman moving toward them with a hand grenade. Another memorable encounter occurred when Kyle occupied a rooftop in the city of Fallujah. As Marines entered Fallujah, he watched a railroad track and a berm rising in front of the city's centre.

The insurgents, perhaps confident that they were unseen, moved toward the Marines in ambush. Kyle fired his .300 Winchester Magnum from a distance of 800 metres, and one insurgent fell dead. Within hours, he had shot down two more while another sniper accounted for two as well. On another occasion, Kyle killed two insurgents riding on a moped after they dropped an IED near an American position. The pair was 150 yards away; a single shot passed through them both.

Chris Kyle became a legend in Iraq and never had second thoughts regarding his service, noting, "It was my duty to shoot the enemy, and I don't regret it. My regrets are for the people I couldn't save: Marines, soldiers, buddies. I'm not naïve, and I don't romanticize war. The worst moments of my life have come as a SEAL. But I can stand before God with a clear conscience about doing my job."

It has been said that the crucible of war will embolden men and women to do things they might not otherwise do. The experience of the sniper is one such example.

ABOVE: A sniper of the 1st Battalion, 23rd Infantry Regiment, 2nd Infantry Division, US Army covers a street in an Iraqi town. (Public Domain)

the back of their minds. He's a serious threat to us." An officer stated matter-of-factly, "We have different techniques to try to lure him out, but he is very well trained and very patient. He doesn't fire a second shot."

Some observers said that Juba was a mythical character, his reputation blown wildly out of proportion. An officer told Stars and Stripes, the army newspaper, "He's a product of the US military. We've built up this myth ourselves." Nevertheless, some contemporary sources say the army chased Juba and forced him to flee from his home turf in the city of Ramadi in Anbar Province – and they conclude that he probably died in combat – real or imagined but in either case unseen.

The sniper can not only kill, but in a stunning moment may also erase an entire Marine battalion's air of invincibility. And certainly, there were times when a Marine sniper made the Taliban weak, trembling with fear as well.

One sniper, who had grown up hunting in Georgia and had a familiarity with firearms well before he deployed to Iraq with the sniper section of a mortar platoon at the age of 20, was forever changed by his wartime journey. During a 2015 interview with Moni Basu of CNN, the young man was frank in assessing his experience in Iraq.

"I enjoyed being on a roof, knowing that any moment now, this could be it," he told Basu. "I enjoyed the thrill of getting a shot out. I liked killing the enemy." He recalled his first kill, saying, "I remember it to this day, like I was still sitting there… I wasn't nervous or anything. I didn't feel nothing."

CRAIG HARRISON

Corporal of Horse Craig Harrison, for more than two years the record holder for the longest confirmed sniper kill in a combat zone, was introduced to the sniper rifle for the first time on the firing range at a British base in Croatia, and the rifle was a Russian Dragunov SVD.

The son of parents who were both dog handlers with the RAFP (Royal Air Force Police), he was born in Cheltenham, Gloucestershire, in November 1974, and joined the British army at the age of 16. He spent 22 years in the army and completed sniper training even though the skill was not necessarily associated with his unit. "My regiment, the Blues and Royals, didn't have a history or culture of sniping in the way that other regiments do, particularly the Parachute Regiment, the Royal Marines and the Special Forces," he wrote in his book The Longest Kill: The Story of Maverick 41, One of the World's Greatest Snipers. "I had to fight to become a sniper and I had to fight to bring my rifle on operations…"

When Harrison dismounted from the Jackal armoured car he was riding in on a November day in 2009, he had no thought that he might make history, but later on he commented that his rifle "would turn the tide of a battle." His Accuracy International AWM (L115A3 variant) sniper rifle was chambered for the .338 Lapua Magnum cartridge, 14.5mm (.588-calibre), and he

ABOVE: Sniper Craig Harrison, while serving in Afghanistan with the Blues and Royals, made two kill shots at great distances. (Creative Commons Mike Searson via Wikipedia)

paired it with the Schmidt & Bender 5-25 telescopic sight. He declared both the best in the world. And he made a strong case for such that day when he killed two Taliban fighters from a distance of 2,475 metres, or 1.54 miles.

"I'd been a sniper for 10 years," he wrote. "I'd been in firefights where my odds of surviving seemed slim to none, but I'd never had to make a shot like this before. I'd never had to shoot so far and to factor in so many variables, while under so much pressure. The pressure of life or death."

Harrison made the shots and became a celebrity… but one who had assurances after returning home that his identity would be kept secret to prevent the risk of becoming a target for terrorist reprisal. A reporter for the Telegraph observed, "Craig was happy to talk to the media when he returned to the UK, and everyone wanted to know about his amazing kill. But he never thought for a second his ID would be released."

Well, it happened in a blunder at the Ministry of Defence, and several years after the long kill he was warned by the authorities that his life and those of his wife and daughter were in danger. He was discharged from the army and compensated financially with £100,000. He has also battled Post Traumatic Stress Disorder in the years since his service.

In his memoir, Harrison mused on the role of the sniper. "To my mind the sniper is the ultimate professional soldier, one of the only true force multipliers in the British Army's inventory. A sniper pair can wreak havoc that is completely disproportional to their number. They can slow battalion advances and turn attacks. They can enhance the defensive battle by making the attackers' lives hell… Snipers don't just kill though. They are trained to observe and report, carry out reconnaissance and can adjust mortar and artillery fire. They are the masters of the shadows."

There it is… the sniper defined… by one of the masters.

ABOVE: A British army sniper camouflaged and holding his rifle prepares to exit a Merlin helicopter at Camp Shawquat, Nad-e Ali, Afghanistan. (Open Government License Sgt Martin Downs RAF via Wikipedia)

ABOVE: A sniper team of the Royal Yorkshire Regiment keeps watch near Kabul, Afghanistan. (Open Government License Lt Col Humphris MBE via Wikipedia)

ABOVE: Rob Furlong used this .50-calibre McMillan Tac-50 sniper rifle to execute his long kill shot in Afghanistan. (Public Domain)

ROB FURLONG

From March 2002 to November 2009, Corporal Rob Furlong of the Princess Patricia's Canadian Light Infantry held the record for the longest distance sniper kill in a combat zone. During Operation Anaconda in the Shahikot Valley of Afghanistan, he made history at 2,430 metres, or just over 1.5 miles. The record shot came just days after comrade Master Corporal Arron Perry had eclipsed the distance record set by US Marine Gunnery Sergeant Carlos Hathcock during the Vietnam War.

Furlong peered through the scope of his McMillan Tac-50 sniper rifle and eliminated the threat to fellow troops posed by a trio of Taliban fighters setting up a machine gun. The sniper progressed through the ritual he had practiced a thousand times and made the kill shot count. "You can teach a certain amount of it," he commented in a 2006 interview with author Michael Friscolanti. "But there is a large percentage that you must have naturally. A good shooter is born. You can't teach someone to be a good shot if they don't naturally have it."

Probably so… sniper training hones the skill, then, which is innate in some. And the praise for the prowess of Furlong and his fellow Canadian snipers came loud and strong from the American troops they had

ABOVE: Canadian soldiers of Rob Furlong's Princess Patricia's Light Infantry patrol in Afghanistan. (Public Domain)

protected so adroitly. One American soldier put it bluntly for all the world. "Thank God the Canadians were there."

Furlong, born on Fogo Island, Newfoundland, on November 11, 1976, possessed those qualities that make the sniper what he is. As a boy he taught himself to fire a rifle ambidextrously, and it followed that he enlisted in the army at age 21 in 1997 after viewing a recruiting tape. Two years later, he was among the Canadian troops deployed as peacekeeping forces in troubled Bosnia.

Despite their heroics, within a relative few months several of the snipers had left the army. Allegations had surfaced that Perry had been guilty of misconduct. None of the charges were proved, but it was a bitter experience for the snipers who had no doubt saved lives. Furlong observed, "It's sad to see what happened over there. It took the shine off what really took place there, and I think in the long run destroyed people's lives."

Furlong and Perry, as well as three other Canadian sniper team members, received the US Bronze Star medal for their service in Afghanistan, but only after their own country's military establishment concurred, having blocked the awards for months. Their medals were presented in December 2003, a full 19 months after their heroism during Operation Anaconda. They were also Mentioned in Dispatches.

In 2004, Furlong went to work with the Edmonton, Alberta, police service. Eight years later, he departed amid controversy involving an altercation with another officer. Today he operates Rob Furlong's Marksmanship Academy in Alberta. The organization offers training, security, and consulting services to the private market and is billed as Canada's only extreme long-range shooting school.

"With my experience in law enforcement and seeing the need for further training in the tactical world, we could bring a police agency up to speed with their snipers in a matter of weeks," he commented. "For civilians we have a marksmanship class on how to handle firearms, use optics and teach them how to target shoot out to 400 metres."

ABOVE: Canadian soldiers train Afghan army recruits during the fighting against the Taliban. (Public Domain)

THE MILITARY SNIPER

CHRIS KYLE

US Navy Chief Petty Officer Chris Kyle discharged his duty during four tours in Iraq and became a legend. His book *American Sniper* and the film that followed brought to a wide audience the life and times of the military sniper.

Whatever discourse surrounds the telling and retelling of his sniper exploits in wartime, there is no doubt that Kyle saved American and allied lives in the most difficult environment one could imagine – the heat of combat when life and death hang in the balance and a decision must be rendered. He did come through the experience a changed individual, and his comments sometimes raised concerns. He has been quoted as saying, "I loved what I did. I still do. If circumstances were different – if my family didn't need me – I'd be back in a heartbeat. I'm not lying or exaggerating to say it was fun. I had the time of my life being a SEAL."

ABOVE: Chris Kyle signs a copy of his bestselling book *American Sniper* at Camp Pendleton, California. (Public Domain)

ABOVE: US Navy SEAL sniper Chris Kyle became a legend after four combat tours in Iraq. (Public Domain)

Nevertheless, he accomplished his mission. His Silver Star citation makes that assertion crystal clear. "…for conspicuous gallantry and intrepidity in action against the enemy while serving as Lead Sniper while assigned to Naval Special Warfare Task Unit-RAMADI in direct support of Operation IRAQI FREEDOM from 24 April to 27 August 2006. Petty Officer Kyle's heroic actions, professionalism and incredible sniper skills had tremendous impact in the success of U.S. and Iraqi Forces in routing the insurgency and seizing key areas of the City of Ar Ramadi, the epicentre of Al Qaeda and insurgent activity in Iraq. During 32 sniper overwatch missions, he personally accounted for 91 confirmed enemy fighters killed and dozens more probably killed or wounded…His engagements directly prevented casualties to U.S. and Iraqi Forces on more than 30 occasions, including enemy rocket-propelled grenade and mortar teams eliminated, five enemy snipers with scoped weapons eliminated, and dozens of insurgent fighters destroyed while actively engaging U.S. and Iraqi forces with small arms.…"

Honest in assessing his purpose, Kyle remarked, "I don't have to psych myself up, or do something special mentally – I look through the scope, get my target in the cross hairs, and kill my enemy, before he kills one of my people."

Kyle was a hero and a controversial figure. No doubt. When he returned home, he settled with his wife and two children in the city of Midlothian, Texas, and became president of Craft International, an enterprise providing tactical training for the private sector and the US military. He was involved in a highly publicised lawsuit with former Minnesota governor and professional wrestler Jesse Ventura among other issues. He was active in assisting veterans who suffered from Post Traumatic Stress Disorder, and in reaching out to one of them, he met his tragic and untimely end.

Kyle and a friend, Chad Littlefield, picked up veteran Eddie Ray Routh on the morning of February 2, 2013, for a visit to a local shooting range. Routh was mentally ill, schizophrenic and unstable, and he murdered both Kyle and Littlefield that day. The bodies were found hours later with multiple gunshot wounds. Routh was tried, convicted, and is currently serving a life sentence in prison without the possibility of parole.

At the time of his death, Chris Kyle was 38 years old.

ABOVE: After a SEAL Team 3 awards ceremony, Chris Kyle (right) and Kevin Lacz wear the Bronze Star Medal. (Creative Commons Lindseylacz via Wikipedia)

THE MILITARY SNIPER TODAY

Even today, the world is wracked with wars and rumours of wars. And where there is armed conflict, the spectre of the sniper is ever present. Lessons learned, in blood, sweat and the climactic squeeze of the trigger, have led to improvements in technology and tactics for the military sniper.

And the sniper plies his trade at this very moment – somewhere amid the unrest that is apparently the lot of humankind. After Russia's invasion of Ukraine in February 2022, the fighting continues, and stories of the sniper filter into the Western media. In March 2023, for example, a video surfaced which showed a single Ukrainian sniper taking aim.

"The clip appears to show the sniper using an infrared scope and depicts Russian soldiers walking down a street before they are picked off," reported Newsweek magazine. "According to the post, the footage was taken by the sniper in Bakhmut, an area that has experienced some of the most intense fighting in the ongoing conflict. In the clip, it is not clear whether the Russian soldiers realize the sniper's position, or even that they are under fire. The video appears to show a total of six Russian soldiers dropping to the floor after being shot."

While Ukrainian soldiers have told reporters that the one-on-one sniper encounters such as depicted in Hollywood films are just fantasy, there is strong evidence that the sniper is performing his task in Ukraine. Such will probably continue in conflicts of the future, particularly given the commitment that appears steadfast within military establishments around the world. Sniper training and the development of sniper rifles and weapons systems are ongoing.

In the United States, numerous sniper schools and training programs are operational. Among them are the Department of Energy Sniper School at Kirtland Air Force Base in Albuquerque, New Mexico, a two-week course that supplies qualified graduates to the Department of Energy security forces, and the FBI Hostage Rescue Team (HRT) Sniper School at the FBI Academy in Quantico, Virginia. Others, such as the six-week Special Forces Sniper Course at Fort Bragg, North Carolina, and the US Army Sniper School at Fort Benning, Georgia, a seven-week regimen, are well known, as is the three-month US Navy SEAL Sniper School based on the East and West coasts of the United States.

The US combat experience in Iraq and Afghanistan exposed a shortage of trained snipers in the ranks of National Guard units that were called up for service, and while the US Army has operated its sniper training program since 1987, the National Guard's delivery of qualified graduates of a two-week phased program at its National Marksmanship Training Center, Camp Robinson, Arkansas, is a more recent development. The US Air Force

ABOVE: A British sniper maintains vigil from a rooftop somewhere in Afghanistan. (Open Government License Sgt Anthony Boocock/MOD via Wikipedia)

Advanced Designated Marksman Course, a three-week program designed to provide new instructors and security personnel for Air Force bases around the world, was originally based at Camp Robinson before moving to Fort Bliss, Texas, in 2008, as the course was renamed Close Protection Engagement Team.

"Day or night, our job is to take out a target before he can fire at one of our multi-million dollar aircraft or kill someone," an Air Force sniper commented. In 2001, the Air Force graduated its first female sniper. "The school was not easy and there were days I wanted to go home," she told author Christian Orr. "I was the first woman to go through; it was because of that and the opportunities it would open up for future women that helped me get through the training and kept me motivated."

ABOVE: US soldiers of the 10th Mountain Division watch the tarmac at Kabul airport in August 2021. (Public Domain)

ABOVE: A Dutch sniper sights his Accuracy AWM rifle in the mountains of Afghanistan. (Creative Commons Ministerie van Defensie)

THE MILITARY SNIPER

ABOVE: Amid a cloud of dust, a sniper of the Royal Dragoons Guards engages the enemy in Afghanistan.
(Open Government License Cpl Barry Lloyd RLC/MOD via Wikipedia)

Sure, the training is gruelling. Former US Navy SEAL and sniper instructor Brandon Webb explained his acquaintance with the rigors of such a commitment. "As a former Navy SEAL Sniper, a basic and later an advanced course instructor, and eventually the head instructor for the west coast SEAL sniper program, I am intimately familiar with the patience and skill necessary to graduate a sniper," he wrote for SOFREP News in a 2021 article titled The Navy SEAL Elite Sniper Program: 3 Months of Hell.

"The 21st-century Sniper is a mature, intelligent shooter that leverages technology to his deadly advantage," Webb concluded. "He has spent thousands of hours honing his skills. He is a master of concealment in all environments, from the mountains of Afghanistan to the crowded streets of Iraq. He is trained in science but, he, alone, is left to create the individual art of the kill. The battlefield to the sniper is like a painter's black canvas. It is up to him to use his tools, training, and creativity to determine how that final shot, and the devastating psychological impact that is ultimately the result of his actions, will play out."

The US Marine Corps has operated its seven-week Scout Sniper School at Quantico for decades, but recent news has the future of the school and its tradition in question. In 2018, the Marine Corps announced the adoption of the Mk 13 Mod 7 sniper rifle, chambered for the .300 Winchester Magnum round, to replace its M40A6 inventory as the primary weapon of its scout sniper. the Mk 13 was already in use with the Marine Corps Forces Special Operations Command.

In the spring of 2023, however, the Marine Corps announced the "immediate transition of Scout Sniper Platoons to Scout Platoons [to] provide the commander with relevant, reliable, accurate and prompt information." The implication was clear – Marine infantry battalions would no longer include sniper elements. The major change is a component of the Marine Corps Force Design 2030 plan that is intended to restructure functionality in the context of modern warfare. The newly created scout platoons will include 26 Marines, a lieutenant, and an infantry gunnery sergeant, slightly larger than the traditional scout sniper platoon of 18 Marines.

The Marine Corps does not intend to turn its back on the sniper concept completely, and filling the void will be the new military occupational specialty of Reconnaissance Sniper, incorporated with the Reconnaissance battalions. Needless to say, an uproar has ensued. "Rather than do away with Scout Snipers…perhaps our senior leadership should invest the little bit of time and effort it would take to better train, equip and organize the highly skilled and motivated Scout Snipers who are already giving their all in defence of our Nation," read a social media post from the USMC Scout Sniper Association.

The British armed forces continue to cultivate the sniper craft, and a resurgence of the sniper's importance has been acknowledge considering the combat experience of recent years. British army snipers typically reside in the recce (reconnaissance) elements of infantry battalions or armoured regiments. Two sniper sections of four two-man teams are standard. Nine weeks of sniper training is provided to candidates from the Parachute Regiment and Household Cavalry at Pirbright, Surrey. Other battalions form a sniper selection cadre which selects and sends candidates to the Basic Sniper Course administered by the Sniper Division, Support Weapons School, at Brecon, Wales.

Royal Marine snipers are trained during 13 intense weeks at the Commando Training Centre Royal Marines at Lympstone, Devon, while specialized maritime sniper teams are fielded by 43 Commando Fleet Protection Group. A section of eight snipers is organic to each Royal Air Force regiment field squadron. Training takes place three times a year for nine weeks at RAF Regiment Training Wing, RAF Honington.

The German Bundeswehr operates a six-week sniper pretraining course followed by four weeks of intensive training at its infantry school in Hammelburg. Among the requirements of the pretraining course is the completion of a 7,000-metre (4.35 miles) run with a 20-kilogram (44 pounds) field pack in under 52 minutes.

Since 2011, the Russian army is believed to be conducting sniper programs at military district training centres, one of which is located at Solnechnogorsk near Moscow. The Russian program is believed to stress artillery spotting, coordination of air support, and counter-sniping capabilities. The British Ministry of Defence estimates that qualified snipers are likely to be grouped into a company of three platoons to each infantry brigade.

The sniper is both reviled and lauded. His exploits thrill, enrage, and strike fear into the hearts of adversaries. When he takes the shot, the aura of the battle is transformed, and when he does not, there are other consequences. When US forces exited Afghanistan in 2021, a Marine sniper watched the crowded gate to Kabul airport, where thousands of people were more than military crowd control could manage.

"Over the communication network we passed that there was a potential threat and that there was an IED attack imminent," the Marine testified later before the US House of Representatives Foreign Affairs Committee. "This was as serious as it could get. I requested engagement authority while my team leader was ready on the M110 semi-automatic sniper system. The response, leadership did not have engagement authority for us, do not engage."

A short while later, the suicide bomber set off his deadly explosion, killing 13 American military personnel.

A single sniper shot withheld…life, death, rules of engagement. Hero or villain? That is for the individual to decide. Nevertheless, the saga of the sniper will continue.

ABOVE: A Ukrainian sniper of the 28th Knights of the First Winter Campaign Brigade aims his Barrett M107A1 rifle, November 2022. (Creative Commons Mil.gov.ua via Wikipedia)

ABOVE: A crowd gathers at Kabul airport on August 21, 2021, as US Marines attempt to maintain order.
(Public Domain)

THE MILITARY SNIPER'S VIEW

He peers intently through the telescopic sight. A flurry, the glare of an opponent's lens, grabs his attention. The suspense of the moment is punctuated by the squeeze of the trigger and the flight of the bullet. The sniper rules the battlefield, dictating the movement of a single individual or large formation of soldiers and their vehicles. He can alter the course of a battle or decide its outcome. The world of the military sniper is secret and shadowy. He has trained for countless hours, and his ultimate test comes amid the tension of the battlefield encounter. The military sniper must be calculating, precise, patient, and even detached from the reality of his mission. Emotion waxes and wanes, but he sets about his task and finds within himself the fortitude to act. Explore the sniper and his role in military history. It is at once startling, disturbing, and compelling.

ABOVE: Silhouetted against the sun a sniper of the British Army takes aim with his L115A3 rifle in Afghanistan. (Open Government License Cpl Rupert Frere RLC via Wikipedia)